Hap~ ~~~~~~~ ~~~~~~~ ~~~~~ ~e.

<u>from</u> ~~~~~~~~~~~~~

Feb-14/08.

SIMMO

CRICKET THEN AND NOW

To my wife Meg and daughters Kim and Debbie,
whose love and support has always been my inspiration

SIMMO

CRICKET THEN AND NOW

BOB SIMPSON

ALLEN&UNWIN

First published in 2006

Allen & Unwin
83 Alexander Street
Crows Nest NSW 2065
Australia
Phone: (61 2) 8425 0100
Fax: (61 2) 9906 2218
Email: info@allenandunwin.com
Web: www.allenandunwin.com

National Library of Australia
Cataloguing-in-Publication entry:

Simpson, Bobby, 1936- .
    Simmo : cricket then and now.

    ISBN 978 1 74175 041 6.

    ISBN 1 74175 041 5.

    1. Simpson, Bobby, 1936- . 2. Cricket players - Australia -
    Biography. 3. Cricket players - Anecdotes. 4. Cricket
    players - Australia - Anecdotes. 5. Cricket - Anecdotes.
    6. Cricket - Australia - Anecdotes. I. Title.

    796.358092

Set in Garamond3 13/17pt by Midland Typesetters, Australia
Printed in Australia by McPherson's Printing Group

Frontispiece: Bob with his daughters, Debbie (left) and Kim, at Sydney Airport after he returned from Australia's tour of England, India and Pakistan in 1964. *Collection of Bob Simpson*

10 9 8 7 6 5 4 3 2 1

CONTENTS

AUTHOR'S NOTE

I am grateful to Geoff Armstrong for his help in the writing of this book. Thanks also to Rob de Ridder for his assistance with the scanning of photographs from my personal collection, and to everyone at Allen & Unwin for their strong support from first draft to final product.

1

ONE LUCKY LITTLE BUGGER

I'm not exactly sure where my natural affinity with cricket came from. Until my two older brothers and I fell in love with the game when we were kids in the 1940s, there was no cricket heritage in the Simpson family. My parents were from Scotland, where Dad had played top-level football for Stenhousemuir and Falkirk in the Scottish League. My parents emigrated to Sydney before I was born, and I can vividly remember following Dad down to Arlington Park, at Dulwich Hill, not far from our home in the suburb of Marrickville, to watch some of his old soccer mates play in the Sydney First Division. To an impressionable seven or eight year old, Arlington Park in those days was London's Wembley Stadium, Glasgow's Hampden Park and the Sydney Cricket Ground all rolled into one. I was amazed many years later when I went back there and saw it was so tiny!

Dad had no cricket blood in him and was probably hopeful that one or more of his children would become a footballer of some ability. But when we took to cricket like so many other Sydney schoolboys did, he was always encouraging us—not least I imagine because we were playing a sport of some kind. I reckon most parents, if they played sport as a child, remember the value of that activity, and are thus happy to see their children going down a similar path. Being the youngest of three boys, inevitably I followed in many of my brothers' footsteps, and I can remember trailing my elder brother Bill wherever he went, especially on Saturday afternoons in summer when he was playing cricket in the local churches' competition.

My great hope in those days was that someone in his team would fail to show and I would be asked to fill in. This happened a few times, mostly when a fellow didn't turn up to field, and I was always thrilled to be out there. Before that, though, my first memory of cricket is a run-out I managed in a game at school when I would have been seven or eight years old. I might have been a 'solid' kid, with a nickname of 'Pud', but I picked the ball up with two hands, ran the batsman out at the bowler's end and for a brief moment I felt like I'd cut Goliath down to size. Another, similar, very early sporting memory is of a rugby match down at a park on the Cooks River at Undercliffe, a suburb not far from home, when I made this big diving tackle. The guy with the ball must have been forty pounds heavier than me, but I nailed him.

My brothers and I shared our bat and we learned much of our cricket on the tennis courts that were situated only a stone's throw from home. Two of the courts were no longer in use, and one day we lugged a concrete block from a nearby quarry to serve as the stumps on the hard clayish surface of the old court (it stayed there for years!). Every afternoon after school I'd be there playing in 'Tests' with our mates and trying to perfect all the shots. The classic old coaching manual *Calling All Cricketers* was my sporting bible, while the records in my well-read copy of the *NSW Cricket Association Yearbook* were my inspiration. I'm sure this early practice helped me to develop my style. The hard ball bounced truly off the clay pitch and—knowing the ball would almost certainly be lost if we hit it over the fence and into the blackberry bushes that surrounded the courts—I quickly discovered the value of keeping the ball on the ground.

Eventually, I imagine because he wanted to see a bit more of us, Dad laid a pitch in our very own backyard, but that was a turf wicket that required more maintenance than the tennis court, so the backyard was always our second preference. Still, it got plenty of use. Both my brothers were leg-spinners who went on to play first-grade in Sydney, Bill with Western Suburbs and Jack for Sydney University.

I later played for Wests, too, but my first experience in Sydney grade cricket was with Petersham–Marrickville. I was fourteen when I first went down to the club for some coaching, being part of sessions that were run by a fellow named Dudley Seddon, who just happened to be one of the most important people in New South Wales and Australian cricket. Mr Seddon had played for New South Wales in the late 1920s in both cricket and rugby league, but his greatest impact on cricket in this country came as a coach and administrator. Legend has it that he'd travel any number of miles to watch and help young cricketers. His knowledge of the game was vast, and from 1954 to 1967 he was an Australian selector. He was a colossal figure at Petersham and then Petersham–Marrickville, and he was certainly very kind and helpful to me throughout my career. I came to appreciate the value of a coach at a very early age.

At the time, my life was not just about cricket. In fact, if I had to nominate one sport as having grabbed my attention it would have been golf. Each Sunday, I would head to the Marrickville course and later to the old Bonnie Doon links to caddy and earn some pocket money. My golf swing came naturally, but even though I yearned to be as good as my golfing hero Norman Von Nida, perhaps because the sport lacked the 'team' element it was never more than 'serious fun'. In summer, it was golf and cricket; in winter, I played golf, soccer, tennis and baseball. That was my form of 'cross training'.

The many miles I walked just to get to my sport, often lugging a golf bag or the Globite suitcase that contained my cricket gear, must have helped build my natural fitness.

It wasn't until I began to rise through the grades at Petersham–Marrickville that I began to really concentrate on cricket, in the main because that was the sport whose heroes were constantly in the papers. For all Dad's love of the game, soccer did not offer the same potentially exciting sporting future as did the summer game. Eventually, I decided to give the round-ball code away and concentrate on trying to make a name for myself as a cricketer.

I tried to make my debut in Sydney grade cricket at the start of the 1951–52 season, when I was fifteen. The Petersham and Marrickville clubs had merged a few months earlier, so competition for places was fierce, but I must confess that having made some runs for Marrickville in the under-16 A.W. Green Shield and under-21 Poidevin–Gray competitions I thought I'd be okay, and as I looked around at the other players at the trials I expected to be picked in second grade. But when they listed the teams, my name was not there. I then looked hopefully at the first-grade line-up, but I wasn't there . . . or in the thirds . . . or the fourths. Finally, I saw my name among the 'train-on squad'. All I could do was keep going to practice and hope to eventually earn a spot in the fours, from where I could work my way through the grades. This I did, finally the call-up came, and after a few games in the fours I was promoted up a grade.

I'll never forget my third-grade debut. I was met by our captain, a tough old bloke whose grey hair made him look 50 though he was probably only 35. Immediately, he said to me, 'You might have scored a hundred in Green Shield, sonny, but don't expect you're going to get 100 today.' I thought he was being pretty hard, but then I looked at the scorebook and saw I was batting eight. I normally batted at No. 3 or No. 4. As it turned out, our top order collapsed, and I was in early enough and got involved in a big partnership. I made it all the way to 98, when suddenly he closed the innings. I'm still not sure about the psychology behind that move, but within a couple of games I was promoted straight to first grade, so the bewilderment was quickly forgotten.

Twelve months later, at the age of sixteen, before I'd made a first-grade century, I was playing for New South Wales against Victoria. Teenagers such as Richie Benaud, Graeme Hole and, most notably, Ian Craig had performed well for New South Wales in the Sheffield Shield, so it had become fashionable at the time to promote talented players as quickly as possible. After Ian, I was the next promising young batsman to come along, and because he had done well, they rushed me into the side.

The gap between interstate and grade cricket in Australia is substantial, but I have come to learn that a batsman who can make runs in club cricket, provided he has the technique and temperament, can do well in the first-class arena. This said, I saw many cricketers with good techniques but poor temperaments who struggled in state cricket. There were a number of players who could bat beautifully for a couple of hours in grade matches on a Saturday afternoon, but couldn't find the necessary application to bat for long periods in four-day contests. I struggled with this to a degree myself, scoring only one century in my first four first-class seasons. Similarly, I saw bowlers who could get away with some poor deliveries at grade level, but were punished when they were inconsistent against the better bats in the Sheffield Shield. There were one or two gifted bowlers who I don't think had to think about their craft until they made the state side, and they struggled as a result. I think this situation of newcomers struggling with a tougher environment is happening today in Test cricket, as the gulf between the domestic competitions around the world and international cricket widens.

I learnt of my selection in the New South Wales team when Phil Tresidder, then a young sports reporter with the Sydney *Daily Telegraph* and later to become one of Australia's most accomplished cricket and golf writers, knocked on the door at home one night as I was getting ready for bed.

'Bobby, you're in the state side,' Phil told me.

'You're joking,' I replied. I hadn't expected the selectors to gamble on me, even though a number of the team's best players were unavailable because they would be playing for Australia against South Africa in the Fourth Test in Adelaide. Arthur Morris, Keith Miller, Graeme Hole, Richie Benaud and Ray Lindwall were in the Test XI, while Ian Craig and Sid Barnes were also unavailable. However, I soon realised that Phil wasn't joking and next day I duly received a letter from Alan Barnes, the Secretary of the NSW Cricket Association, congratulating me and stating officially that I was in the New South Wales side to face Victoria at the Sydney Cricket Ground the following week. I immediately felt overawed, and my nervousness didn't subside until I went to Shield practice on the Thursday before the game, and formally met some of my new team-mates. I was certainly the youngest player in the side, but there were a few guys who weren't that much older than me, and of course I'd come into contact with many members of the side in grade cricket, so I realised there was no need to feel so uncomfortable. This said, I addressed all my seniors as 'Mr' or 'Sir'. When I was sixteen or seventeen, if I found myself sitting next to Keith Miller in the dressing room, there was no way I was going to blurt out, 'Hey, Nugget, how ya goin'?' Today, when I go around coaching kids, they all say, 'G'day, Simmo.' That's one of the ways the world has changed.

I will never forget my first ball in first-class cricket. Jack 'Snarler' Hill, who would soon be picked for the 1953 Ashes tour under Lindsay Hassett and in 1955 would go to the West Indies with Ian Johnson's team, was a crafty wrist-spinner who'd been playing for Victoria since straight after the war. Before I went out, I was warned to play forward to Hill at all costs, because only that way would I nullify much of the zip he generated with his top-spinners. So out I went and immediately played back, the ball fizzed through, and with a late jab I managed to get an inside edge and the ball flew past leg-slip. I was lucky . . . and off the mark . . . but as I turned for two, Hill snarled at me, without even a hint of a smile, 'You lucky little bugger!'

My first-class career was one ball old, and I'd already learnt the value of listening to good advice, and also that I was now in a tougher sporting environment than I'd ever been in before. For the next 50-plus years in cricket, I'd keep on learning, and love every minute of it.

2

CLASSIC MILLER

One day in 1954–55, the New South Wales cricket team of which I was an 18-year-old member found itself in Maitland, a country town around two hours drive north of Sydney. We were on our way up to Brisbane for a Sheffield Shield match against Queensland.

At a reception put on especially for the players, our captain Keith Miller rose to his feet to reply to the toast to our team that had been given by the Maitland mayor. He began, 'Lady . . .' Keith had spotted there just one woman in the hall, 'and gentlemen. It is indeed, Sir, wonderful to be in your, er . . . city. The boys have enjoyed their stay in this lovely, um . . . town . . . the people of your borough have gone out of their way to entertain us . . . and we will always remember our stay in this, uhhh . . . district. I assure you we will welcome the chance to come back to . . . er . . . where the hell are we anyway?'

I think of that function often whenever I'm asked to make a speech of my own. For anyone else, such an introduction would have been a public relations disaster. I'm sure I'd have been escorted back to my chair, or probably out the door, in no time flat. But that night in Maitland was classic Miller. His delivery was pitched just right, with so much panache the locals loved him for it.

Keith was actually known for his ability to remember names, and those few he couldn't remember, he always called 'Hap'. Short for Happy. He was an extraordinary man and a sublime cricketer, and like just about everyone my age, who grew up in the years immediately after the Second World War, he was one of my favourite players as a kid. I can vividly remember my first experience of him as captain, a year before that trip to Maitland and Brisbane. It was just my third Shield match, and as you can imagine I was more than thrilled to have Keith as my captain; the previous season, when I made my debut, the Test stars were away and Sid Carroll was the New South Wales skipper. From the moment we left the dressing room until we reached the centre, I kept pace with my great and shrewd leader, and then I stood near the pitch to await my instructions. At last Keith decided, and with a flourish and a toss of his mane, announced, just as cricket folklore says he did, 'Scatter.' Or words to that effect. There was a spot vacant at fine leg, so I headed there.

The top seven in that New South Wales batting order—Arthur Morris, Jim Burke, Ian Craig, Miller, Jim de Courcy, Richie Benaud and Ray Lindwall—had all played Test cricket. Alan Davidson was unavailable, otherwise the innings would have started with eight straight Test guys. With 'Davo' out, I was at No. 9 in the batting order, and the second spinner. We were such a strong and experienced team, everyone knew where to go except me.

It was in somewhat similar circumstances to that first experience of Keith's leadership methods that I began my career as a slip fieldsman in first-class cricket. I was the New South Wales 12th man for a time in that 1953–54 season, and one day during our match against Victoria in Sydney I was summoned onto the field to replace an injured player. Of course, I was delighted to be in the action and away from the boredom of the dressing room. I headed straight to the skipper and enquired, 'Excuse me, Mr Miller, where would you like me to field?' Mr Miller seemed somewhat preoccupied and with hindsight I wonder whether he was thinking about something other than cricket. Eventually, he said, 'Oh, I don't know, laddie. There is a hole over there. That will do for you.'

That hole was first slip. In the next hour I took two reasonable catches, one off the bowling of Keith, the other off Richie, and my fielding fate was sealed for the rest of my career.

In those early days, I think Keith rather fancied me as a leg-spinner. In that game in Brisbane, my first experience of him as my Shield captain, we were playing on what was then a typically dry Gabba wicket, the sort of surface you might see today in Bangalore. Keith opened the bowling with Lindwall and Jack Clark, a right-arm fast-medium bowler from the Paddington club, but after just five overs, Keith brought Richie Benaud into the attack. In his book *Benaud: On Reflection*, Richie remembers saying to Keith, 'But "Nugget" [as the experienced men called him], the ball's still new,' to which Keith replied, 'Don't worry about that, it'll soon be old. Just think about the field you want.'

The look on Richie's face betrayed the fact that he wasn't convinced, so Keith added, 'It's all right. It'll spin like a top for an hour. We've got a great chance to bowl them out.'

It took no time at all for Richie to prove that Keith had read the wicket exactly right, and soon my captain was walking over to me with the ball in his hand. 'Your turn to bowl, young Bobby,' he said.

Somewhat shocked, but delighted, I got through my first three overs. But then Keith walked over and enquired, 'Why am I yet to see your excellent wrong 'un?'

'I seem to have lost it for the time being,' I replied.

'In that case,' he said dismissively, 'you can piss off until you find it.'

So it was sadly back to the outfield for me, from where I saw Richie take five wickets before lunch. But for a couple of missed chances, we might have knocked them over in the first two hours, but after the interval the pitch flattened out and Ken Archer and Peter Burge made hundreds and brought Queensland back into the game. Meanwhile, I resolved to rediscover that googly and then be ready to bowl to Keith every time he batted at the nets. Eventually, he conceded my wrong 'un had returned, and later that season he brought me on second change in the second innings against Western Australia in Sydney and I took 5–37 from 9.7 overs.

Keith was an especially great bowler. While many have suggested he was laidback and a bit laconic in his approach to the game, I beg to differ. He was actually as dedicated and ambitious as any player, but he never liked to show this trait. He could also be riled into action, such as the day South Australia's dynamic opener Les Favell tried to hit Richie over the top but instead skied the ball to at cover. With the great Miller circling underneath it, we all clearly heard Les's squeaky voice calling to his partner, 'With this old bloke under it, we'll look for two!'

Keith duly made a mess of the catch, something he very rarely did, and Les couldn't help himself. 'Bad luck Nugget,' he said with a grin. 'I thought you were in trouble.' Our captain was furious, and grabbed the ball so he could bowl some of the fastest bouncers I have ever seen.

To me, Keith always seemed happier if he could play down his talent and influence. In November 1955, New South Wales were playing South Australia at the Sydney Cricket Ground and in the evening of the first day his fourth son was born. Keith, of course, was delighted and celebrated into the early hours of the following day.

He was late waking up the next morning, somewhat hungover, and then forgot to pick up one of his team, Peter Philpott, on the way to the ground. After doubling back to collect 'Percy', they found themselves with little time left before the 11 a.m. start of play and, as is inevitable whenever you're running late, traffic seemingly blocked every escape route. There was no way Keith was going to make it in time until a policeman on a motorcycle appeared. Keith explained the situation and with their escort's siren blaring, they reached the SCG just as we were about to walk out to begin the second day. The previous night Keith had declared our innings closed at 8–215, hoping to get a few overs at the South Australians before stumps, but there had been time for only one Pat Crawford over before the umpires offered the visiting batsmen the light. They were resuming at 0–2.

Breathless as he entered the dressing room, Keith threw on his cricket gear and with shoelaces dangling caught up with the rest of us about halfway to the wicket. He immediately sought out Alan Davidson, who had been preparing to bowl the first over of the day, to inform him that he would have a couple of overs 'to get the booze out of his system' and then Davo would take over. Just 14.3 eight-ball overs later, we walked off the field after South Australia had been bowled out for 27. Keith had taken 7–12. South Australia followed on and he bowled just six overs in the second innings, taking 0–19. His job had been done, and we eventually won the game by nine wickets. He was unique and eccentric, and a truly great cricketer who had that rare talent, particularly with the ball, to change a match in a couple of overs.

•

I think it's also important to remember that he wasn't perfect. I remember going out to bat in a grade game between his club, Manly, and Petersham–Marrickville when I was just seventeen. It had rained overnight and the wicket was wet. Miller actually arrived early for the match, which I would learn was unusual, and he took the new ball, belted them in short and I would either occasionally try to hook the ball, or just dodge the bullet any way I could. It was surely just a matter of time before he'd dismiss me, but then, after about four overs, he did the strangest thing—he took himself off and didn't bowl again for the rest of the day. I would have thought, being such a dangerous bowler as well as the Manly captain, Keith would have helped his team a bit more that day.

Whenever I see old black-and-white film of him in action, I am reminded just how easy and beautiful a bowling action he possessed. Off only about fifteen paces, he could, when the mood took him, bowl as quickly as anyone. His high, pure delivery meant he could get the ball to bounce sharply, and also gave him the rare ability to bowl perfect outswingers. I reckon every budding fast bowler should be shown his action, and that the biomechanics who these days seem to have a mortgage on theories about bowling methods should accept the Miller model as being one of the best ways to bowl.

In my view, Keith was a better bowler than batsman. His 170 Test wickets at 22.98 and 2958 Test runs at 36.98 support this, though I know not everyone will agree with me. He was a stylish batsman, good enough to score seven Test hundreds, but he was not always happy against pace bowling, as we found out one day in Sydney about ten weeks after he'd been delighting the people of Maitland with that 'where the hell are we, anyway' speech.

New South Wales were playing Victoria and in those days the SCG pitch was lively. Three weeks earlier, Frank Tyson and Brian

Statham had spearheaded England to an emphatic victory in the second Ashes Test, bowling Australia out for just 228 and 184. Here, Sam Loxton was leading Victoria in the absence of usual skipper Ian Johnson (the then Australian captain), and while as far as I knew Sam and Keith were good mates, there was a bit of rivalry between Keith and a few members of the Victorian team, which might have dated back to the late 1940s when Keith transferred from Melbourne to Sydney. Certainly, Keith and Ian Johnson weren't the best of friends, and this was a time when many members of the press were campaigning for Miller, not Johnson, to be leading the Australian side.

Perhaps it was Johnson who had urged Johnny Power, a pretty quick fast bowler, to pepper Keith with bouncers when he came out to bat. I was at the other end, on the way to my maiden first-class hundred, so I had a close-up view of the action. In those days, there was no restriction on the number of bouncers that could be bowled per over.

After three overs of non-stop rib-tickling and no runs being scored, Keith strode halfway down the wicket, drew a line across the pitch, looked at Power, pointed to the bowler's half of the wicket, and said: 'Laddie, that is your side and the other is mine. You should bowl in mine from now on.'

Fast bowlers are stubborn. Power continued—probably with some prodding from Sam Loxton, who was always a combative cricketer—to land his short ones on his side of the wicket and into Keith's ribs. No bowler had ever gone to this extent to take on the great Miller for fear of retaliation. Our captain was dismissed soon after for a duck, and afterwards, as it generally did in those days, the mood on the field settled down. It was the only time I saw Keith even rattled, but in the Victorian second innings, a few of the batsmen looked a little white-faced as they faced up to our hero at his finest. He took 5–38 as the match was won by nine wickets.

No one ever had Keith Miller down for long. He was a magnificent player, the best all-round Australian cricketer I have ever seen.

3

THE LEARNING GAME

As well as being a great batsman, Neil Harvey was always very helpful to me. On my first tour with the Australian team, to South Africa in 1957–58, I really wasn't good enough to be there. I was getting out too easily. 'I'm not good enough, I'm not going to stay in the side,' I said to Harv. 'What can I do?'

'Just look around the side,' Neil replied. 'Tell me, where do you think there's a vacancy?'

I thought about it and realised that there might be an opportunity shortly with at least one of the opening bat positions. Jimmy Burke and Colin McDonald were established at the top of the batting order, but both had been around for quite a while, and I sensed that 'Burkey' was struggling a little.

'Do you think I've got the technique?' I pestered Harv.

'Yes you do,' he replied kindly. 'But you've got to be more selective in the shots you play.'

From there we sat down and went right through my game, a process that for me continued over the following eighteen months. I felt much better about myself and my cricket after that chat with one of the game's greats.

Neil really was a brilliant left-handed batsman. I vividly remember the 167 he scored against Jim Laker in Melbourne in the Second Test of 1958–59, my one Test of that summer. You could see him taking out all his frustrations from his and Australia's failures against the great English off-spinner in 1956, getting down the pitch to Laker further than I've ever seen any batsman go before or since. Mostly, he was getting to the ball on the full. Years later, when I became a coach, I always remembered that knock, explaining to young batsmen, 'When you go down the wicket you go down to get the ball on the full, not the half-volley.' Harv was also a good all-round player against the quicks. His footwork was magnificent, just brilliant. I'll never forget those square cuts of his. That he was giving me this advice suggested he understood the art of batting, that it wasn't as simple as just going out there and belting hundreds. I'm not sure I realised that before this tour.

I would have liked to have been a batsman in the Harvey mould. I had been very much a stroke-maker as a teenager. If anything came within sight, I wanted to whack it for four. Now I had to ask myself: 'If you are going to be an opening batsman, where are you going to score your runs?' I decided I would no longer try to hook or pull the fast bowlers. With the square cut, though, I felt the odds were in my favour if I played the shot correctly: don't try to hit it too hard, don't lean back when you play the stroke—if you get a top edge it'll fly over the slip cordon. I was good off the pads and hip, so if the bowlers strayed onto the leg stump I'd deflect and drive them away. I was a good runner between wickets, so I'd look for every quick single I could find. There'd be no more big wind-up drives, but I'd still look to get on the front foot and use the pace of the bowling to time the ball to the boundary.

I needed a game plan for each situation, to work out the bowlers. If there was a left-hand swing bowler on, such as Alan Davidson, I'd aim to get forward as much as I could. If he pitched short, I wouldn't stay forward, but I wanted to focus on hitting the ball with the full face of the bat to the V that was shaped by mid-off, my bat, and mid-on. By getting forward, I'd stop the bowler from swinging the ball as much as he wanted. For every bowler, I worked out the best way for me to play him. The intention was not to make me robotic, but if I had a plan it was so much more likely that I would play the appropriate shot than if I'd never thought about it. There's a big difference between premeditation and planning.

After the South Africa Tests I went back to playing Sheffield Shield for Western Australia. Here I applied my new batting principles with some success, though in 1958–59 I was still in the middle order. It was only at the beginning of the next season, when Jimmy Burke retired from Test cricket and Western Australia's long-time opener John Rutherford gave Shield cricket away, that I slotted into the top of Western Australia's batting order. I'd moved to Perth in 1956, after missing selection for that year's Ashes tour. I was still opening up when I retired from Test cricket in 1968.

•

The 1957–58 tour of South Africa was as happy a time as I ever had in cricket. The catalyst for making it so pleasurable and successful was the attitude of Neil Harvey, who had been strangely passed over for the captaincy after Ian Johnson and Keith Miller retired in 1956 and had every right in the world to be upset that he hadn't been given the job. The average age of the touring party was 24, and even some of the older blokes, such as Wally Grout and Ken Mackay, had played little Test cricket. As clearly our best player, Harv could have been a poor influence on us young fellas had he taken the decision badly, but instead of carrying on, he was brilliant, which was terribly important from day one as it turned out. Ian Craig, the Board's choice as skipper at age 22, had been working in London and would be travelling from there straight to South Africa. Our manager, Jack Jantke from South Australia, had a heart attack just before our departure date and couldn't accompany us. So Harv, the vice-captain, was left in charge and got everyone organised. Then, once we settled in, he was the bloke who made sure everyone looked up to the captain.

Harv's respect for the game and its traditions was never better captured than in an event that took place away from the eyes of the press and public. During the series, Ian Craig's form was ordinary, to the point that at one stage he decided to drop himself from the Test XI. However, Peter Burge, the third selector, was very quickly told by Harv that one should never drop the Australian captain, under any circumstances. That was it: 'Craigy' was outvoted. Harv would have cherished the captaincy, but only through honourable means.

This was a tour where some great players finally had the opportunity that they'd been craving and they took it brilliantly. We won the series 3–0, after starting as rank outsiders. Alan Davidson was no longer in Lindwall and Miller's considerable shadow; instead, for the next six years, he was the best new-ball bowler in the world. Richie Benaud was the No. 1 spinner in our side, and in this rubber the most influential cricketer on the park. Burke and McDonald were a terrific opening pair, the youngsters added vitality, we all loved playing tough and there was hardly a weak link in the field. Away from the park, there was a fantastic spirit within that team, which Craigy, Harv and Richie fostered magnificently. I remember Burkey on the piano and his brilliant impersonations, going to the movies with 'Slasher' Mackay, spending many enjoyable evenings in the homes of South African cricket fans, the Christmas team dinner with the boys, the visits to the game reserves on the Sunday rest days, and the baseball . . .

Back in 1935–36, a tradition had started when the Aussie tourists played a local South African team in a charity baseball game. Most of our team played baseball back home. It was a tradition we continued on our own tour more than twenty years later, with Harv as our pitcher, Craigy at first base, Richie at second, Burge at third, Les Favell as catcher and me as shortstop. Davo was in centre field, as magnificent as ever. Our win was so decisive that the home team asked for a re-match, which was organised for just before we sailed home. This time they threw their best provincial team and their ace pitcher at us, and for six innings we struggled to get bat on anything but his curve ball. But this meant he had to throw his fast stuff, and by the seventh his arm was falling off and we came through. Winning had become a habit for us.

I started off that tour by dropping seven catches. In the thinner air, the ball was coming on to me a lot quicker than I expected and it took me two or three weeks to sort it out, but during the Test matches I caught anything that came above grass level, which was lucky, because that was the only thing that kept me in the side. I had to learn to be patient, to be aware that the ball was coming on to me quicker and higher, and adjust by really concentrating on getting side-on to everything instead of taking the ball in front of me. It was about being *technically* right, because the thin air had thrown my instincts out, and the way to perfect that was to take hundreds and hundreds of catches at practice. Twenty-eight years later, when I was working with the Australian team, I did much the same thing with David Boon and Geoff Marsh under a big old oak tree at Hamilton in New Zealand. Every morning, we practised catches—short-leg catches, nicks, anything. It was a matter of concentrating on the right technique and doing it repeatedly. You can't teach someone to be a great fieldsman, but you can teach them to be more than competent. South Africa is where my fielding drills started.

The techniques of catching weren't all I learnt. My success as a teenager had me falsely assuming that I was naturally gifted, but listening to Harv and observing him out in the middle (especially seeing him field so brilliantly, getting to everything without ever needing to dive) was inspirational. Seeing Slasher play within the confines of his talent and have a big impact on the series was a real education. It was important that I understood my own game and knew what I could and could not do. Furthermore, I was learning that 'talent' is such an overrated word. It's really no more than a good night your mum and dad had nine months before you were born. 'Talented' cricketers do possess some good genes they inherited from their parents—but they still have to work hard and be smart if they are going to take advantage of them.

The 1957–58 South Africa tour was really when I started learning about my game, and I enjoyed the process. I loved improving and enjoyed doing things right. Much later, after I retired and was analysing the game from the press box, I began applying my accumulated knowledge to other cricketers' games and found that I could help them out.

•

I'd originally moved to Western Australia for the opportunity. At that stage I was a regular member of the NSW team, but I was lucky if I batted higher than No. 7 and bowled a few overs. I knew if I joined the Western Australian team I would probably bat as long as I possibly could in both innings and bowl as much as I wanted to. I sought advice from Dudley Seddon, who thought it was a good idea. What I didn't realise was just how fortunate I would be to go to a place where the venues suited me down to the ground. The wickets were fast and bouncy, and the light was so much better than anywhere else in Australia. Perth and Johannesburg would have to be the two best places in the cricket world to see the ball. You can almost read the brand as it comes to you. I felt my path to becoming a Test regular would be a comfortable one.

By the start of the 1959–60 season, things had gone a little awry. I'd played just one Ashes Test in the previous season and then missed selection for Australia's tour of India and Pakistan. I'd played a season for Accrington in the Lancashire League, and toured South Africa with a 'Commonwealth XI'. I was a married man with a pregnant wife, and basically broke; there were times in England when if I hadn't earned a 'collection' through my efforts on the field we wouldn't have eaten very well. Collections involved someone from the club going around the crowd seeking money from the spectators so that a player who had put in a good performance would be rewarded for his efforts. I probably received about 90 quid from collections during my time at Accrington, which helped enormously because the money was tight. However, I had to be a little rueful, because I'd been told that back in the halcyon days of the League, in the years after the Second World War, the top professionals sometimes received upwards of £50 a time from the big crowds that saw them play.

For all this, I was encouraged. My concentration had improved in the League, as I batted against good bowlers such as Pakistan's Fazal Mahmood and England's Johnny Wardle. I also played a couple of innings against Neil Adcock, the outstanding South African fast bowler, which suggested I was a much better player than I'd been two years earlier. When I returned to Perth for the first practice of the new season, one team-mate came up to me and said, 'Jeez, your game's tight now'. I was practising the same way I batted out in the middle, always determined not to get out. In fact, I can remember Des Hoare, one of WA's opening bowlers, saying to me in the nets one day, 'I don't think anyone's got you out here all season!'

What I had to do was make it impossible for the selectors not to pick me, and I went a long way towards doing that by averaging more than 300 for the 1959–60 first-class season. The personal highlight came in Sydney when I scored 98 and 161 not out against a full-strength New South Wales team that included Benaud and Davidson. Then I went to New Zealand with an Australian Second XI and scored what I consider to be the best hundred of my life— 129 not out at Dunedin, an innings in which I timed the ball perfectly and scored the runs quickly enough for us to win the game with plenty of time to spare. That was important, because my team-mate Ronnie Gaunt and I had the next match off and we wanted to play some golf at Christchurch, but to do that we had to catch a 4 p.m. plane so we could start our round as scheduled first thing the following morning. As I stood on the first tee, in my mind, my dream of becoming a Test opener was close to being fulfilled.

4

FACING HALL WAS HELL

It was 11.01 a.m. one Saturday, early in November 1960, when I first saw Wes Hall as a bowler on a cricket field. At that moment, Hall was stalking the area around the start of his 30-yard run-up. He was impatiently waiting to deliver his first ball in Australia.

A week before, injury had forced him out of the West Indies' initial first-class game of their tour of Australia—against Western Australia in Perth, a match in which I went on to score 87 and 221 not out. There was much disappointment that he had missed that match, for his reputation as being the planet's fastest bowler had preceded him. The locals were aching to see him on their bouncy WACA wicket, though I, as an opening bat, was not quite so keen. Now, in this match between the West Indians and an Australian XI, he had his chance, having been delayed one more day after our captain Neil Harvey had sprung a surprise on the Friday by sending the tourists into bat.

Colin McDonald, perhaps the pluckiest and, at that stage, the best opening batsman in the world, had taken centre and was now ready to assess first-hand whether the frightening tales of Hall's pace were true. I stood at the other end, knowing that another productive batting performance would just about lock up a spot in the Australian team for the first Test. Since being dropped during the 1958–59 Ashes series, I had spent two years reorganising my game so that I would be able to cope with the rigours and demands that the opening berth posed.

The umpire called, 'Play ball.' As he did, I turned to look once again at Hall's huge frame away near the sightscreen, and noticed that in the bright Western Australian sun beads of perspiration had gathered on his forehead. One yard . . . two yards . . . in he ran and immediately I was struck by the thought, 'What a magnificent athlete!' As he accelerated, a sense of power was evident, and as he neared the crease at a speed which I had never seen from a fast bowler, I knew that here was something very special.

McDonald stood in his impassive way . . . earnestly watching, waiting . . . until finally Hall, in a dramatic, explosive, leaping delivery stride, let the ball go with as ferocious an intent as I have ever seen. The ball was short, as so many deliveries from Wes Hall were, and it scorched into the fastest wicket in Australia and then reared high above McDonald, who never came out of his crouch. Gerry Alexander, the wicketkeeper, flung himself desperately down the leg side, trying to climb a ladder which wasn't there, but the bullet cleared him by at least six feet. One bounce, and the ball crashed into the boundary fence.

The usually unflappable McDonald, with nearly a decade of opening in Test cricket behind him, looked down at me and in mouthing one word . . . 'SHIT!' . . . expressed clearly what lay ahead for batsmen across Australia that season. At the other end, a thought quickly flashed through my mind: why on earth would I want to open the batting against a bowler of this frightening pace? From this day on, I had three measures for quick bowling: fast, very fast and . . . OH SHIT!

The celebrated Australian cricket writer and commentator A.G. 'Johnnie' Moyes, in his book of that season *The West Indies in Australia*

1960–61, wrote of my brief innings: 'Simpson's long run of success stopped when he was caught by the second of the leg-slips after a most unhappy few minutes.' In fact, I was dismissed by Hall's opening partner Chester Watson when the innings total was 8 and I was yet to score, but there was no doubt in anyone's mind who was most responsible for my dismissal. In the scorebook, Hall finished with four wickets for the innings, including McDonald and Norm O'Neill, beginning a series of battles between himself and the Australian batsmen that would become a feature of that memorable summer.

As it turned out, I did regain my Test place at the top of the order for the series, and now, looking back, I regard the way I helped take the fight up to Wes Hall throughout that season to be one of my proudest achievements. The series ended in victory to Australia, but only after some truly magnificent and highly dramatic cricket was played by both sides, and such was the popularity of the West Indians—and Wes Hall in particular—that an estimated 500,000 Melbournians lined the streets of their city to pay homage and honour to the tourists after the final Test.

In many ways, Wes Hall was the 'father' of modern-day fast bowlers. He was the first man to successfully introduce the long run-up, which is the hallmark of many fast bowlers today. Whether this approach is to the advantage or disadvantage of cricket in general is to be argued, but it was Wes Hall who so brilliantly introduced it into Test cricket. Such was his popularity in Australia that season, I can't recall him being heckled by the crowds for taking so long to complete an over. 'They liked the look of this big chap with his lovely approach to the wicket; his readiness to chase the ball on either side of the wicket; his demeanour when he bowled a bouncer or got one to rise from a length,' wrote Moyes of Hall's bond with the Aussie fans.

As a cricketer, I saw 'Big Wes' as a superb, exuberant, all-round athlete, who has a tremendous love for the game and the people who play it. I am proud to say that he remains today one of my very closest friends. He probably aimed more bumpers at me than any other fast bowler, but never in all those tense encounters, in many places throughout the world, did I ever resent him in a way that I resented some other fast bowlers. Even after I hit him for four successive fours while playing for a Tasmanian Combined XI in Hobart that season, when I then had to duck hastily under the most unforgivable of all balls from fast bowlers—a bean-ball—I quickly accepted his apology. 'I'm sorry, it slipped,' he said immediately. With other pacemen, I might not have been nearly as forgiving or willing to believe that it was indeed an accident.

Wes has a sense of humour all of his own. I well recall once playing for New South Wales against Queensland in Brisbane in 1961–62, when Wes was playing for the 'banana-landers'. It was the first over of the match and the Gabba wicket was lively. The fourth ball cut in off the pitch much too quickly for me, and as I played back and across it struck me a cruel blow, flattening my protector. I collapsed in a heap on the ground, writhing in agony with tears streaming from my eyes. Finally, with my eyes still blurry from the after-effects of the blow, I looked up to see the huge frame of what could only be Wesley, gazing down at me. His eyes were wide, the gold chain that always hung around his neck was glistening in the sun, a half-smile was breaking across his face, and there was a query on his lips. 'Man,' he said, 'if you can use my flat tonight, you've got it!'

I cannot imagine the same humour coming from some of the ill-tempered, bad-mannered fast bowlers around today. These self-styled bullies seem preoccupied with wanting to make cricket their own property.

Sometimes, though, the humour worked the other way. In 1962–63, Wes was bowling for Queensland against the touring M.C.C. team, and opening the batting was the Rev. David Sheppard, later to become the Bishop of Liverpool. Quickly, a bumper was fired down, but after Rev. Sheppard ducked underneath it he looked up to see Wes in a bit of bother, his hand over his face. It turned out that the tiny gold cross that Wes wore on his gold chain had flicked up as he let go of the ball and caught him in the eye.

Having made sure he was okay, Rev. Sheppard looked at the chastened fast bowler and said, 'Remember Wesley, the good Lord always looks after his own.'

Rev. Sheppard went on to make 94, while Wes never again wore that cross. Ironically, years later, the fast man became a lay preacher.

When people talk of the great fast bowlers of cricket history, Wes Hall must be up there near the top of the list. His career record of 192 wickets in 48 Tests is enough to give him that honour, but it is even more remarkable when you consider that for his first 23 Tests, between 1958 and 1962, in which he took 116 wickets at just 21.87, he carried the West Indies attack on his mighty shoulders. He was the only fast bowler in the team until Charlie Griffith burst on the scene in England in 1963. His remarkable stamina alone astounded us that first summer we saw him—it was not just a matter of seeing him out for four or five overs and taking advantage of what would follow. He was used unmercifully for the first four Tests by Frank Worrell but never once, even when weak from injuries, did he shirk his duties. Just how many more wickets he might have taken, if only he had had more adequate support from the other end, is open to conjecture. Undoubtedly, it would have been many.

Pace alone was not the sole reason for Wes's success. His magnificent action allowed him, when he kept the ball up, to also bowl a wicked outswinger, an unplayable ball for a man of such pace. He also had the uncanny ability to get the ball to kick up higher from a good length than any bowler I have seen. I recall no less an authority than Sir Donald Bradman stating during that 1960–61 series that no one, in his experience, was able to extract the same lift from a good length as Wes Hall.

There was nothing subtle about Big Wes. He was a genuine express bowler, a man who solved all problems by sheer pace and ferocity. There were never any half-measures with him, particularly if he got the flow into his run-up that he wanted.

Occasionally, though, he struggled to get that run-up right. Very early on, I picked that invariably when he was in full flight I would get an extremely rapid ball that pitched short of a length. If he missed his run-up, however, he had a tendency to overpitch and I waited on this moment, to get onto the front foot and spank him through the covers. It didn't happen often, but it did happen, though sometimes it didn't work out as I'd envisaged, and I have a reminder of this hanging on the wall of my study at home—a photograph of me pushing forward from the bottom half of my body, but at the same time trying to extract my head away from what is obviously a searing bouncer. Obviously, I had misjudged his intentions; having recognised a stutter in his approach to the wicket, I was endeavouring to get forward for the drive.

As a batsman, Wes's every stroke—even every movement—was exaggerated. He came over as clownish as he took great joy from swinging wildly and exuberantly at deliveries, but he was often a deceptively dangerous clown. It is usually forgotten that in the Tied Test at the Gabba, as well as bowling heroically to take nine wickets and play a starring role in the last over drama, he scored

50 and 18 batting at No. 10. In the first innings, Wes and Gerry Alexander added 86 for the ninth wicket; in the second, he and Alf Valentine added 31 for the final wicket. By holding us up on that last morning (and then coming out to destroy the Australian top order) he set the stage for all that followed.

One day during the series, Wes went for a big, big drive, but things went wrong: the ball was struck by the very bottom of the bat and the blade disintegrated into ten pieces. The look of wonderment and amusement on the big man's face as he kept holding the handle but nothing else in his hands is one of my fondest memories. The Australian team was close to rolling around the ground with laughter. But that was one of the few times on the field that we had any reason to laugh at or with Wes Hall.

Such was his ferocity and pace with the ball that season that it is possible that I faced the fastest deliveries ever bowled. Only Jeff Thomson at Bridgetown in 1978 ranks up with Wes Hall's fastest. Wes was so quick when everything clicked that he could make his own pace and extract life from the deadest wicket. I believe he was at his most rapid on a dead SCG pitch—in those days a dull, grey, lifeless, spinner's paradise—and at the MCG on the final day of the Second Test. On the latter occasion, Australia needed just 67 runs for victory, after bowling the West Indies out for 181 and 233. As I went out to open the batting with Colin McDonald, and pondered our small target, I thought to myself, 'Well, Wes shouldn't be too interested today. He'll probably just go through the motions and save himself for the next game.'

How wrong I was. Apparently, Wes had told West Indies team manager Gerry Gomez, 'If you want to see fast bowling, you'd better keep an eye on me.' Very quickly, there were three Australian batsmen back in the pavilion, two to Hall, one to Chester Watson.

Wes found pace and lift I have never seen equalled, extracting this venom from a wicket that our fast bowlers had struggled to obtain any life from. He bowled unchanged, undaunted, and never at any time looked like dropping below a near-lethal pace. In the end, the fire of Wes Hall was dampened a little that season—not from any reduction in his desire, but through overwork and some nagging injuries. By the last Test he was almost bowling off one leg and a shorter run, but was still able to get the odd ball to fly.

I suppose Wes and I did have some onfield 'feuds' going, both in Australia in 1960–61 and in the Caribbean in 1965. At the MCG in 1960–61 I managed to hit 27 off him in two overs. But I also remember that at one stage during the Tasmanian Combined XI game in Hobart, Alf Valentine, the excellent left-hand Jamaican spinner, strolled up to Gerry Connor, the batsman at the other end, and whispered, 'Man, don't go down that end, there's a war on!' Gerry obviously took that suggestion to heart, because he seemed more than happy to remain at the bowler's end. But on that occasion, and after all the other fierce encounters, our relationship was always one of mutual respect on the track and one of great friendship off it. We occasionally played in the same team together away from the conflict of the Test arena, and I always enjoyed this immensely. Whenever I have travelled to the West Indies, he has always been the first to invite me to his home and to show the hospitality with which he has become synonymous.

One of the most impressive aspects to Wes Hall's life in cricket has been the responsible attitude he has always displayed towards the game. Even with the adulation and hero worship he has received from all corners of the cricket world, he has never lost the humility that seems to be the hallmark of so many fine people. I have no doubt that as great as he was a fast bowler, he is an even greater human being. He is a man of immense kindness and is gentle to a fault . . . but only off the field! I will never forget him, back in the early 1960s, cuddling my daughter Kim when she was only a baby, at a time when out in the middle it seemed he was always trying to knock my block off. I often wondered how the fans would reconcile his fiery on-field persona with this fun-filled man cuddling a tiny figure into his massive but very gentle frame.

5

BOYS ON TOUR

We often travelled by train in England when we toured there in 1961 and the programming was so tight that there were times when the first two days would start early so day three could finish early so we could catch the train to the next venue. And there was some horrendous travelling; sometimes we crisscrossed the country instead of just hopping from a county to the one next door. And the tour didn't end with the final Test; instead we played Essex and Hampshire, a match against the 'Gentlemen of England' at Lord's, two festival matches, and concluded the tour with a game against the Minor Counties at Newcastle and finally a game in Scotland and two matches in Ireland. The first of these festival games was at Hastings on the south coast, and then we headed for Scarborough in Yorkshire, where we played the following day. To do this last trick, the third day at Hastings ended at 4 p.m., and we hopped on a coach to London so we could catch the train to York. When we arrived there in the early hours, they unclipped our carriage and left us in a siding so we could get some sleep. At 7 a.m. we were woken for breakfast and then we caught the bus to Scarborough, where we fielded first in front of 15,000 people and John Edrich and Peter May scored centuries. We ended up winning that game by three wickets, after 1499 runs were scored in three days. The next day we were at Newcastle, again fielding on the opening day.

The travelling could be arduous but it also brought the boys closer together. Ken Mackay, much better known as 'Slasher' because of his often negative play on the field, was just wonderful, particularly with the more inexperienced players. No one ever told him that he was in charge of the young blokes but that's the way it was, and it meant that some problems that had apparently occurred with previous Australian teams in England, where the younger players were made to feel a little alienated, did not occur. I was one of the group who spent most of our time going out to dinner with Slash, who was a man who loved the movies, Elvis, and talking cricket. On the field, he had a terrible batting style and was an ugly bowler, but still he made himself into a vital and very popular member of the Australian team. His courage is typified by the fact that when he and Lindsay Kline batted for almost the entire last session in Adelaide earlier that year to draw the Fourth Test against Frank Worrell's West Indians, Slash took the last ball of the game, a riser from big Wes Hall, on the chest rather than risk lobbing a catch to one of the close fielders. His skill was probably best seen in South Africa in 1957–58, when he topped the batting averages and confounded their star off-spinner Hugh Tayfield so thoroughly that the whole team's dread of quality spin bowling was swept away.

Neil Harvey was on his fourth Ashes tour, and you'd have to go a long way to find someone who loved London more than he did. Harv had a list of contacts from his previous tours, so he was able to get us tickets to many of the London shows, and if he couldn't help there were high-flyers from the Lord's Taverners who were eager to be of assistance. On one occasion, not only were we invited to the London Palladium, we were actually introduced, one at a time, from the stage; our names were read out, and we stood up, turned, gently bowed and sat down hoping we'd performed the formalities right. Everything seemed to be going well until they introduced our manager, Mr Sydney George Webb QC from Sydney. Syd stood up, turned, bowed and as he did so Bill Lawry dropped a fart cushion on his seat. The entire audience broke up after they saw the reaction of the team, but for Syd it was merely water off a duck's back.

'Bloody Lawry,' our manager would often moan—unless he was crying, 'Bloody Misson!' One day we arrived at Kings Cross Station to catch a train to some county game, and there was a notice positioned prominently: 'Would Mr Sydney Webb, manager of the Australian cricket team, please report to the station master.' Syd was very pleased, explaining that clearly we were going to get the 'VIP treatment'. Like a colony of penguins, we followed Syd to find the station manager, but when we finally got there none of the station staff knew anything about it. I think they might even have reprised that joke before Syd wised up.

The most celebrated con occurred at Clarence House, home of the Queen Mother. It was a small affair, just the members of the England side, our squad, a number of officials, and a few members of the Royal Family, including the Queen, Prince Philip and Princess Margaret. Most of the chat was about horses, which I know nothing about, and I ended up having a very long conversation with Lord Snowdon, who seemed to be no fan of the racetrack either.

Near the end of the night, Frankie Misson decided that the royal spoons would be safer in the manager's pocket. Soon after, just before the function was due to end, Frank took it upon himself to explain to the Queen Mother that our manager had a habit of souveniring things to which he wasn't entitled. Her Royal Highness twigged straight away. When it came time for our farewell, the mood was formal as we lined up, one man next to the other, before saying, 'Thank you Ma'am, we've had a wonderful evening,' as we bowed and left the room. Soon it was Syd's turn, and quite beautifully he added to his farewell, 'I only wish, Ma'am, we had something more tangible to remember the night.'

With a smile, the Queen Mother replied, 'Well I believe you may well have that something in your pocket.'

Sydney George Webb QC put his hand in the pocket of his suit, sheepishly pulled out the cutlery, and I swear you could see him mouth the words 'Lawry' and 'Misson' through gritted teeth.

Syd had a very stylish crocodile-skin briefcase that he used to carry everywhere, except for the two days on tour when he was terribly flustered because he couldn't find it. No one was going to tell him that it was on a hook on the dressing-room ceiling, about four metres from the floor. I don't know how Frank and Bill got it up there, but there was no question that Syd was both relieved and exasperated when he finally found it. Fortunately, it never took long for any displeasure to settle, and at the end of the trip Syd thanked Bill and Frank for making him feel part of the team. He got into a bit of a power play with Richie on that tour, as the two argued over who should be talking to the media about official tour matters. However, though I'm not exactly sure what the controversy was about, my memory is that most of the players sided with Syd in his battle with Richie. I thought he was just a nice man. After we returned to Australia, I wouldn't know how many members of that team Syd helped with their legal matters. As far as he was concerned, they were forever part of his family. He was marvellous to us, though we'd given him hell.

•

A bit more than two years later, after Ian Meckiff was no-balled for throwing at the start of South Africa's first innings of the First

Test of 1963–64, in Brisbane, there was a lot of criticism of Richie for not bowling Ian at the other end. It reached the point that our captain received death threats, and we needed a police escort to get to and from the ground.

Late in the Test there was a rain delay, so we were all off the field. Unbeknown to the rest of us, Bill Lawry had purchased a pistol replica (and the caps to go with it) from a nearby joke shop. In those days at the Gabba, next to the dressing room was a nice little area where we had our meals, and everyone was sitting in there waiting for the match to restart, just having a cup of tea and a yarn. Bill, meanwhile, had asked our masseur, a bloke called Jock, to help him out. He gave Jock the pistol and a copy of the Melbourne sports newspaper, *The Sporting Globe*, which carried a boldly headlined front-page story asking why Meckiff hadn't been bowled from both ends. Jock fronted Richie, calling him a bastard for not doing as the *Globe* (and plenty of others) wanted, but Richie was only half-interested until he noticed the gun hidden under the paper. Jock fired it maybe three times, and the captain jumped at least a mile while one of his opening batsmen was laughing uproariously in the background.

Perhaps Bill's biggest coup came in Richie's farewell Test match, later in that summer of 1963–64. By this stage, I was the captain, Richie having stood down earlier in the series. Now to appreciate this story you need to know that Richie is a very fastidious man. When he entered the dressing room in his playing days he would invariably remove his jacket first and put it on a coat-hanger. Then his tie would come off, to be placed neatly over the jacket. Then the shirt, which went onto a separate coat-hanger. His trousers would be slipped smoothly onto a third coat-hanger, while his socks were turned inside out and then folded together and placed on the bench in his locker. His expensive slip-on leather shoes were placed below his seat—not under, but left out just a little so that later, after practice or the day's play, he could step straight into them.

It was during Richie's last practice with the team that Bill said to me, 'Simmo, do you mind if I slip off just a bit early?'

I said, 'No Phanto, what's up?'

Bill was called 'Phantom' because of his liking for the comic hero. 'You'll see, skipper,' he said quietly, 'you'll see.'

'Okay,' I said. 'Away you go.'

I knew he was up to some sort of mischief, and watched as he headed not for the home dressing room in the Members Stand, but for the groundsman's room. There, he found for himself two six-inch nails and a hammer. Then he returned to the rooms, where he hammered the nails through the heels of Richie's shoes and into the wooden floor.

After practice, Richie had his shower and then his post-practice routine began. Once he had towelled himself dry, the shirt would go on first, then the underpants, then the trousers. Everything was just where it was supposed to be. Then he sat down . . . one sock on, then the other . . . and then he slipped into his shoes . . . stood up . . . and he wasn't going anywhere.

Usually unflappable, he tried to get moving without anyone noticing, but it was no use, by this stage the whole team was in on the joke. As the room filled with laughter, all he could do was mutter, 'Bloody Lawry!'

Sydney George Webb QC would have been proud of him.

6

THE GRIZ AND THE FAV

'I don't know what you think of Simmo, and I don't care. He has been appointed captain and as such he has my total loyalty and support.'

That was how the first team meeting after my appointment as captain of Australia during the 1963–64 series against South Africa began. The speaker of those words was Wally Grout.

For me, they capture the personality, dedication and spirit of the great wicketkeeper. Straightforward, sometimes blunt, Wally seldom left anyone in doubt about his feelings. His toughness and loyalty to Australian cricket and his mates was legendary, and he was the first person in my experience to make 'never give a sucker (particularly if he's a keeper) an even break' his sporting creed.

Wally's nickname was 'Griz', short for the 'Grizzling Grunter'. Despite this, to his mates he was an ideal travelling companion who enjoyed life to its fullest. He was also as quick with his tongue as with his gloves, as he amply demonstrated one day in South Africa in 1957–58. In the Third Test, at Durban, during a very long and tedious partnership between Jackie McGlew and John Waite, suddenly there was a burst of applause for some inexplicable reason. McGlew turned around to Wally, who was standing over the stumps, and in a quizzical tone suggested that some sort of record must have been established.

'I bet it was a long-playing one,' the Griz muttered. This was his third Test, though he was ten months past his 30th birthday and had first played Sheffield Shield cricket way back in December 1946. For many years in Queensland, he'd been understudy to Australia's No. 1 keeper, Don Tallon, and even when he was picked for South Africa, after Gil Langley retired, he was no certainty for the Test team. Legend has it that the choice for the keeper's spot between Grout and South Australia's Barry Jarman in the First Test came down to one vote, that of his state comrade Peter Burge, who was the third selector on tour. Skipper Ian Craig preferred Barry, vice-captain Neil Harvey went for Wally, and Peter eventually chose Wally, not because they were both 'banana benders' but because he thought Wally was fractionally superior keeping to the spinners, and with Richie expected to do a lot of bowling that was important. Wally promptly set a new Test record by taking six catches in the home team's second innings of the Johannesburg game, four of them from Alan Davidson's bowling, and poor Barry didn't get a chance to be his country's first-choice keeper until after Wally retired nearly a decade later.

Again in South Africa, this time at the Kruger National Game Park, we were stopped by other tourists and asked rather abruptly whether we had seen any lions. The Griz quickly replied: 'Yeah, two beauties about a mile back.' As the grateful group reversed their jeep and scurried away in a cloud of dust, hot in pursuit of their cherished quarry, we said to Wally: 'What goes on? We haven't seen any lions?'

'Not true,' he snorted. 'We passed over two railway lines back down the road.'

Based purely on glovework, Wally Grout was the best wicket-keeper I have ever seen. I say this not living in the past and with due respect to men such as Alan Knott, Rod Marsh and Ian Healy, who I admired tremendously. Grout, however, was a freak and his instinct for the impossible was legendary among his team-mates. His ability to make difficult catches look so easy often masked his phenomenal skill, while his only concession to showmanship was that, after bringing off a brilliant catch, he'd offer a twirl of the arm as he gleefully threw the ball in the air.

For me, three catches best demonstrated his greatness. The first was when he held a nick from the West Indies' Conrad Hunte at the Melbourne Cricket Ground in the second innings in 1960–61, taken after Hunte, who was past his hundred, tried to slash a head-high full toss from Norman O'Neill through point. He got a faint edge, and Wally, who was standing close to the stumps, took it cleanly.

The second great catch occurred at Karachi in 1964. After a tough tour of England we had to battle through a four-Test program—three in India and one against Pakistan—on the way home. Wally suffered a hairline fracture of his jaw in the First Test against India, at Madras, and missed the following two Tests. Then, on the opening day in Karachi, we took a hiding, with the Pakistan openers breaking record after record, a wicket not falling until Abdul Kadir was run out for 95 in the last hour of the day, with the score just one run short of 250. Another wicket fell at 266, but 'Billy' Ibadulla looked like he was going to bat forever, and when Graham McKenzie wearily began the final over of the day, Ibadulla was 166 not out, and all we could think about was getting off the field and having a good lie down. Perhaps not surprisingly, Graham's line was astray, he drifted one onto Ibadulla's pads and the

Pakistani opener glanced one off the full face of the bat. He must have thought he'd finish the day unbeaten on 170, but Wally flung himself wide down the leg-side to bring off a one-handed blinder. He might have been nearly 38 and nursing a recently cracked jaw, but he still had the drive not to give any sucker—least of all a bloke who'd batted all day in front of him—an even break.

His third great catch occurred in Adelaide in 1965–66, when England's Colin Cowdrey propped forward and inside-edged Keith Stackpole's quick top-spinner onto the flap of his pad, from where it flew up shoulder-high to Wally, who nonchalantly accepted the catch standing over the stumps. If anything the ball was keeping a bit low on this fourth day, and Cowdrey had been out there for two-and-a-half hours for just 35, as he tried to force a draw. I thought this was the greatest wicketkeeping catch I ever saw, because it required lightning-fast reflexes and beautiful quick, soft hands. I'm not even sure Wally would have had a clear view of the ball as it took the edge. It all happened so quickly, yet Wally made it look so simple that the press of the day described it as an 'easy' catch.

Describing Wally as an 'athlete' is a little difficult. He wasn't a natural at anything other than wicketkeeping, and running a lap in quick time was a marathon. Yet the transformation when he put on his keeping gloves was amazing. Standing back, he covered an incredible amount of ground, and he expected his slip fielders to do the same. I quickly learnt to give him room and though he was often accused of stealing from me, we had an agreement: first in best dressed. He might have 'poached' a couple over the years, but I can't remember him missing any that I would have caught. One day at Lord's, a batsman top-edged a hook over Wally's head, and I knew instinctively that as the first slip I was the closest to where the skier was going to land. I took off as fast as I could, ran about 20 or 30 metres, took the catch, and was then astonished to find our keeper right behind me. I fancied my pace, but Wally had kept up with me!

While he was brilliant standing back, over the stumps he was fantastic. Peter Burge knew his man when he voted for him before that Jo'burg Test all those years ago. Wally's stumping capability on both sides of the wicket was safe, sure and bullet-fast. He was also a magnificent reader of the game, and the help he offered to Ian Craig, Richie Benaud and myself when we were Test captains was enormous. His death, less than three years after his farewell Test, was a tragedy. We had sensed that he'd experienced some health problems in the West Indies in 1965, but nothing prepared me for the news in November 1968 that he had passed away. I'd always thought he was indestructible.

•

Wally Grout was wicketkeeping in a Test at Madras in 1964, when one of the funnier lines I heard during my Test career was delivered. On the final day, the Indian batsmen were struggling to save the game and one of them, Hanumant Singh, the Prince of Banswara, was going along very slowly. He seemed to be getting a lot of help from the umpires, who were certainly treating this man of Indian royalty with the utmost respect. At one point, a special team-mate of ours named Johnny Martin was refused an obvious out, when an appeal for a clear gloved catch to me at slip was turned down, and for a brief moment he was totally exasperated. Then he turned and quipped down the wicket, 'Hanumant, if my name was Sir John Martin you'd have been out long ago!'

Everything Johnny said and did had a happy feel. Of all the cricketers I ever met, no one graced their sport and life with a greater love, humility or zest than Johnny Martin.

Johnny's nickname was the 'Fav', short for the 'Favourite'. His team-mates actually bestowed the name on him after a long-time New South Wales selector named Albert Vincent was heard to remark to a bystander, 'That little Johnny Martin is a particular favourite of mine.' Of course, Australian cricketers being Australian cricketers, that was enough for the ribbing to start, and even though his new moniker was conferred on him in a facetious manner, I think everyone realised that no one could have named him better.

Johnny was one of those rare characters who entered his sport with an almost naive love and enthusiasm for it and never lost it.

I first met him in 1954 when he came down from a tiny New South Wales hamlet called Burrell Creek to try out for my grade club Petersham–Marrickville. We quickly learned that Burrell Creek is located about 30 kilometres from Taree, with a population that, back in Johnny's day, seemed to vary between one and 100— according to the story he was telling at the time. His reputation as a big hitter and an unorthodox 'chinaman' bowler had preceded him, and as he approached the nets with his bow-legged rolling gait I remember thinking that I had never seen any one so obviously from the bush. But he bubbled with enthusiasm and confidence, and after he bowled just one delivery, I knew that here was a rough but rare diamond in the making.

His unusual ability won him immediate selection in our first-grade team and started for me a cherished friendship as we both battled our way up the cricket ladder.

While bowling was his forte, batting and the hitting of sixes, I was soon to find out, was his passion. In just the second match of that summer, he blasted several out of the ground, but what was intriguing afterwards was discovering that he was keeping count: he knew exactly how many sixes he'd hit to that point in his career.

He never changed. My first question to the Fav was always, 'How many?' He would always quickly tell me, then give me the rundown as to how he'd added to his tally.

Sometimes that tally increased rapidly. Pound for pound he was one of the biggest hitters I have seen, with perhaps his most enormous tonk being the one that deposited a ball from Western Australian leg-spinner John Rutherford onto the roof of the old Bob Stand at the Sydney Cricket Ground in November 1957. Old-timers afterwards reckoned it was one of the biggest hits ever seen at the SCG. I didn't see it, because I was in South Africa with the Australian team, but we heard about it soon enough. It was one of those sixes so huge and so memorable that people kept talking about it. Another time, in a grade match at Pratten Park in Sydney, he put Alan Davidson into the backyard of one of the houses that bordered the ground, clearing the actual boundary fence by a long, long way. I think Garry Sobers was the only other bloke who hit Davo that far.

Johnny's batting was thrilling and entertaining, but it was his uncanny bowling ability that soon won him acclaim. With a jaunty, longer than normal run-up, he had a superb action for a spinner. He gave the ball a real tweak and his sharp spin and beautiful flight meant he had the rare ability to dismiss any batsman at any time. He made his first Test appearance at the MCG in the Second Test of 1960–61, against the West Indies, and marked his debut by taking three wickets in four balls. And not just any wickets: Rohan Kanhai misread the left-hander's wrong 'un and skied a catch to Frank Misson; then Garry Sobers edged a catch to me at slip; two balls later, Frank Worrell was undone by another wrong 'un and I had my second catch of the innings. Earlier, in our first innings, Johnny had come in at No. 10 and added 97 with Ken

Mackay, making 55 himself, including a six off Worrell to bring up his fifty that cleared the longest boundary at the ground. He was actually dismissed going for another big hit soon after Slasher was bowled by Sonny Ramadhin, which left Misson undefeated on 0, and afterwards Johnny was asked why he'd thrown his knock away. Frankie had never been dismissed by the West Indies, he explained, and he didn't want to upset his record!

A little-known fact from that great series was that Johnny played in three Tests, and Lindsay Kline, who also bowled chinaman, appeared in the other two. But Lindsay's two Tests were the most famous ones—the Tied Test in Brisbane, when he played the shot to Joe Solomon that led to Ian Meckiff being run out, and the draw in Adelaide, when he batted with Slasher for 100 minutes to save the game. Johnny took 43 first-class wickets that season to Lindsay's 32, but the Victorian was preferred when the selectors picked the team to go to England. Johnny had to wait until 1964 before he got his Ashes tour.

His record in first-class cricket was excellent. Only six bowlers have taken more first-class wickets for New South Wales than Johnny's 293—Greg Matthews, Geoff Lawson, Arthur Mailey, Bill O'Reilly, Richie Benaud and Mike Whitney. He played only eight Tests, but I think he was unlucky, in part because Richie, obviously, was in front of him but also because he was seen to have the 'the wrong style'. Chinaman bowlers have always been seen as loose cannons of a kind—a point accentuated during the early 1960s because Richie was always super-accurate—so he was never allowed to achieve his full potential at the highest level. Johnny was one of the old-fashioned spinners who gave the ball air and lured his victims into indiscretion; he was also a bloke who liked to test his skills against the opponents and, at the same time, have some fun.

I will always recall his skills with much admiration, but the thing I think of first when I remember Johnny is his bubbling personality. He was the ideal tourist—always ready with a song, a terrible and generally corny joke, or the right word of encouragement at the appropriate time. If he was lumbered with the job of 12th man he was superb. After the toughest and darkest session, the players looked forward to returning to the room and to the encouragement of Little Johnny. He always met the team at the door with a cheeky grin, his fingers laden with the favourite lit cigarettes of the smokers (right brand to the right bloke). Behind him, everyone's preference in drink had been neatly lined up as well.

On tour, he endeared himself to everyone and enjoyed immensely being introduced as the 'Mayor of Burrell Creek'. For me, Johnny and that little village will be forever linked. For one cricket season, so he wouldn't have to catch the overnight mail train down every weekend to play grade cricket, he'd found a job in the city, but he couldn't settle and soon went back to his old ways. In 1958–59, he moved to South Australia, so he wouldn't have to compete with Richie for overs when playing for New South Wales, but that didn't work out either: he was always drawn back home. One of my fondest memories of the 1964 Ashes tour was introducing the team to a distinguished audience at a swank luncheon for nearly 1000 people at the Savoy Hotel in London. There was royalty (including the Duke of Edinburgh), knights of the realm, high-ranking ex-military officers, well-known sportsmen, prominent actors and politicians of all persuasions there, and Johnny, who was no giant, brought the house down when he climbed up on the table with a huge grin so he could acknowledge the applause after I asked him to stand on a chair so everyone could see him. As he said later, with a hint of a grin, 'Not bad, eh, for a boy from Burrell Creek?' He was the first to call thirteen years later, to offer encouragement after I announced that I was returning to Test Cricket during the World Series Cricket years, and he promptly offered his services as well. He was still taking wickets and hitting sixes up at Burrell Creek, so why not?

The Fav had a couple of heart attacks, one in 1971 when he was just 40, the second in 1984. When I saw him not long after the second attack, he was his usual whimsical self, thrusting his spinning finger at me and quipping, 'Not bad, eh, Simmo—50,000 overs without a rebore!' I couldn't help thinking how unfair it was that his finger didn't need any attention, but his heart, the biggest part of him, apparently did. He died eight years later, way too early, aged just 60. I don't know if St Peter asked him how many sixes he'd hit when Johnny made it to the Pearly Gates, but if he did Johnny would have known, and it would have been plenty. And in no time, I'm sure, he'd have been one of St Peter's Favourites.

7

UMPIRES, WET AND DRY

As well as being one of the greatest games in history, the famous Tied Test at the Gabba in 1960–61 was also a very important Test for me—my first game back on the international scene after almost two years in the 'wilderness'. It was just as significant a game for another fellow who would see a lot more Test cricket through the 1960s—umpire Colin Egar. This was Colin's Test debut, an amazing way to start. He was at the bowler's end for the final over, but even though three wickets fell in the space of six balls he didn't have to make a decision, with Richie Benaud walking after he was caught behind off the second delivery of the over, and then Wally Grout and Ian Meckiff were run out at the keeper's end.

One of the most famous stories to come out of that last over is of Frank Worrell walking back with Wes Hall, as Big Wes prepared to bowl to Lindsay Kline. There were a maximum of two balls left to be bowled, the scores were level, and our last pair was at the wicket. 'Remember, Wes,' Worrell is reputed to have said, 'if you bowl a no-ball, you'll never be able to go back to Barbados.' Wes was so startled he made sure he put his back foot a good yard behind the crease, which would have pleased Colin Egar. Imagine the pressure this Test debutant would have been under! What if Wes had overstepped? Imagine a dramatic Test like that ending with the ultimate anticlimax—a no-ball call from some umpire few people had heard of—and no slow-motion replay to show whether the umpire got it right. Actually, what would have happened is that everyone would have assumed Colin knew what he was doing, and backed him 100 per cent. In the years to come, Colin would confirm that he was exactly the right person to be at the bowler's end for that incredible final over.

Colin was the first and one of the very few umpires of my experience who actually attended net practices—and not just as a casual observer. He was there to spend a couple of hours standing at the bowler's end. He even did this one day after he had retired, because he'd been invited to officiate in a 'veterans' series. When I asked him why, he replied, 'I need to get a bit of practice and the feel of things again.'

I thought then, and still think now, how wise and simple. Yet I have hardly seen an umpire before or since who was similarly inclined. Colin Egar's methods make so much sense to me. If more umpires went to practice, they'd gain the feel and instinct for what will happen out in the middle. Another benefit would be that the players would appreciate their input. If an umpire at practice said to a bowler, 'I'd be no-balling you for overstepping if you bowled like that in a match,' the bowler would be mad not to pay attention.

Over the years, one of the difficulties I have noticed with umpires—even at the highest level—is that they have a problem in understanding the mechanics of the game. Decisions are made that knowledgeable observers know instinctively cannot possibly be right. A classic example of this comes when a left-handed batsman is given out lbw to a right-handed off-spinner bowling from around the wicket. This bowler really has only two chances of achieving such a decision: one, if the ball pitches on the middle and leg stump, the batsman goes back and the ball straightens; two, if the batsman doesn't offer a shot and the ball doesn't straighten but continues on before it hits the pads. Otherwise, in this situation, it is technically impossible to give the batsman out lbw. Yet, too often, umpires shoot the finger up without proper consideration or because they don't understand the simple mathematics of angles. If they had trained at the nets with the players, life would be much easier for them.

Instead, as I understand it, only Simon Taufel among current umpires attends players' practice sessions. The others study their rule books, attend blackboard lectures and pass their examinations. Practical experience is gained only in the middle, when the pressure is always on. How much easier it would be if Colin Egar's methods were adopted. The umpires could then gain a better appreciation of what umpiring truly involves, without the stresses that come from the players' constant appeals.

Of course, many umpires handle that responsibility well, but not all of them. I remember the umpires we had in a match in the West Indies in 1978 who fell into that latter category. For two days in Grenada, we played on a wicket that could only be described as a minefield. It exploded almost every delivery and the score after the second day was two broken hands, numerous bruises and countless abrasions. On the third morning, the match was delayed after water seeped through the covers. Damp spots were evident, but the run-ups and footholds were dry and in my opinion—and not just because we were bowling—the wicket was fit for play.

Finally, after two inspections by the umpires but no resumption in play, I expressed the view that the wet spots shouldn't stop play resuming. 'Oh no, Mr Simpson,' one of them replied, 'it is not the wet spots that worry us but the dry spots around them.'

Thirteen years earlier, in Kingston, Jamaica, we ran into an umpire named Owen Davies—a Welshman by birth and the manager of a local banana plantation—during the First Test. As was the policy in the Caribbean at that time, there were two 'home' umpires officiating; it wasn't a question of appointing the two best umpires in the West Indies, rather the two best umpires from Jamaica. Mr Davies was one of those two umpires.

We were playing under the new no-ball rule, whereby no part of the front foot was allowed to touch or go over the popping crease. This rule had been brought in essentially to prevent bowlers from 'dragging' their back foot over the bowling crease as they delivered the ball. (The bowling crease is the line on the pitch through the centres of the three stumps at the non-striker's end. The popping crease runs parallel with the bowling crease, four feet or 122 centimetres in front of it.)

From our side-on position in the pavilion, we could see that the front feet of Wes Hall and Charlie Griffith were landing at least a foot in front of the popping crease. We asked the umpires to have a look at it, but nothing changed. Eventually, it was the usually mild-mannered Brian Booth, our vice-captain, who fronted Owen Davies to remind him firmly that we were playing under the new no-ball rule. 'I know we are,' the ump told Brian. 'But I'm not bothering about it. I think it's an unfair rule.'

Later in the same tour, the Australian team travelled to British Guiana (now Guyana) for the Third Test, and arrived to find that the local umpires were on strike, because only one of their members had been selected to officiate in the Test. The view across most of the Caribbean was that there weren't two umpires in British Guiana good enough for Test cricket. Consequently, the most experienced umpire in the West Indies, Cortez Jordan from Barbados, had been brought over. But the locals wouldn't cop Jordan, and officials from the British Guiana Umpires' Association instructed their man, Cecil Kippins (who had Test experience and would actually stand in the last two games of this series), to boycott the Test.

This decision was confirmed less than 24 hours before the Test, at which time I was told it would be possible to get someone from nearby Trinidad, but that there was no longer time to bring in Douglas Sang Hue—probably the best umpire in the Caribbean—from Jamaica. With all this in mind, I gave the authorities a list of umpires we would accept and identified just one man who we said was unsuitable. In the meantime, just in case the Trinidad umpire couldn't make it on time, it was agreed that the former West Indies captain Gerry Gomez—who was then a West Indies selector and a member of the West Indies Cricket Board, and had managed the West Indies team in Australia in 1960–61—would be named as the 'stand-in umpire' who would officiate until the man from Trinidad arrived. Gomez had an umpire's certificate, but had never stood in a first-class game. He was also working as a radio commentator, providing summaries after each day's play.

Next morning, I was amazed when I arrived at the ground and was greeted by umpire Jordan and by the fellow we had said was unsuitable. I headed quick smart for the local officials, who explained that none of the other umpires could be found in time, so we'd have to make do with the umpires now on hand. That was totally unacceptable, we explained firmly, and the compromise was that Gomez, who I knew as an honourable man, would stand for the entire Test. I'm fairly sure this provided the only instance of a Test umpire, at the end of the day and while still in his umpire's kit, vaulting the fence so he could offer his opinion of the day's play to his radio audience. As it turned out, we lost the game, but no fault could be found in the performance of umpire Gomez.

In South Africa in 1966–67 we found that the local umpires were under enormous pressure. So much pride was placed in a home-town victory—as if this were some sort of affirmation of the worth of their political system and way of life—that it proved too much for some umpires. I felt the umpires on that tour were some of the worst I ever encountered during my international career. The great irony was that the worst decision of the whole series went our way, when Mike Procter was given out lbw in the Fourth Test. If there had been another set of stumps next to the ones that were there, the ball still wouldn't have hit the wicket.

In the Fourth Test in Johannesburg, with South Africa leading the five-match series 2–1, we were losing. After two days, we'd be dismissed for 143 and South Africa were 7–266 in reply, with their wicketkeeper Denis Lindsay, who was in magnificent form, 111 not out. After a rest day, we woke on the Monday morning to find that it had been raining for much of the night and the ground was saturated. There seemed little chance of any play being possible for the day. The rain cleared in the late morning, and there was an inspection at noon, after which the local ground officials opened the gates and let the spectators in, even though the umps had said they wouldn't even look at the pitch again until 3 p.m. With the prospect of a South African victory pretty strong, if not that day then definitely the next, a crowd of over 14,000 was soon ensconced in the stands, with many of them heading straight to the bar. The pressure to get play underway began to build.

Eventually, at 4 p.m., play resumed. Without doubt, this was the wettest Test field I ever saw—when our slip cordon took up its position, our boots were instantly covered in mud and water went up to our ankles. Facetiously, I regret to say, I asked the umpire to get some more sawdust (plenty had already been brought out for the bowlers) so we could build mounds so that our fieldsmen could at least stand above the water level. Without a hint of embarrassment, the umpire said, 'Okay.' So back on came the sawdust man, and some of Australia's finest cricketers began building little sawdust castles before play could begin. The irony was that South Africa finished with a first-innings lead of 189 and Bill Lawry was bowled by Mike Procter before stumps, but the scheduled fourth day was washed out completely and on day five, with us just two wickets from an emphatic innings defeat, the rain came back and the Test was drawn.

Not all umpires have the skill or imagination of an official the Australian team encountered in India in 1969–70. After a confident appeal for a catch behind the wicket off John Gleeson's bowling, the umpire took a long time to make a decision. So long, in fact, that Gleeson, who thought it was a clear-cut decision, had to appeal him again. Still the umpire waited, until he finally gave the batsman out and then quickly apologised for the delay. The strong headwind Gleeson had been bowling into had slowed the noise of the snick reaching him.

But even this bloke wasn't as good as the umpire we ran into once when the New South Wales team was playing in the town of Cessnock, in the Hunter Valley a couple of hours north of Sydney, on the way north to play a Shield game in Brisbane. Late in the match, our captain Keith Miller threw the ball to Bill Watson. Now Bill was a fine opening batsman who played for Australia in the mid-1950s, but he couldn't bowl a hoop down George Street. Still, like most opening batsmen of that time, he fancied himself as a leg-spinner. Delighted to be finally able to show his wares, Watson offered up one of his slow 'donkey drops' and, to everyone's amazement, the batsman played back, missed and was struck on the pads. Delighted with this remarkable development, 'Blinks' (as he was nicknamed by Keith, who was fascinated by Bill's nervous blinking whenever he faced the bowling) shrieked an appeal.

After much deliberation the umpire shook his head. Not out! Poor Blinks couldn't believe it. 'Not out!' he cried. 'Good Lord, the batsman played back, it was my top-spinner (truth was, Blinks never spun the ball), it pitched on middle stump, hit the batsman below the knee and would have hit the middle stump halfway up. He must have been out!'

The umpire took another long look and said slowly, 'Granted Mr Watson, granted. But unfortunately the ball wasn't travelling fast enough to disturb the bails.'

If we had umpires like that today, there'd be no need for television replays or analysis from expert commentators.

8

STATISTICS AND THE DON

Statistics can tell many stories and not all of them are true, but it is impossible to argue with Sir Donald Bradman's cricket record. Just how good was he? A comparison with Allan Border, who when this book was published had scored more runs in Test cricket than any other Australian, offers some idea. The great AB scored 11,174 Test-match runs in 265 innings at an average of 50.56. The Don played 80 innings for 6996 runs at an average of 99.94. If he had played as many innings as Border and maintained his near-century average he would have scored well over 23,000 Test runs. Of course, such a comparison is an inexact science—perhaps if his workload was greater or he'd faced the same bowlers Allan did, Bradman might have slowed down a little. Then again, if he'd had more innings when at his absolute peak—say between 1930 and 1932 when he scored 2330 Test runs at 129.44—he might have scored even more.

The closest I ever came to seeing Bradman bat was in 1946–47, when my elder brother took me into the old Sheridan Stand at the Sydney Cricket Ground to watch the second day's play in the second Ashes Test. As we set off for the day, we knew that with England 8–219 overnight it was almost certain that the Australian captain would be batting at some stage, but then the clouds came over the ground and only an hour and a half of cricket was possible. My main memory is of the rain pouring down. Australia was 1–27 at stumps in reply to England's 255, and the following day, Bradman and Sid Barnes started a famous partnership that eventually added 405 for the fifth wicket. Both men were dismissed for 234. Sadly, the Simpson boys from Marrickville could only afford to attend one day of the Test and we had to make do with listening to this wonderful batting on the radio at home.

Today, The Don's remarkable career batting average, and his equally extraordinary ability to turn hundreds into double—and even triple—hundreds, still dominates the cricket record books. Given the volume of cricket these days, a number of players have scored more Test runs than Bradman, and Sachin Tendulkar, Sunil Gavaskar, Brian Lara, Steve Waugh and Ricky Ponting have scored more Test hundreds. But still no one has come close to his record twelve Test double centuries; no other Australian has done so on more than four occasions. However, it is not his cricket that I will remember most about him, but his open friendliness and generosity of spirit.

Sir Donald never lived in the past. 'We have had so many great cricketers,' he would say, 'but though we must treasure our heroes and friends of the past, we must also respect and enjoy the talents of the present, for they will be the future heroes and icons.' He was a generous marker of modern cricketers and always argued that a champion of one era would be a champion of any era.

I first met Sir Donald in 1954, when Keith Miller brought him into the New South Wales dressing room at Adelaide Oval. Of course, he was a demigod to an impressionable 17-year-old such as me, so I was awestruck, and battled to say more than 'Yes, Sir' or 'No, Sir'. I remember him congratulating me on being selected for first-class cricket at such a young age and wishing me well in my career. I recall, too, being very impressed by the serene confidence he possessed as he mixed with men he had once played with, such as Miller, Arthur Morris and Ray Lindwall, and also youngsters such as Ian Craig and me. What struck me most, though, was that he seemed so small alongside Keith Miller.

As my career progressed and I made the Australian team I was able to benefit greatly from Sir Donald's counselling. In 1958–59, I was in and out of the Test team, and during the Sydney Test, when I was 12th man, I spent a lot of time talking to him in the dressing room as we watched the cricket. In those days, the only people in the room when the team was fielding were the 12th man, a masseur or physio, and the room attendant. So when, as he had previously arranged with our captain Richie Benaud, he came into the room before lunch or tea to see whether Richie wanted to meet with him during the break, it was a wonderful opportunity for me to have a chat. As I would discover often over the years, Sir Donald was always happy to talk cricket, and we chatted every day during that Test. This was more than enough time for me to gain an enormous respect for him as a judge of cricket and a man of vision and integrity. Here was a legend of the game, who was also an Australian selector and senior figure on the Australian Cricket Board of Control, but he would never have entered the room without seeking the captain's permission. I do remember as clearly today as I did then the answer he gave when I asked if he would score as many runs in the cricket of the late 1950s as he did in his day.

He took some time reflecting on the question, before replying, 'Yes, but it would take me longer to score the runs.' He then explained why, listing defensive bowling, better fieldsmen and poorer batting pitches as the main reasons. In his view, the batting surfaces of the 1930s were the best for scoring runs on. In comparison, many of the pitches of the 1950s were more uneven. This was typical Bradman. Whether you asked him a question in person, by phone or by letter, you always received a full and reasoned reply.

For a while, this was the last opportunity I had to spend time with the great man, as I was dropped from the Australian squad after this Test and didn't return until the celebrated series against Frank Worrell's West Indies team in 1960–61, after I turned myself into an opening batsman. During this time the question of bowlers throwing rather than bowling had become one of the most debated issues in cricket, and in Adelaide during that 'Calypso Summer' I was one of a group of Australian players invited to dinner at Sir Donald's home. It was a typical cricket night, until our host produced a hand-wound projector on which he had ready to show us a compilation of the run-ups and deliveries of a number of bowlers, both past and present, whom he believed had problems with their actions. I'm not sure if I had ever watched slow-motion replays before. I came to learn that this was typical Bradman. He had prepared instructive and telling evidence to back his judgement that cricket did have a chucking problem, and his desire that those with illegal actions be forced to fix their problems or be thrown out of the game. Sir Donald was a stickler for the laws of cricket and felt strongly about them being flaunted.

I have no doubt it was at this evening, as Sir Donald unravelled for me the mysteries of a bowler's action, that my strong views and knowledge about illegal-action bowling were formed. I had many evenings such as this over the years with Sir Donald and his wife Jessie, and never came away from any of them without having learnt a little more about cricket and life.

Our relationship became closer when I was appointed Australian captain. He was still the chairman of selectors, so we spent more time together and I was allowed to share more confidences. However, once the team sheet was handed over, Bradman believed the captain was in charge. He would always make himself available at lunch or tea, but if you didn't want to discuss anything he would leave the team alone to take his own meals. It was this type of non-intrusiveness that made him so respected and appreciated by the team.

Over the years, there was some media speculation that he was too aloof. From my experience, this couldn't be further from the truth. Sure, he wasn't one to barge in and impose his views on you, but if you asked he was as generous and helpful a person as I have ever known.

At the same time, he didn't resent it if you didn't accept his counsel—as I found out in my first year as Australian skipper, when I was having problems against South African paceman Peter Pollock. I did seek The Don out for help and he suggested that I was pushing forward too much and that it would be better if I went onto the back foot more. Naturally, I tried to put his advice into action, but it felt awkward and seemed to be upsetting my rhythm. When I discussed this with the great man, he simply replied, 'That's fine, Bob. You must not change your natural rhythm. Go back to your own style.'

Perhaps the most influence Sir Donald had on my career was to convince me that I should return to Test cricket during the first season of World Series Cricket. I had been out of first-class cricket for ten years and was nearly 42, and even though I was still scoring runs regularly at first-grade level in Sydney, international matches were obviously a different story altogether. One day, over lunch, he urged me to make the comeback, comparing my position to his in 1946, when he opted to play on after the Second World War. At that time, he hadn't been keen either, but decided he had to make the commitment because, after the war, both cricket and the people of the world needed a boost. He felt then that he had a responsibility to play his part and believed strongly that I was needed now to counter the threat to the game we both saw being posed by Kerry Packer's commercial interests. Such were his powers of persuasion that by the end of that lunch I committed myself to the greatest challenge of my cricketing life.

Whenever I played golf with Sir Donald I saw some of the determination that must have been one of the chief reasons he became such a great cricketer. In the 1960s, we played off about the same handicap, but even when our round was a social two-ball and a good chance for us to get away and chat about cricket, he wasn't prepared to give an inch. I was no better. Maybe it was my Scottish family background that made me as stubborn and competitive as The Don.

Golf and family were our shared passions away from cricket. In the early 1990s, I went to see him and took my then six-year-old grandson Ashley with me. Even at that stage, Ashley was a lovely swinger of a golf club, and he sat quietly while much of the conversation revolved around golf. Next day, perhaps not surprisingly, Ashley excitedly told his mother, 'I met the best golfer in the world yesterday!'

Thinking back, he might even have been right, for everything Sir Donald did was outstanding. Who would dare argue that the great man, if he had concentrated on golf instead of cricket, would not have been a champion?

A few years earlier, after I had become coach of the Australian team, I had asked Sir Donald to attend a team dinner the night before an Adelaide Test. He graciously agreed with one proviso: he didn't want to make a speech, but would be happy to answer questions. It evolved into a wonderfully unique occasion with light banter between the guest of honour and the team. It was also, in a way, a time for reflection. I have never forgotten Sir Donald's parting message to us. I hope no one else in the game forgets it either: 'Remember that you are all custodians of cricket and when you leave the game it should be better for your presence.'

•

Sir Donald was undoubtedly the most knowledgeable person I met on the subject of cricket. Over the years he was very, very helpful to me. Any query I put to him received a full and concise explanation, such as the time during the 1958–59 season when I asked him how the eras compared in terms of the speed of scoring. This is the reply he sent me:

> If you want to start an argument amongst a group of cricket enthusiasts, just make a categorical statement that the rate of run-getting is faster today than it was 30 years ago. But, if you want to escape from the argument unscathed, arm yourself with facts—not fancies.
>
> The first thing to do when someone asks a question on scoring rates is to make sure you understand what the question means or even perhaps from what angle the questioner desires the reply.
>
> This business of scoring rates sets a superb example of how misunderstandings can occur. For instance, let us just take what appears to be a simple question: how do scoring rates today compare with those in the earlier part of this century? The average layman would say that was a straight question, but let me illustrate how complex it is.
>
> Firstly, by 'scoring rate' do you mean runs scored per day? Because if you do it will be necessary to have a faithful comparison

between the number of hours play per day. These have not been by any means uniform.

Secondly, you must compare the type and quality of bowlers. Thirdly, you must have regard to the state of the pitches and whether the outfields have been slow or fast. Fourthly, you must know whether field placings were defensive or not. Fifthly, you must know whether the pitches were covered against rain or left uncovered and the various ramifications of such rule changes.

Before running out of numbers let me go on to mention other relevant facts.

There was a period when Test matches were limited to three days and there was also a period when they were played to the finish. Surely, it is obvious that the duration of a match must have a bearing upon the tempo with which it is played.

What about the size of the wicket? It has constantly been increasing until today when a batsman has to defend a wicket, which is the largest in history. Surely, the larger the target one has to defend a wicket much more. It is then likely that the batsman's scoring rate will drop.

What about the lbw law? That was altered in the 1930s. It now gives the bowler certain advantages, which undoubtedly play a part in restricting run rates.

The taking of a new ball after so many overs has varied over the years. Originally, the fielding side only had one new ball at the start of an innings and used it until the innings was concluded. In the 1940s, a new ball could be taken after 40 eight-ball overs and it was in fact frequently taken after less than 100 runs had been scored off the previous ball. This meant a predominance of fast seam bowling and pushed the slow bowler into the background, resulting in a decline in the scoring rate.

What of the boundaries? There was one season where the Adelaide Oval boundary was reduced to a maximum of 75 (and later 80) yards, thereby cutting perhaps 30 yards or so from the old length of the drive. That season's scoring rates cannot fairly be compared with a normal year when the boundary all round was the fence. There have been variations in the boundary distances in England also.

The size of the ball is now smaller than it used to be. I could go on almost indefinitely, but just one final point. In a season where the principal bowling attack is in the hands of such men as Tyson, Trueman or Bailey who may take up to seven minutes to bowl one (eight-ball) over, how can the number of overs bowled in a day possibly reach the proportion that you would get with slow bowlers like Grimmett and Mailey, who would get through an over in less than three minutes?

Surely the foregoing remarks will be sufficient to justify my belief that: it is impossible to have a true and fair comparison of scoring rates between different eras, and the nearest and fairest approach to a true answer, particularly from the batsman's point of view, is to take the number of runs scored per 100 balls bowled.

If that theory be accepted, one can produce some interesting statistics, but again they must be taken having regard to many of the special factors already outlined, and isolated instances must not be used to try, invalidly, to prove a point . . .

With The Don's comments in mind, I offer you just a few figures:

The series between Australia and the West Indies in Australia in 1960–61 is always hailed as one of the most exciting of all time. However, if you reduce it to mere statistics, it was actually a triumph of character, zest, style and personalities, more so than hectic scoring rates. The West Indies' scoring rate for 100 balls bowled during that series was 45.7, a mere 0.2 greater than Australia's rate against England in England in 1961—a difference of perhaps two runs in a whole day's play. Australia's scoring rate against the Windies in 1960–61 was 40 per 100 balls, or only 0.2 runs per 100 balls less than its rate against England in Australia in 1962–63, a series which is regarded as one of the most boring in Ashes history.

Once again, statistics can tell many stories. But what these run rates underline for me is the fact that attractive cricket cannot be judged solely by the speed of scoring. In my view, a run orgy against inferior bowling is up there with the most boring things in the game. Attractive cricket comes from personality, character, style and a host of intangible factors associated with quality and close competition. The publication of a mass of statistics can often mislead. The visual enjoyment of the day's play you are watching is the thing that counts.

9

CRICKETERS OF THE 1960s

If I could have transported myself from the early 1990s back to the mid-1960s, and served as the Australian Test team's coach, Grahame Thomas was the player I would have most liked to work with. Grahame was a superb, naturally gifted batsman who had a lot of things going for him, but with hindsight his shot selection was poor. He could pound the ball around and sometimes look spectacularly brilliant, but too often he tried to play *too many* shots. Someone should have said, 'Listen Grahame, if you want to be a regular run-getter, make the shots you're best at your "bread and butter", and leave the others until you've passed your hundred.'

Of course, that was similar to the principles I applied to my own batting, but I just didn't have the perception in those days to identify other people's technical deficiencies as well as I could my own. That's where someone like Neil Harvey was so special and so rare, and I was lucky he took the time to help me when he did. It also underlines, in my view, why the role of a coach is so important and shouldn't be undervalued. It is when you get away from the atmosphere of a team that things become clearer. This is why a gifted player sometimes needs to get dropped before he can stop and really come to terms with what is right and wrong with his game. Until then, mistakes are usually repeated while team-mates keep assuming the player will 'work things out'. As I've said, I learnt more about cricket after I retired from the game, when I could watch the goings-on closely and dispassionately from the press box. As a coach, I was an observer—not a talker—during matches. Only then could I watch a player who was struggling or not getting all he could out of his game and instinctively think, 'That's not right. What's going on?' Further analysis would home in on the problem; remedial work in the nets would usually fix it.

Back in the 1960s, I didn't have that instinct. And there was no Neil Harvey in the team, so Grahame was left to do the best he could, which was such a pity. He was a unique talent who should have scored more runs than he did.

Another fellow I would have liked to coach was Doug Walters, mainly to make sure no one else tried to get hold of him to change the way he played. My whole philosophy on coaching is that you take the natural talent and a cricketer's natural way of playing the game, and then try to build on those gifts and make the cricketer more consistent. Dougie was often criticised for having a poor technique, but there was much to like about the way he played, and his Test career average of 48.26—better than Lawry, myself, O'Neill, Booth, Ian Chappell, Redpath, Cowper and all the other Australian batsmen who played between 1964 and 1969—suggests there actually was a certain consistency to his game as well.

A few fast bowlers, notably Mike Procter, John Snow and Bob Willis, found him out at times, but he was hardly the only one who had to battle against such outstanding bowlers. And Dougie had his good days against them too, such as at Old Trafford in 1968 when he scored 81 and 86 against Snow in his first Test in England, or in 1974–75 when he hit Willis for six off the last ball of the day in Perth to reach a century in a session. Dougie was wonderfully confident when he first came into the Australian team in 1965–66, armed as he was with a rare ability to score quickly whatever the circumstances. His front elbow might not have been pointing up the pitch when he defended, in the way some English textbooks wanted it, but he could adjust so brilliantly to different conditions, always react quickly, put the ball into gaps and run magnificently between the wickets. He was also one of the great players of spin bowling, in the Harvey class. People in Trinidad still speak about a century in a session he scored there in 1973, on a first-day pitch that was spinning like a top, in which he made Lance Gibbs look second rate. The way Doug's heels clipped together like a soldier on duty when he played his on-drive was unique, but if you watched closely he was still beautifully balanced, head over the ball, just like any coach should have wanted. Only a fool would have tried to change him, or tried to get someone else to bat like him.

He was also a much better bowler than most people realised, finishing his career with 49 Test wickets at a good bowler's average of 29.08. One day I asked him why he didn't get more, and he replied with a grin, 'Simmo, you wouldn't bowl me!' But then we realised that I only captained him in three Tests. His first series was 1965–66, but I missed two Tests because of a fractured wrist and then chicken pox, and he missed the 1966–67 series in South Africa and the first half of the series against India at home in 1967–68 because he was completing his National Service. In 1977–78, he was in the World Series Cricket camp when I came back to Test cricket.

We certainly could have used Dougie in South Africa in 1966–67, and not just for his batting. I'm sure Graham McKenzie, who often had to carry our bowling attack on his considerable shoulders, would have appreciated him.

Big 'Garth' was a wonderful bowler who has been terribly under-appreciated by cricket pundits, especially when you consider that except for right at the start of his career, when Alan Davidson bowled the first over, and then for a couple of seasons in the mid-1960s when Neil Hawke was in stirring form, he didn't get a lot of support from the other end. In my view, Garth should be rated alongside Glenn McGrath in the history of Australian cricket, just behind Davo, Dennis Lillee and Ray Lindwall.

Garth had a short run-up and a beautiful, loping action, all power at the point of delivery, that allowed him to swing the ball away from the bat and also bowl a very sharp bouncer. Best of all, he never got tired. If I was coaching fast bowlers and wanted to cut my message down to one sentence, I'd say flatly, 'Bowl like Graham McKenzie.' He was a man who rose to the occasion. In South Africa, when the rest of us were struggling, his bowling was magnificent—he had a couple of South Africans in real trouble with his quick stuff, and I remember he dismissed 'Tiger' Lance a couple of times with perfect fast bowling: in at the ribs . . . another short ball . . . another short ball . . . then one pitched up . . . out!

There was nothing flamboyant about his bowling. He was quicker than McGrath, more dangerous with his bouncer, and otherwise of the same style—no nonsense, just doing the job. When asked to bowl, whether it was his first over or his twentieth, Garth always acknowledged the request with a shy smile, a raised right hand and a bent pointer finger. He was just as unflappable off the field. I remember we were staying at a hotel outside Bristol in 1964, and had just set off on our bus to the ground when someone shouted, 'There's Garth, walking up the street.' We'd forgotten him. The bus stopped, he looked up at us and then coolly climbed aboard. No panic.

He could bat a bit, too, best exemplified by the famous innings he played at Old Trafford in 1961 when he held up an end while Davo batted us back into the Test. Garth opened the batting for Western Australia a couple of times, once scoring 51 against South Australia after losing his opening partner (me, lbw to Peter Trethewey) for 6.

Just as Garth was so dependable as our strike bowler, to me Ian Redpath became the 'Mr Reliability' of batsmen. Here was a cricketer whose performances were best when things were going wrong. Between 1966 and 1970, Australia was thrashed twice in South Africa, and both times 'Redders' averaged in the 40s. From 1969 until he retired at the end of the 1975–76 season, he never had a bad series, yet he also never received the recognition he deserved. His omission from the 1972 Ashes tour might have been the worst decision by selectors ever. In his final Test series, against Andy Roberts and Michael Holding, he opened the batting and scored three centuries.

He was a special character, a sensible man who was always committed to the team and the cause. He appreciated the honour of being in the side. You could always tell how he was going by how far he crouched in his batting stance. If his bum was pointing a long way out, he was struggling, but as he gradually stood taller you could tell his confidence was returning. There was a style about his batting, but also a genuine toughness. But I remember him as the ultimate team player. I think it is because of Redders and Bill Lawry that I've always reckoned that Victorians become Australian cricketers faster than any players from other states. Sometimes, for example, I could sense that the Western Australians were still Western Australians, even though they were now in the Australian team set-up. Same with some Queenslanders. In my experience, it was never that way with the Victorians.

Redders' first tour with the Australian team was the trip to England in 1964, and he ended up hitting the winning runs at

Headingley in what proved to be the only victory of the series. We'd been tagged as the worst team ever early on that tour, but the team bonded together as well as any group of blokes I've known, and everyone chipped in to make the tour a success. It would have been natural for a bloke to revel in his own success after he played the shot that retained the Ashes. But that wasn't Redders' style. He came off, grinning from ear to ear, and stopped on the steps up to the dressing rooms to say, 'That was for you, skip.' I've never forgotten that.

My vice-captain on that 1964 tour was Brian Booth, who like Redders played an enormously influential but underrated role in this era of Australian cricket. Brian was also a very stylish batsman, very strong in the forearms and wrists, but it was his off-field influence that I remember most, particularly on that tour when he could always be relied on to fix a problem or sort out a player who had become disheartened, perhaps because of injury, perhaps because of some perceived injustice. Of course, that happens on every tour, but Brian was the best bloke I ever knew for finding the right solution. I can't think of one squad Brian was involved in where the team spirit wasn't outstanding.

Brian is a committed Christian but he never allowed his religious beliefs to disturb the normal running of the team. He never objected to blokes swearing or telling dirty jokes, but he had such a dignity about him that if he did decide to have a quiet word with a young player who might have been out a bit late a bit often, the message always hit home.

He didn't make his Test debut until he was 27, on the 1961 Ashes tour, fully five years after he represented Australia in hockey at the Melbourne Olympics. Today, you're almost a prodigy if you're 'only' 27, but back in those days it was considered to be a very old age for a debutant. Dougie and Garth were both teenagers when they made their Test debuts, and Redders was 22 when he scored 97 in his first innings, against South Africa at the MCG in 1963–64. Brian quickly made up for 'lost' time by being just about Australia's best batsman in his first two complete series. He scored two hundreds against Ted Dexter's Englishmen in 1962–63 and two more against South Africa a year later. After that, the runs dried up a little, and in the West Indies in 1965 Charlie Griffith's bouncers affected him as much as anyone. Brian scored a gutsy 117 against Charlie in the Second Test, but very few after that and in the following season, after captaining Australia twice when I was unavailable, he was dropped from the side. That was one of those situations where the selectors had to make the change—we were a Test down with two to play, and Brian was averaging 16 with the bat for the series—but I bet it caused them plenty of angst, before they finally signed off on the decision.

Like Dougie, who came from Dungog in the upper Hunter Valley of New South Wales, Brian was a product of the New South Wales countryside, from a village called Perthville out near Bathurst. He tells some interesting stories of life in the bush, of cycling fifteen miles each way to play in cricket matches when he was twelve or thirteen years old. I'm not sure if too many kids would be prepared to do that sort of thing today.

10

MUCH BETTER THAN AVERAGE

One of the admirable traits of cricket supporters in India is their love of the game and all who play it. The people of India hero-worship their own, but they also appreciate the overseas stars. In addition, they love and respect the players of the past.

Even today, a decade after my full-time coaching career finished and nearly 30 years after my last Test, I am immediately recognised and greeted with almost embarrassing affection when I land in India. I must say I always greatly appreciate this reception, but I also have to accept that my popularity is understandably overshadowed by how some other former players from India have been lauded.

The late Ken Barrington was one of their favourites. They responded to his wonderful cricket ability, and also to his sense of humour, friendliness and ability to interact with them even in the tightest situation. I also sense that they appreciated that for his greatness as a run-getter—you can mount a strong case that he has been England's most successful batsman since Sir Leonard Hutton—they also warmed to the fact that he was somewhat underrated by many critics.

I am biased in thinking that Ken might have been cricket's *most* undervalued great player, partly because I became a close friend of Ken but also because I rate so highly the qualities such as guts and determination that Ken and so many of the genuine cricketers of the world stood and stand for. Look at his record against Australia, in particular, and tell me why he never achieved the lasting fame he obviously deserved.

Wally Grout, the great Australian wicketkeeper, once remarked, 'Whenever I saw Ken coming to the wicket I thought I saw a Union Jack trailing behind him.'

On many occasions during the 1960s, Ken carried the weight of England's chances on his shoulders. In Ashes Tests, he played thirteen matches at home between 1961 and 1968, scoring 1065 runs at 59.17. In Australia, he played two full series—1962–63 and 1965–66—and scored 1046 runs at 69.73. He scored hundreds in his first Test in every overseas country he played in, except Australia, where he started with 'only' 78 at the Gabba in 1962–63. In Tests in India he averaged 96.29, scoring three hundreds in six Tests. In fact, he averaged more than 50 against every Test opponent, except South Africa, who restricted him to an average of 49.45 in fourteen Tests, and the West Indies, who clearly targeted him as England's most important batsman in England in 1963 and 1966. Yet Ken scored three of his best and bravest hundreds against the Windies—two in the acrimonious 1959–60 series in the Caribbean and another at Port-of-Spain in January 1968. The players of his generation admired and respected a real competitor, a true Englishman who fought for his country as hard as they fought for theirs and then smiled his broken smile over a beer afterwards.

As I said, it always seemed to me that he never received the recognition he deserved. Part of that was probably because of his adopted style of batting, which was admittedly very unglamorous, and his perceived lack of urgency at the crease. He was even dropped by England for batting too slowly after making 137 in the First Test against New Zealand at Edgbaston in 1965, perhaps because

England were expected to wallop the Kiwis in the 1960s and Ken's seven-and-a-half hours for his runs in that match was too much for some to take, even though his individual score was 21 runs more than New Zealand scored in their first innings, which suggests there might have been a little in the wicket and that batting might not have been that easy.

Simply rattling off the bare statistics of a long innings rarely reveals the entire story. For example, when I made 311 at Manchester in 1964 to secure the Ashes for Australia it was considered an ultra-slow innings. We declared our first innings 58 minutes into the third day of that Test, at 8–656. In 1993, Allan Border's Australians batted for 40 minutes into the third day of the Fourth Ashes Test, at Headingley, before declaring at 4–653. We did receive more overs than AB's side, but at the same time, the wicket on the first day in 1964 was a lot greener than the one at Leeds 29 years later. Times and expectations change. Some so-called 'attacking' players were not as quick-scoring as their image suggests. A pleasing style often gives a false impression of speed—and poor Ken Barrington certainly couldn't lay claim to that.

Ironically enough, he was a thrasher when he began with Surrey in the County Championship, a batsman who went after everything he could reach. While that method worked he was praised, but when the same flashing stroke got him out he was accused of being irresponsible and inconsistent. So when he struggled in his first two Tests, in 1955, and then was not selected in the next four years, he changed his approach and became a really tough customer to remove.

The most stark change he made was to open his stance so that sometimes his left shoulder pointed in the direction of mid-wicket. Consequently, he always looked as though he would be easy meat for an inswinger—but he never was. Even Alan Davidson found him difficult to dislodge. Ken's stance and method of playing back and across should have left him as a lay-down misère for a bowler of Davo's class, but Ken's record in the two series in which he faced the greatest left-arm swing bowler of them all (1961 and 1962–63, when he passed 50 seven times in 19 innings) says otherwise.

Sometimes after 1959 Ken did show glimpses of his old attacking self, and when he did he could be quite devastating. He was a great hooker in the safe, short-arm-jab mould and a wonderful square-cutter of the ball. Because he employed such an open stance, he needed the ball to be pitched really well up rather than be just slightly overpitched before he could go for the big drive, but he was still able to smash it through the offside when the opportunity presented itself. Being a leg-spinner himself—and always ready to talk about the art—he was a very competent player of wrist spin, unlike most of his countrymen, who usually have no idea. He might even have been the first English leg-spinner to learn how to bowl a flipper, after watching Richie Benaud in action on a tour to South Africa and Rhodesia with Ron Roberts' International Cavaliers in 1960.

We Australians virtually adopted Ken on that tour. I think he liked our egalitarian approach to the game and he repaid us by scoring more Test runs against us than any other batsman of the time. His image as a dour man at the crease was nothing like the Barrington we players knew off it. He was always good for a laugh, a practical joker, impersonator and a wonderful 'mangler' of the English language. According to Ken, target shooters used 'high-philosophy bullets'. Another time, he woke having 'slept like a lark'. And he described the players at a buffet in Pakistan as 'a swarm of lotuses'.

Ken also had high ideals about the game he loved. He was one of the few players prepared to come out publicly against the highly controversial bowling action of Charlie Griffith when the topic was political dynamite in the mid-1960s. That issue took a lot out of Ken emotionally, but he felt an important principle was at stake.

He had a mild heart attack during a double-wicket tournament I helped devise and organise in Australia in 1968–69, after which he announced his retirement from first-class cricket. However, he stayed involved in top-level cricket with managerial and quasi-coaching roles with England teams on tour during the second half of the 1970s and into the 1980s. In 1981, he was in Barbados as assistant manager of Ian Botham's team when he suffered a second heart attack and died in the arms of his wife Ann.

It says a lot for the respect in which he was held that the ultra-competitive Fleet Street contingent on tour agreed to delay publishing the news of his death until it had been broken to his son Guy, who was studying at boarding school.

One thing I'll never forget about Ken is that he loved to chat between overs when he was batting. The trouble with this from our point of view was that the conversations were going way too long because we just couldn't get him out. Eventually, it was decided that we had to make sure he had nobody to talk to. I loved the bloke, but gave instructions, 'Don't let Kenny feel too much at home.'

Not that it seemed to affect him. Wrapped up in that Union Jack as he always was, he knew just what we were doing.

•

I'm sure Ken Barrington was the hardest bloke to get out in the 1960s. He wasn't the most flamboyant, but from the very first ball he was a bloody rock. But, of course, he wasn't the only champion of the time.

The two batsmen from the 1960s who can match Kenny for career batting average are South Africa's Graeme Pollock (60.97 in 23 Tests) and Garry Sobers (57.78 in 93 Tests). Sobers was undoubtedly the best all-round cricketer I've ever seen. He could do it all. It didn't matter where he fielded, he was brilliant. He was a lively fast-medium bowler who swung the ball a lot, almost as much as Alan Davidson. He had actually started in Test cricket as a 17-year-old orthodox left-hand spinner, and later he became a fair chinaman bowler, but it was at batting that he was most destructive. A little like Pollock, Sobers never aimed to get his front foot right to the ball like they ask you to do in the textbook, but I can't remember him driving at balls and getting caught. They both kept their heads very steady—that was the 'platform' from which they threw the bat at the ball.

Garry built a reputation for being able to play all types of bowling, and from my experience that was unquestionably true. Yet it is also a fact that I had a little success against him, because he had trouble detecting my wrong 'un. I dismissed him in both innings of the Fifth Test in Melbourne in 1960–61, caught by Wally Grout on each occasion. Yet I'd hardly say he had a weakness against wrist-spinners, because at other times in that series he demolished Richie, which could pose problems for me as the first slip. Richie had an excellent top-spinner, but Garry was just flaying the bat at it, and it kept going for four; my fear was that he'd nick one and it would fly in my direction. I wouldn't have had a chance, but fortunately every ball hit the middle of the bat.

What I liked most about Garry as a cricketer was that he tried so hard all the time. He was dominant when he played for South

Australia, never once shirking his responsibility and they ended up winning the Sheffield Shield in 1963–64, the first time they'd won the trophy for more than a decade. For a man who reputedly had a casual attitude towards life, he sure cared about cricket. Maybe as a captain he used to drop off to sleep a little, but he still led the West Indies to series victories over Australia and England, and his all-round performance against the Poms in 1966 must be regarded as one of the most phenomenal in history. I covered it for the *Evening Standard* and saw him score 722 runs at 103.14 including three hundreds, take 10 catches and 20 wickets, and win all five tosses.

The funny thing was, as good a batsman as Garry was, back in 1960–61 we thought Rohan Kanhai was better. I reckon the Kanhai we saw that summer was as technically good a batsman as I have ever seen.

When we first saw Pollock we thought getting him out would be easy, because he played with his pad too far away from the ball, and he seemed fairly limited on his pads. But he was freakish in many ways—the manner in which he kept his head still, swung through the line and always middled it. I'm glad no one tried to change him, or perhaps he was strong enough and confident enough to go his own way. I was struck by the way he *always* hit the ball through the gap and how, if you dropped a delivery a fraction short, he would always smash you to the boundary. It was that inevitability about his batting that set Graeme Pollock apart. Kenny Barrington might have been harder to get out, but Sobers and Pollock were the ones most likely to hit you for four. All three were champions, the best of their time.

11

NOT QUITE A CRICKET REVOLUTION

In May 1977, the story got out that the boss of the Nine television network in Australia, Kerry Packer, had secretly signed most of Australia's best cricketers and many exceptional overseas players to participate in a series of cricket matches that would compete with, rather than complement, the traditional Australian season. It is not my intention here to go back in detail over that often acrimonious time (I wrote a book about the subject, called *Simmo*, which was published in 1979), but I do think it's appropriate to record a few thoughts, some of which, obviously, are offered with the benefit of hindsight.

I know most people will think of me as a strong 'traditionalist', at least in part because I came back after nearly ten years out of Test cricket to lead Australia in its home series against India, a rubber that had to directly compete with the first season of World Series Cricket (WSC) 'Supertests'. But I don't think of myself as such a stalwart for the old days. Indeed, my conclusion to the hubbub that was WSC is that it was a revolution that didn't go far enough. If we were going to have all the publicity, all the hurt, all the breaking down of friendships and assaults on the traditional way of doing things, shouldn't the changes have been more . . . revolutionary?

In the end, what happened? Mr Packer got his television rights. The Australian Cricket Board (ACB) kept what it most treasured:

control of the game in Australia. A few star players were well looked after financially, but many of those who weren't quite stars, but were also very important to the game, were left thinking, 'What has changed for me?' They were paid more money—though not a lot more—and had to play a lot more cricket to earn it. The cricketers did not get genuine representation on the Board, just a gesture that they would be kept informed. 'Peace' broke out in 1979 for the ACB and WSC, but within five years senior members of the Test team were threatening not to tour the West Indies unless their contracts were improved. One of the players' chief complaints from pre-WSC days—that they weren't receiving an appropriate slice of the profits—was still unresolved, and wasn't really settled until 1998, when the Australian Cricketers' Association and the ACB finally signed a memorandum of understanding. If WSC had really been all it was cracked up to be from the players' point of view, that would have happened twenty years earlier. The only difference this time was that Channel Nine pretty much stayed out of the fight.

People also like to pretend that WSC invented one-day cricket; but that's not right, they just exploited it to the max. Night cricket was fantastic, but surely it would have happened anyway, eventually, as it was doing at the time in other professional sports in Australia such as Australian football and rugby league.

When I look back on my comeback, I think I did as well as I possibly could. I scored more runs in the Test series against India that 'traditional cricket' put up against WSC than in any other Test series I played in. During that season, we more than held our own against the Packer cricket, even though there was no doubt the quality of players in WSC was superior. There was something about our cricket—the magic of the Indian spinners, Bishan Bedi, Bhagwat Chandrasekhar and Erapalli Prasanna; the intrigue of promising young Australian batsmen such as Peter Toohey being fast-tracked into Test cricket; Jeff Thomson versus Sunil Gavaskar and Gundappa Viswanath; the story of my return; the fact we were playing on the traditional Test grounds whereas WSC was taking place at football stadiums, trotting tracks and showgrounds—that, in that season, I believe we won the public relations battle.

However, the following year, people came to realise that the Packer boys' cricket was fair dinkum, night cricket became a wonderful point of difference for them, and as Australia crashed to defeat in the 1978–79 Ashes series, WSC finally built up a momentum that was irresistible. Eventually, the Board had to cave in, before they went broke. Purely from their perspective, the deal they brokered was not too bad: the only people who got burned completely were the ABC, who no longer had the television rights, and some of the young players who suddenly found themselves on the scrapheap as the WSC players moved back into positions of authority within the Australian Test team.

The Board was very keen for me to play that first season, 1977–78. There was a tour of the West Indies scheduled for straight after, but I wasn't keen to go, mainly because I didn't think I could ignore my sports-marketing business for so long (having already left it largely unattended during the Australian summer), and also because I wasn't sure if, at 42 years old, I'd be able to contribute with the bat as well as I would have liked. At that stage our expectation was that the WSC West Indians, including all their fast bowlers, would be playing. In the end, though, after we won an exciting series against India 3–2, I felt I had to go, because I would have been letting down the young blokes who'd worked so hard to get us that series victory, and also because I'd gone so well in those Tests that I could hardly use lack of form as an excuse for staying at home.

We certainly weren't the strongest Australian team in history, but those Indian spinners certainly knew how to bowl on any type of wicket, so to come out with a win was very satisfying. The series had offered something refreshing for cricket fans—different tactics and an alternative style to what they'd become used to in recent seasons, when fast bowlers such as John Snow, Lillee and Thommo, Andy Roberts and Michael Holding, and Imran Khan had all performed superbly. Nine years later, during the Australian team's tour of India, I invited Bishan Bedi to meet the boys and have a bowl at them in the nets. He was almost 40 but still fantastic. Dean Jones came out after batting against him and said, 'That old so and so can bowl. Every time I went down the track he had the ball on a string and just pulled it away from me. I never got to him!'

In the West Indies, the Packer players did appear against us in the first two Tests. My perception was that Andy Roberts in 1978 wasn't any faster than Wes Hall or Charlie Griffith in 1965, but my reflexes weren't quite as sharp as they could have been, in part because of my age but more so because I wasn't used to that sort of bowling, and I didn't score any runs against him, Colin Croft or Joel Garner. I hadn't faced genuine fast stuff since Peter Pollock and Mike Procter in South Africa in 1966–67. When I had last been to the Caribbean in 1965, it had taken us a couple of Tests to get used to Wes and Charlie, but by the Fourth Test we scored 6–650 against them. I'm not saying that a similar batting revival would necessarily have occurred in 1978, but I'm sure we would have improved. Instead, their WSC men fell out with their board, and we had the better of the final three Tests against a much-weakened Windies side.

Several positives should have come out of that tour for Australian cricket, but unfortunately most of them eventually came to nought.

Chief of these was the case of Jeff Thomson, who was fantastic throughout the tour. I thought we worked very well as captain and vice-captain, but not long after we returned home he announced he wanted to join WSC; the Board wouldn't let him and he missed the 1978–79 Australian season. I don't think he was ever the same bowler again.

I remember the Board's horrified reaction when I suggested the great fast bowler be made vice-captain. 'Why do you want Thommo?' one prominent and very agitated administrator asked me.

'Because he's a leader,' I responded, 'a bloke the players respect.'

I wasn't suggesting Thommo would be the next captain, but I was certain that making him vice-captain would help get the very best out of him. Sure enough, the fans in the West Indies witnessed some of the fastest bowling ever seen in those parts.

Graeme Wood and Craig Serjeant batted beautifully in the Third Test, at Guyana, when we made 362 to win, still the fifth highest successful fourth-innings run chase in Test history. And we got those runs after collapsing to 3–22. Wood and Toohey were equally as impressive in the final Test, which ended in controversial circumstances when the crowd rioted after Vanburn Holder was correctly given out caught behind late on the final day, while Graham Yallop often batted with great courage, especially at Port-of-Spain when he batted three and scored a stirring 81 in the second innings against a fired-up Roberts, Croft and Garner. (During the following Test, in Barbados, Graham became the first man to wear a helmet in a Test match.) However, in the years to come, once WSC and the Board joined forces, none of these batsmen ever completely fulfilled the potential they showed on this tour. Graham had a couple of good years, and Graeme Wood went on to play 59 Tests (averaging just 31.83 with the bat), but the truth is none of them improved much after that tour. In the case of Serjeant and Toohey, they went backwards. I often wonder whether, if I had stayed on as captain (and as something of a coach, too), their careers might have evolved differently. Ironically, this lack of development happened with the young WSC players, most notably David Hookes, who was a technically flawed batsman who just needed time to get his game in order. Instead, he became one of the rebels' most publicised figures, and never recovered.

In the weeks after the West Indies tour, there was much conjecture as to whether I would remain as captain. Eventually, I asked the Board whether they wanted me to continue. I felt in my heart that I was capable of scoring enough runs to justify my place in the side, and on that basis I was keen to bat on. Unfortunately the Board decided they couldn't guarantee my selection in the team, so I decided to retire for the final time. At the time I thought they were wrong to cast me aside, and I still think that now. The fight with WSC was far from won (though I think some Board members thought it was) and there was no obvious man to take over the captaincy.

From day one, I felt sorry for Graham Yallop, who became the new skipper. I remember him calling me after it was revealed I was retiring, to say he hoped it wasn't true. This was hardly a man aching for the top job. He received little help from his selectors, who at a time when they needed to show faith in young players, kept making changes. Even Allan Border got dropped. If only they'd understood that in such circumstances, when young players are being inconsistent, it's a bit like solving a jigsaw puzzle—some pieces fit, others don't, but once you've chosen a piece you must give it every chance to fit in. That's what Australia did in the late 1980s, when we backed hard-nosed cricketers such as David Boon,

Geoff Marsh and Steve Waugh, and what England did before the 2005 Ashes series. In both cases, the eventual results proved the policy right.

There were a number of lessons to be learned from the cricket war of the 1970s. That was just one of them.

12

THE THIRST FOR KNOWLEDGE

As a teenager in first-class cricket, I used to learn plenty from observing at close quarters great players such as Keith Miller, Ray Lindwall, Arthur Morris, Len Hutton and Alec Bedser, but the moments I found most helpful came when I was in the dressing room during a match and suddenly an experienced player would be sitting next to me, keen to talk cricket. I didn't learn much once stumps had been called, because over a beer the dressing-room chat tended to veer away onto other subjects, but during the day there were many times when a giant of the game was happy to sit there and comment on the action as it transpired out on the field, or recall an incident from earlier in the game and make a telling and insightful comment. Senior players were similarly helpful at the nets, advising on the right line to bowl, or perhaps stressing the importance of practising as if you were out in the middle. 'You're not here to give him a hit,' someone might say if you were bowling at half-pace, or 'You've got to be more selective in your shot-making,' if you'd spent your fifteen minutes in the nets flashing at everything. These conversations helped shape my cricket thinking.

I think of those times when I contemplate the decline of West Indies cricket in the last decade. One of the features of that fall has been the manner in which their past players have usually been quick to comment on the shortcomings of their successors. Much of this criticism has been valid, but I sometimes wondered whether some former players needed to be a little generous, if not now then back in the time when they were still playing. Could they have done more back then to ensure that the West Indies remained a strong team after they retired?

I believe one of the problems that eventually beset the Windies was simply that they were too successful for too long. A seemingly unending stream of blitzkrieg victories created the false impression that the champagne would bubble forever. The youngsters who came into the team in the early 1990s and beyond were brought up only on wins at international level, and seemed to believe that as long as they were born in the Caribbean they'd be victorious, too. How wrong they were.

What was forgotten was that almost all the greats of the past had served an apprenticeship, generally in county or league cricket in England, before they made the West Indies team. But as the quality of league cricket declined and the county scene closed its doors to unproven players from overseas, this crucial opportunity to learn was lost. The only hope was that the Test players could become teachers to the next generation, but that does not seem to have happened. Instead, while the natural talent of the young players from the islands remained, their work ethic was poor and attitude dismissive, and gradually things slid from bad to worse. I saw this first-hand when I did some coaching work in Jamaica around 2002; eventually, we decided to bypass players aged 18–22 years because they had been 'lost' and instead focused on those aged 16–17 years. When my consultancy ended I stressed it was vital that the Jamaican authorities introduced a coaching system that suited the natural instincts and flair of this young group of naturally gifted cricketers. The last thing they needed was a highly technical program that sought to turn them into robots.

Those kids in Jamaica were lively, instinctive and very keen to learn, and as I saw them in action my mind went back to 1985–86, when I was the coach of the New South Wales Sheffield Shield team and had been invited to link up with the Australian team, again on a consultancy basis, to see if I could help the squad at a time when it was going through a very difficult period.

After a tour of New Zealand with the Aussie team I wrote a report for the Australian Cricket Board. Part of that report reflected on the significance of peer influence in the Australian team set-up and also its impact on Australian cricket in general; another section dealt with matters of coaching that reveal a little of my overall coaching philosophy and a little of what was wrong with the Aussie team of the mid-1980s. A very important observation at the end reveals much of what makes coaching good cricketers such a joy. The report read this way . . .

Australian cricket has probably gone through more changes and turmoil in the last 10 years than in any other decade in the history of the game. Invariably, the major ones to suffer in conflicts are the direct combatants, in this case the players.

While the crises created through WSC and the South African defections may have assisted the players to receive greater payments, the infighting and selfishness has destroyed some of the great strengths of Australian cricket. This is particularly seen in the diminishing role of the Australian captain within the team and the almost total destruction of peer influence within Australian cricket.

The Australian cricket captain always held a rather unique and envied position in Australian sport. While obviously answerable to the Australian Cricket Board, he held an almost autonomous position. For instance, when on tour he was the centre-pin around which the tour revolved. He generally handled the press, spoke first at functions. If only one speech was to be made, he delivered it. With the help of his senior players, he supervised practice and assisted in the development of the skills of the players in the team. He also became something of a father confessor to his charges.

This system worked wonderfully well, for the players responded to the fact that a fellow player, not an official, was in charge. Generally, a very close relationship was allowed to develop within the team. In addition, I believe a far greater team involvement was possible under this system, with various members being given the responsibility to handle the physical training and fielding sessions, etc. Instead of just being a team member, they became an important cog in the team and generally responded to the extra responsibility.

Traditionally, the senior members of the side took over the coaching of the newcomers. This generally wasn't on an organised or even spoken basis—it was just something they accepted as their role and responsibility to the team. For instance, Neil Harvey played a vital role in my own career, assisting me on the techniques of the game and advising me to open the batting, for he saw not only that I had the skills for the position but also that my opportunities were better there to secure a permanent berth for myself, and that it was also in the better interests of Australian cricket.

There was never a big thing made of this peer influence and, in fact, it was not until I looked back on my career when I was captain that I even realised the pattern that had developed.

Unfortunately, due to many circumstances, peer influence has virtually disappeared, much to the detriment of Australian cricket. Perhaps the saddest aspect is not only has it nearly gone at the top level, but also in the grade and district ranks. Whereas most district teams had a couple of old hardheads who ran the team, kept the youngsters on the straight and narrow, and also coached them, these days very few of these senior players remain and as a result the youngsters are left to make their way on their own.

At the top level, it is probably easier to explain why things have changed, with so much turmoil over the last decade or so and players appearing often to be preoccupied with sorting out selfish off-field matters such as contracts, conditions, etc. At the lower level, there is no easy explanation, except perhaps that these days no one seems to have or want to make the time necessary to put something back into their cricket. Whatever the reason, there is no doubt in my mind that the decline in peer influence has played perhaps the major role in the decline of Australian cricket.

I say this having been so closely involved in Australian cricket for such a long period and in particular during the last decade. There is no doubt in my mind that the players of today are still being blessed with the same amount of natural skill that any previous era had, but unfortunately we are not turning this skill into winning performances.

Obviously, the decline in peer influence is not the only reason for the disappointing performances in recent years. Unfortunately, in this same decade there has been a sad withdrawal from teaching the skills and basic fundamentals of cricket and a concentration on what I consider lesser needs, such as an over-emphasis on physical fitness, diet, motivation, etc. No one believes in physical fitness more than I do, but when fitness is presented as a cure-all and a way to instant success, but is not aligned to skills, then I am concerned.

Over the last ten to fifteen years too much emphasis has been placed on physical training and valuable practice time has been wasted by good intending, but unfortunately ill-advised coaches and administrators who believed that extra fitness was a sure-fire magical way of ensuring success. Undoubtedly this has affected our cricket, with the development of skills and techniques almost neglected in the quest for greater physical strength.

Physical fitness is critically important, but it should be mainly the player's responsibility to get himself fit in his own time, so that the limited time available for group training can be utilised to develop the essential skills and techniques needed to meet the demands of cricket at its highest level.

Unfortunately over the last decade or so, many of the Australian teams have been in the hands of people whose skills lie on the physical-training side, and naturally they have concentrated on areas they are comfortable with, rather than the more demanding development and improvement of cricketing skills. While physical fitness, diet and motivation are all important, they should not be the dominant factors in the development of skills and should not be seen as instant ways of ensuring success.

Australian cricket at all levels has more designated coaches now than at any time in the history of the game, and yet there has never been a period in my experience where the players so urgently need coaching. This is clearly shown by the amount of time that I spend with the Australian team undertaking simple but necessary corrections to their techniques.

Even basic fundamentals such as turning blind and going down to field the ball on the wrong knee are commonplace. Such obvious fundamentals should have been spotted and attended to at school level, or in grade ranks at the worst.

That players have been allowed to proceed to the Test level is a sad indictment of our system and must be remedied urgently.

While we have an excellent scheme to encourage coaches to improve their skills, it would appear that there is a shortcoming which allows players to progress with such simple obvious flaws. I have little doubt that all the coaches who have had something to do with the players who have reached Test levels would know the right and wrong way to execute the manoeuvres that I have mentioned, but nothing has been done to change the players.

Picking up and correction of mistakes is to me just about the major part of coaching. It is not that difficult to do and I believe that all of our coaching manuals and training classes for coaches should include a segment on this subject. It is not much good having an extensive coaching system if the coaches are not capable of remedying simple basic fundamentals.

Interestingly enough, I have found in the two years I have had with New South Wales and the six months coaching Australia that the players relish learning and correcting problems in their technique—particularly when it is explained to them why what they are doing is wrong.

While it has been suggested often that the youngsters of today don't take kindly to advice, my experience has shown that they thirst for knowledge. It is up to us to provide this knowledge so that they can utilise the natural skills they have been blessed with.

Bob Simpson
17 February 1986

13

THE TOUGHEST TEST

'A tie! A tie! Is that better than a draw?' Dean Jones screamed at me as I raced onto the field at the end of Australia's Test against India in Madras in 1986.

Immediately, that line took me back to the First Test at the Gabba in December 1960, after the West Indies' Joe Solomon had thrown out Ian Meckiff to end cricket's first Tied Test. Back then, as in Madras, in all the excitement many players didn't know what the result meant.

I was the only person involved in both of these two dramatic matches. In the twenty years since Greg Matthews dismissed India's No. 11 Maninder Singh with the second-last possible ball of the Test in Madras, to force that remarkable tie, many people have asked me which of the two games was more exciting.

Both Tests ended with a ball to spare and, of course, both were remarkably tense and thrilling contests. But in so many ways they were different, not least in the fact that while the Gabba tie is a treasured memory in cricket folklore, the Madras match is hardly as iconic. It would be nice if both games were as well remembered, for they both deserve to be.

In Brisbane, we fell to 5–57 chasing 233 for victory on the final day, but then Richie Benaud and Alan Davidson mounted a superb recovery, and by the second-last over we needed seven runs to win, with twelve balls to get them and four wickets in hand. We expected to win. But then Davo was run out for 80, Richie caught behind for 52, and two more run-outs denied us victory. Initially, at least, we were very disappointed not to be one-up in the series.

In Madras, we'd set the pace in the Test from ball one, and Allan Border had made two declarations as we set India 348 to win on the final day. By my calculations, that was an impossible task on a wicket that had threatened to spin from just about the opening over. After all, at that time only four teams had ever scored so many runs in the fourth innings to win a Test. Even today, it's only been done on six occasions. Before this game, I had said to Allan, 'If we're going to make anything out of this Test series we've got to win this match.' I thought he agreed with me, but when it came to that final morning he still took some convincing before he headed off to inform his counterpart, Kapil Dev, that we were declaring on our overnight score.

In our dressing room straight after the Test I was able to say, 'Well, there you are fellas. I told you before play today that India wouldn't get 348 to win this game. Right, wasn't I?'

It was a close-run thing. Sunil Gavaskar made 90, and India reached 6–331 well into the final session. After five days playing under the most trying conditions I have ever encountered—on a red and dusty 'field', temperatures in the high 40s, with humidity always around 100 per cent, and a nauseating smell from the old Buckingham Canal surrounding the ground wafting across the field—I thought we were gone. In the end, a tie was a relief. It had been tougher than Brisbane, but just as exciting.

I have no doubt that watching a tense finish from the pavilion is more of a strain than being in the middle, for you can do nothing about what is happening out on the field. There is little you can do but support the troops and worry. This is where I spent both last days of the Tied Tests. At the Gabba, I'd been the first wicket to fall in our second innings, caught for a duck by Lance Gibbs off a Wes Hall riser. The Test at Madras was my first as official coach of the Australian team. (I had toured with the team to New Zealand earlier in the year, but that was in a consultancy role, to see if a full-time coaching position would suit me.)

As coach, it was always my policy to never interfere or offer advice to the captain while the game was actually in progress. But this did not stop me from mentally captaining every over from the pavilion. Sometimes, inevitably because you are removed from the pressure of all that goes on in the field, the 'correct' strategy is so much clearer from that 'comfy chair'. However, on that last day I wouldn't have changed a thing. Allan did a superb job.

In other ways, though, a coach can be a great help. During the final session, our left-arm spinner Ray Bright, who had been struggling with the heat throughout the Test, was forced to leave the field. It was not the first time he'd had to come off on that fateful day. Ray is one tough character, so when he muttered, 'Sorry coach, I'm stuffed,' I had two reactions: to offer sympathy to a brave warrior, and to bluntly remind him that Australia still needed him.

After a long drink, Ray sauntered over to me and said, 'What do you reckon, Simmo?'

'AB and Australia need you badly out there,' I replied, 'if that's at all possible.'

Ray stopped for a moment, and then turned around, grabbed his hat and went back onto the field. In the final hour, he took three crucial wickets and, with Matthews, brought Australia back into the game.

Matthews bowled practically unchanged throughout that day. In his own idiosyncratic way, during the afternoon he'd rest between overs just outside the boundary fence, sitting on a tiny stool in the shade of the stand. Where he got that stool or where it went I have no idea, but in these days of high-priced memorabilia I'm sure it'd be worth a dollar or two. (I do know Steve Waugh snared a couple of stumps at the end of the game, giving one to Greg, and that Allan Border got his hands on the ball.)

I'm not sure many people appreciate just how tough cricket is when it is played under the conditions our Tied Test heroes conquered that day in Madras. After 30 minutes in the field, the players' clothes were wringing wet and also filthy with red dust. Bowlers' sweat-drenched socks squelched moisture through the eyelets of boots, while distressed batsmen changed their gloves every twenty minutes, and still struggled to keep a slippery grip on their bats. Dehydration was almost impossible to avoid; concentration was demanding. In the dressing room, every player had a job to do and it seemed that, more often than not, team manager Alan Crompton, NSW Cricket Association secretary Bob Radford (who was travelling with the team) and I were the lone supporters sitting in the Australian section of the viewing area outside the dressing room. Physio Errol Alcott had never been busier, while the rest of the squad were zooming on and off the field to meet the requests of the players, or were racing around the boundary to get drinks to fieldsmen. David Gilbert, the 12th man, assures me he was on the field 17 times in the last 20 overs of the match, surely a world record.

I am normally a quiet, calm watcher of cricket who likes to write letters to calm my nerves. But that was an impossible task in Madras during the Tied Test, because even under the stands the perspiration left you limp and soaking wet. Anyway, who could stay calm in this cauldron of excitement? At the start of the day there were probably around 5000 people in the M.A. Chidambaram Stadium; by the final hour the attendance had built up to maybe 25,000 and the crowd roared and cheered and blew their whistles every time one of their heroes scored a run. If a four was struck, the noise was thunderous; when a wicket fell, the silence was palpable. Players who had never shown a moment's superstition became obsessive, as sitting on your hands, staying in the same seat or standing in the same spot became the norm when something good happened. The hardest part is watching—which is all you can do.

Tension affects everyone in a different manner. Players who normally cannot stop talking become mute, while other quiet watchers become chatterboxes. Some can't watch directly and instead follow the play by listening and feeling the hysterical excitement or stark disappointment of the crowd, which means those who do dare to watch are obliged to answer the inevitable question: 'What's going on now?' In Madras, the drama was played out in slow motion, with the last 20 overs taking more than two hours. This only added to the tension. It was around 5 p.m. when last man Maninder went out to join Ravi Shastri, with six balls to be bowled and four runs to win. At this point, I turned to Alan Crompton and Errol Alcott and said with a dry grin, 'How nervous do you reckon this bloke would be?' Because Shastri was on strike, 45 not out, India were probably slight favourites. At the Gabba in 1960, with one eight-ball over to go, Australia needed six to win with three wickets in hand. It looked like we were going to win, though I can't remember feeling confident at the time.

While the drama on the field in Madras mounted, life continued in the viewing area as Alan was suddenly harried by officials who were rather incongruously reminding him that the two teams had to leave soon for the plane to Hyderabad, the venue for our upcoming one-day international. Did they expect us to stop the match to catch the plane? As it turned out, the flight was delayed from its scheduled 5.30 p.m. departure by nearly four hours.

It was 5.19 p.m. when Matthews bowled the match-tying ball to Maninder. Earlier in the over, Shastri had scored a two to backward square and then accepted the single that tied the scores, which didn't upset us as it got the No. 11 on strike. I think the fact that Shastri took that single says something about Indian cricket—that they were happy with the tie rather than going for the win. When umpire Vikramraju gave Maninder out lbw, I dashed out onto the field with Alan and Errol, which is when I ran into Dean Jones.

In the dressing room, the players slumped into cane chairs or their kitbags, while the rest of us applauded their efforts. I made sure the players acknowledged Allan's efforts as captain, while outside the fans who had congregated in big numbers cried out, 'Well played, Australia!', and when they got a glimpse of the captain chanted, 'Border! Border! Border!' I sidled up to Bob and asked him if he could use his contacts at the Madras Cricket Club to quickly organise some beers for the boys, which Bob, the master administrator, was somehow able to do. At the airport, our fellow passengers seemed delighted they'd been made to wait three-and-a-half hours, as it meant they were sharing airspace with the heroes of the day. Both teams were given rousing cheers as they stumbled to their seats. Later, when we arrived at our hotel in Hyderabad, the hotel had French champagne waiting for us, which we gladly and proudly drank. It wasn't until a couple of days later, when we checked out, that Alan Crompton received the bill!

The hours after this amazing final day's play were a time for reflection. For me, I think the over-riding memory was the scene on the field straight after the game—not just Dean running up to me, more the atmosphere that engulfed the ground late that afternoon. It was crazy—that same concoction of confusion, exhilaration, incredulity and joy that we'd felt in Brisbane. In Madras, for the Australians, there was quickly also exhaustion. Most of all, there was a certain pride to have been a part of it. I was grateful to have been there.

14

SELECTION MATTERS

I have always felt that the Australian selection committee I was part of from 1987 to 1995 worked fantastically well. Chaired by one of the fairest men you could ever meet—my old opening partner from Western Australia, Laurie Sawle—the committee was dedicated to the Australian cause. Laurie and I were joined in 1987 and 1988 by Jim Higgs and Greg Chappell, with John Benaud replacing Greg from the start of the 1988–89 season.

Whenever I think of Laurie and that selection committee, I remember a flight we shared to Perth for a Test Match one season immediately after the side for the next match had been announced. As word came through over the intercom that we were commencing our descent, I turned to my mate of 30 years and said, 'You must be looking forward to getting home and being with your wife and family.'

'Normally I would,' he replied. 'But you do realise there is no Western Australian in the team?'

I hadn't. Throughout the two-hour selection meeting that had taken place earlier that day, I had never sensed that the chairman was angling for a player from his state. As a former Western Australian player I knew how parochial the WA public is, and how critical they would be that their selector hadn't obtained a place for at least one 'sandgroper' in the national squad. Fortunately for

Australian cricket, Laurie was bigger than that sort of thing. In his own quiet way, he was a very strong man, who always preferred to find a consensus among his committee rather than simply put a difficult selection to a vote. In all my time as a selector, I can only recall one occasion when Laurie had to stop the debate and use his casting vote.

That came in 1989, when we sat down to pick the team for the upcoming Ashes tour. We were torn over the final fast-bowling spot. Having decided to include Tasmania's Greg Campbell on the basis of his enormous promise to back up Terry Alderman, Geoff Lawson and Merv Hughes, the choice came down to Mike Whitney or Carl Rackemann. 'Whit' had topped the season's first-class averages and taken nine wickets, including 7–89 in the first innings, in Australia's most recent Test, against the West Indies at the Adelaide Oval. 'Mocha' had struggled in the past with various ailments, but at his best he was an outstanding paceman, and having missed Queensland's first three Shield games of the season he'd been consistent and injury free for the remainder of the summer. Both men deserved the trip. I was one of two selectors who went for Whit, in my case because I believed we needed a left-hander. The other pair, however, preferred Carl. Allan Border was still to come in as captain and give his views on the squad's make-up, and when he did he said, 'Rackemann is the right choice. Whit doesn't swing the ball.'

Laurie Sawle, as chairman, promptly announced, 'Okay, that's the way we'll go.' So Mocha got the trip, and though he didn't play in a Test he was terrific throughout the tour.

I had first been offered a position on the selection committee when I took up the Australian coaching role in 1986, but I felt then that it could get a little awkward, being close to the players as coach one day and then having to sit in judgement on them the next. It took me twelve months to realise that while this situation was a reality, as coach I was also in a unique position when it came to assessing the relative merits of players. In essence, the many advantages of the coach being a selector outweighed the few negatives. I knew I'd have to be careful not to let the fact that I liked or disliked a bloke affect my analysis, but I had been confused by several selections that had been made and realised that some big decisions were needed if the Australian team was to dig itself out of the deep hole it was then in. I wanted to be part of those moves. In the end, I think I saved more players in my time as a selector than I dropped, but that was never my intention, and while I never betrayed confidences between me as coach and a player, I did always offer full and honest appraisals of players' performances to my fellow selectors.

From day one, there was criticism of the fact that the coach was on the selection committee. Some of it came from players who'd missed out, some from ex-players who believed there was no need for a coach at all. Ian Chappell was always arguing this case, which I always found peculiar given that from 1969 to 1975, because the captain, vice-captain and a third senior player made up the selection committee on tour, he was always one of the selectors when the Australian team he was a member of went overseas. If Ian really believed that a coach shouldn't have been a selector because players would consequently be reluctant to discuss their problems with the coach, he probably shouldn't have been putting his hand up to select Test XIs on tours in the years when the captain and vice-captain were the closest things the team had to a coach.

The only time I wished I wasn't a selector was when I had to tell a bloke he'd been dropped. However, it was always better that the coach/selector do it. Calling Geoff Marsh when he was left out in

1991–92 was awful, because he had been so strong for so long and had been such an important part of the rebuilding program that had begun in 1987. I'll never forget how hard he worked on his game—a bit like I'd done nearly 30 years earlier—learning to bat within his limitations. And yet in the end I reluctantly agreed with the rest of the selectors that his recent figures just didn't stack up. I was the last of the selectors to come round to this view—it is terribly hard not to get loyal to certain people when you admire their guts and determination, and the way they motivated the team—but, with hindsight, they were right and I was wrong. This was actually a classic example of where the selection committee worked well; with four strong characters involved no one opinion or philosophy was dominant. My understanding is that this has continued since 1995. Anyone who thinks that one person dominates the Australian selection committee has rocks in their head.

•

Of all the selections we made between 1987 and 1994, I think the first one—the 1987 World Cup squad—was the best. The team had been struggling since Greg Chappell, Dennis Lillee and Rod Marsh retired in early 1984, and its performances in the previous two years had been dreadful. My view in 1986 was that there were too many players in the side who were content just to do enough to stay there. They didn't seem bothered to push the perimeters of their talent— instead, bad habits were everywhere. Further, there was a lot of poor humour in the squad—the kind of cruel jokes that can be funny when you're on top but terribly hurtful if you're the recipient and you're struggling. The attitude to practice was, 'Oh no, not another one.' It was astonishing how many players were exhausted at 5 p.m. but energised at seven. Worst of all, this environment had been around long enough to be entrenched. There seemed to be no joy in being an Australian cricketer, and that annoyed the hell out of me. It wasn't cool to be proud.

The selection panel of which I was now a member decided that a revival was not going to happen overnight, and came up with a list of around sixteen players who we'd focus on. The fourteen-man World Cup squad came out of that group. Further, we identified a core of five cricketers—Allan Border, Geoff Marsh, Steve Waugh, David Boon and Craig McDermott—around whom we'd build the Test and one-day teams. These guys were all talented cricketers, but more importantly they were ambitious and mentally tough men who treasured wearing the baggy green. Each of them would make a terrific team-mate. We never said outright to these blokes, 'Your place is assured,' but I think they sensed our support, and typically they set out to justify rather than exploit the confidence we were showing in them. McDermott was the only one of the five who wasn't a permanent fixture in the team for the next four or so years, but even he had his good days, and he eventually became a quality fast bowler. Soon, Dean Jones, Merv Hughes and Ian Healy were incorporated into the nucleus. By 1989 we had a dedicated team that had a genuine toughness about them. They wanted to avenge what had occurred in the previous Ashes series in Australia. Guys such as Border, Boon, Marsh, Hughes and Waugh felt badly about being beaten by England in 1986–87, they really did. The 1989 Ashes victory was no real surprise to us selectors, although even we didn't believe that the boys would win so decisively.

Greg Chappell was the person who first brought Heals' name to our attention. We hadn't been totally happy with either Tim Zoehrer or Greg Dyer, who had kept wicket for Australia in 1986–87 and

1987–88 and wanted to go in a different direction. Jim Higgs had seen Heals and was impressed, and Allan Border supported him, and after I made a couple of phone calls I was keen to go along with them. But after a few weeks in Pakistan on Heals' first tour, I was thinking, 'What the bloody hell have we done?' The poor fellow had a shocking tour, and not just because he put a few chances down in the Test matches. During fielding drills, I found it way too easy to confuse him because his footwork wasn't right. However, his work ethic was excellent from day one and he had nice hands, so there was definitely plenty to work with. When I reported back to my fellow selectors that, yes, Heals had not had a good tour, I was still able to talk positively about him. It was easy to support his retention in the side, and to his enormous credit, he really got stuck in and became a genuinely great wicketkeeper.

Of course, Heals achieved his greatest fame keeping to Shane Warne, which was appropriate in a way, because the two of them had both been shock selections when they first played for Australia. Heals had played just six first-class games before he was selected, and Shane seven. Four years after Shane's debut, another bowler came out of the blue, who also went on to a stellar career. I was no longer a selector by then, but I have no problem identifying a brilliant and perceptive choice. When he was first picked, as a replacement for Craig McDermott at the 1996 World Cup, I had to make sure I had things right. 'I've checked,' I told the boys after the news came through, 'his name is Gillespie.' The following day manager Colin Egar and I were at the airport armed with a photograph of our new recruit to make sure we collected the right person. It all seems so ridiculous now, given Jason Gillespie's distinctive appearance and his superb record for Australia. 'Dizzy' won me over very quickly. He was just fantastic—no one worked harder than he did.

Dizzy would have fitted right into the 1987 World Cup squad, because he's a busy cricketer and that team was made up of busy cricketers. By 'busy', I mean you could sense the urgency in them, hear their encouragement for each other, see through their body language that they were up for the contest. When the guys from 1987 ran between wickets, they hustled. When they backed up their mate in the field they did it enthusiastically and consistently. I used to keep saying, 'All we need is three or four per cent improvement in everyone and as a team there'll be a huge improvement.' The targets AB and I set for them were realistic. The spirit out in the field was as terrific as the work ethic was off it.

Before the 1987 World Cup, I purposely took the team to Madras, the scene of the previous year's Tied Test, for ten days of solid hard work. The weather is terrible there in September–October—outrageously hot and humid—but I knew that if we approached it right, we'd come out of it super fit, super strong and mentally alert. We spent a lot of time duplicating what we would be doing in the matches, either batting and bowling with conviction in the nets, or completing fielding drills designed to mimic match-day situations. For the games, I stressed that a missed single was a crime, and urged the boys to score off as many deliveries as possible. To me, that was more important than hitting fours and sixes. I had also discovered that the team that scored the most singles in a one-day match usually won.

We won our first game, against India, by a precious run, and the camaraderie afterwards was as buoyant and heartfelt as I can ever remember. Word was out that the Aussies had changed, that we were strong. In our third encounter, a rain-affected match against New Zealand, Steve Waugh bowled brilliantly at the death, Geoff Marsh took a great catch, and again we prevailed by a very narrow margin. The next morning, at 7 a.m., we were out on the lawn at the front of the hotel practising our fielding. The Kiwis walked past . . . and I couldn't help loving the looks on their faces: 'Jeez, those bastards are keen.'

Australia weren't easybeats anymore, and we haven't been since.

•

Back in the 1960s, there were a couple of times when as captain I tried to influence the selectors. On one occasion I took the direct route, fronted the selectors, and failed miserably to get what I wanted. The other time, earlier on, I'd gone another way and things worked out well.

In 1966, I was keen to have Grahame Corling selected for our upcoming tour of South Africa. This was the only time I ever rang a selector, in this case Sir Donald Bradman, and said, 'We've really got to take this bloke.' Unfortunately, I got nowhere. Grahame had been struggling with shin soreness but I knew he had recovered and was starting to get back among the wickets. He had bowled brilliantly in England in 1964, getting Geoff Boycott out all the time, usually caught Simpson at slip, which is the way you want to get them. Grahame bowled at brisk pace, and at his best had a really good outswinger and a surprising bouncer. Instead of him, the selectors took Neil Hawke, who was carrying a football injury, to South Africa, a decision that left our attack terribly undermanned. That tour was probably Graham McKenzie's greatest, but we would have been much more competitive if Grahame Corling had been bowling at the other end.

Eighteen months earlier, I was desperate for Norm O'Neill to make the Australian team for the tour of the West Indies. I knew how good a batsman Norm could be, and was also keen to use his experience in the Caribbean, but his recent form had been moderate and he hadn't scored a Test century for more than two years. Not long before the team was due to be announced, New South Wales played South Australia in Sydney and Grahame Thomas and I both scored centuries in the first innings, after Norm had been trapped lbw by Neil Hawke for a duck. Norm was batting three for us at the time, with Peter Philpott as a makeshift opener, and come the second innings we needed 276 to win outright with not much time to get them. I kept thinking that Norm needed a score to get in the side for the West Indies, so after I cleared it with Grahame (who was a certainty for the tour), I suddenly announced, 'Oh Normie, mate, you're opening the innings with me today. Go and put the pads on.' Then, as we walked out to commence the run chase, I added, 'Norm, we're going to run the pants off these blokes. I'm going to do all the calling. Is that okay?'

Norm was not the greatest judge of a run, and he was a notoriously nervous starter. 'Yeah, that's fine, Simmo,' he replied.

We went out and got the runs in 43 overs. Norm finished with 133 not out and I can still remember the look on his face when I called him for a couple of really short ones. The best part of the story was that when the team for the West Indies was announced, he was in it.

•

Australians are at their best when they hustle, and if one man best captured the way hustle came back into fashion with the Australian cricket team from 1987 it was Dean Jones. 'Deano' loved playing for Australia and competing at the highest level, and wasn't scared to let his team-mates and opponents know it. His attitude was infectious, whether in the nets, during fielding drills or out in the middle. He loved running the first run hard, backing up his mates in the field, diving on a dry, hard ground to turn a four into a three, or converting a comfortable single for the opposition into a run-out chance for us.

Deano was a delight to coach. The work I did with him during the India tour in 1986 was as rewarding for me, and I think for him, as anything I was ever involved in. From that memorable Test in Madras, when he defied the heat and humidity to score 210, in one of the greatest innings ever, Dean was an integral part of the Test and one-day sides. His role in the World Cup win in 1987 and the Ashes victory in 1989 should never be underrated.

Off the field, his hyperactive nature could drive people mad. Maybe once a fortnight on tour I'd have to say, 'Deano, it's time for a chat.' He'd always reply, 'Oh Christ, not that time already is it coach?' We'd sit down, have a talk and he went back to being the bloody good cricketer we needed him to be. He just wanted to be noticed, and I think he enjoyed the discipline I brought to the Australian set-up.

That double century in Madras was the best Test innings I saw as Australian coach, and his unbeaten 102 in a one-day final in Auckland in 1990 was the best one-day innings of my experience. He took Richard Hadlee to pieces that day. That was the only time I saw Hadlee without a clue where to bowl the next ball. Dean could go over the top, but at his very best he was a superb technician who prided himself on his orthodoxy. He was dropped from the Australian Test team in 1992 because he had moved away from technical efficiency and consequently was getting out in the most extraordinary ways. He was still scoring a few runs, but often streakily, and too often it just didn't seem as if his brain was in the right gear. The mood in the room when he was batting was, 'Which crazy way is Dean going to get out now?' I found it really sad, because I love the bloke and wanted him to get his game back in kilter. But whereas in India in 1986 he had been a terrific listener, by 1992 he seemed convinced he could do things that were actually beyond even his considerable talent. Good young players such as Damien Martyn, Justin Langer, Matthew Hayden and Michael Slater had arrived on the scene, and the selectors decided it was time to move on.

Being a selector requires a sharp mind, good all-round knowledge of the game, compassion, bravery, and an all-encompassing love for the sport. A selector has to look to the future, something I thought the selection panel I was part of always did well—and something Trevor Hohns, who took my spot on the selection panel, did superbly in his years as chairman of the panel from 1996 to 2006. It is more difficult to be a selector today than it was even a decade ago, because not only does being dropped from the team mean a player has lost his prestige, but his financial security has also been put at risk. Obviously, everybody wants to play on longer these days to make as much money as possible. Seven to ten years as an Australian cricketer should ensure you are set up for life.

Yet Trevor and his team seemed to get most of the really awkward decisions right. The selectors terminated the one-day careers of Mark Taylor, Ian Healy, Michael Slater and Steve Waugh, but continued their Test careers. The suggestion was also given to Ian Healy, Mark Taylor and David Boon that it was time for them to retire. As it had been with the wicketkeeping position in 1988, with Dean Jones in 1992, and with plenty of other cases too, the desire was always to bring new blood into the team at the right time. It seemed to me, watching from the sidelines, that Trevor's clear thinking and shrewd leadership was definitely in the Laurie Sawle class.

15

BIG MERV

Of all the cricketers I coached, Merv Hughes might have been my favourite. He has a well-deserved reputation as the lovable rascal of Australian cricket, but more than that he was one of the most underrated bowlers in the history of the game. There was a lot more to Big Merv than a hefty body and trademark moustache—for an important period in Australian cricket, from the time he took 13 wickets in one Test against the then mighty West Indies in late 1988 through to the end of the 1993 Ashes series, he was the heart of the side, in many ways its inspiration. Put a ball in Merv's hands and he was always going to give you 150 per cent, whether he was fit or ailing, bowling uphill or into the wind, on helpful tracks or on the ones that broke other fast bowlers' hearts. There were times when I was Merv's biggest critic, but I was also his No. 1 fan. He was a great bloke to have in the side because he had a knack of making those around him respond and offer a little bit more than they might otherwise have had.

If you'd walked through a local park and seen Merv staggering in to bowl from that long run of his, more tiptoeing than striding to the crease, you'd have been inclined to scoff. 'No way mate, give it away,' you might have told him. 'You'll never get anywhere bowling like that.' Yet for a time he was one of the most feared fast men in the world. Batsmen might not have rated him the quickest or the most athletic of bowlers, and some were inclined not to rate him at all because he did not look the part of the well-oiled, fast-bowling machine, but then they were confronted by the body language and quickly found that Merv would always come at them with everything he had. 'I don't want you there and I am going to do everything I can to get rid of you,' Merv said to them all, without even opening his mouth. Of course, he could also say his piece; the gruesome old 'mo' would quiver away and his many fans in the outer loved the idea that their man was getting stuck into the enemy.

The thing is, he was smarter and shrewder than pacemen are supposed to be. I think the reason he attracted the public affection that eluded many of his Australian fast-bowling contemporaries—men such as Craig McDermott, Terry Alderman and Geoff Lawson—was that as well as being an outstanding wicket-taker (as McDermott, Alderman and Lawson also were), there was always a bit of a twinkle and a grin in what Merv did.

'How many left?' Merv might have asked the umpire.

'Three,' was the reply.

'Is that three gone, or three to come?'

Whatever his reputation, Merv was nobody's fool. In the dressing room, he may not have a lot of what my generation calls commonsense, but he was rarely short of a comment or an escapade to liven up the mood. Having him around was an experience; he was a terrific influence and a monumental pest. As far as his playing weight was concerned, his problem was that he was a glutton. Merv was not averse to hamming it up at a bar, playing to the gallery who assumed that because he was there and a bit over the top, he had to be well into the booze. He did like a drink or two, but never a dozen, and he was just as likely to go on the wagon for long periods if it meant his kilos were more under control.

While he was involved with the Australian team, it was food, not drink, that added centimetres to Merv's waist. I don't know how many times I told him about it—and if I did that, then team physio Errol Alcott did so countless more—and every time he assured me he was going to be strong. 'My brain keeps telling me that what you say is right,' he'd explain. ' "You're being silly," it'll say. "Stop eating so much and you'll last a lot longer." But then my gut butts in and says to my brain, "Oh, bugger off!" '

During one Test match in Adelaide, Errol and I were into him mercilessly, watching what he ate, trying to curb his insatiable appetite. Then he went missing during a tea interval, which was unusual for Merv, who was always noticeable, until one of the players dobbed him in. We found him in a toilet cubicle. Sitting on the seat and eating the biggest plate of sandwiches I had ever seen.

Merv was a bigger nuisance than the flies and he loved it. I tried to make sure I was never sitting in front of him on a flight, because if that was where you were seated there was absolutely no chance of a quiet journey. Even before the plane was setting off from the terminal to get ready for take-off his long, hairy arm might be reaching over to give your hair a ruffle or your ear a quick clip. Perhaps he'd settle for a sudden pounding on the seat from behind, or would lean forward to tell you another of the world's corniest jokes.

'Simmo, do you want the good news or the bad news?'

'Whatever you reckon, Merv.'

'My old man's going to have a brain transplant. But he's thrilled to bits, because he's going to get my brain. He reckons it's never been used before!'

On the field, Merv was a formidable performer, no doubt about that. He was not in the Australian team just for his bonhomie, he was there on merit. On the 1989 Ashes tour he did not take a swag of wickets—19 in six Tests, which is good but not outstanding as far as statistics go—but he did get so many of the crucial, tough wickets. Terry Alderman, who snared 41 scalps, was outstanding and rightly received a lot of the kudos, but if Allan Border was ever in a corner he knew he could throw the ball to Merv and, more often than not, his man would take the important wicket. Consequently, the impetus we built up from the start of that series was never lost.

What captain could ask for more? Merv was also a great fieldsman, a fact often overlooked because he invariably patrolled the outfield where match-turning dramas rarely occur. However, if the ball went in the air, I would as soon have Merv underneath it as anyone. At practice, I would stretch him hard, perhaps giving him ten high catches in a row. He was always right under the last one, sweating his guts out, and ready to go for the eleventh if that's what I wanted.

He became the spirit of the team, because he was never down. In the dressing room, if we were struggling, Merv might start telling the most ridiculous or outrageous jokes. In a one-dayer at Edgbaston in 1993, Robin Smith belted us all over the place and England finished with 5–277 from their 55 overs. In reply, we lost three wickets before our total reached 100, before Allan Border and Mark Waugh commenced a crucial partnership. For one solid hour, Merv kept these jokes going and the team was in uproar, laughing like mad. The England supporters in front of us couldn't understand why we were so chirpy when we were in so much trouble, and even our captain out in the middle looked up at one point and threw his hands out, as if to say, 'What's going on?' This was Merv's way of saying, 'Hey, come on fellas, we are still in this. Everything is going to be all right.' We won the game by six wickets.

Merv was a big, brave and very resolute man. Perhaps not *exactly* a coach's dream, but the kind of personality any sensible coach and his team values very highly. He had a passionate desire to play for Australia—another characteristic that made him a powerful Test cricketer. I will never forget Merv's fabulously assertive performance against the West Indies in Perth in 1988–89, when he went into battle for the entire nation after Geoff Lawson was felled and badly injured by a Curtly Ambrose bouncer. The big man captured 8–87, including a hat-trick, in the Windies second innings (having already taken 5–130 in the first), but was more concerned with Lawson's wellbeing and the fact that we'd lost the match. Then there was Adelaide in 1989–90, against Pakistan, when Merv bowled on a right knee that would have put most fast bowlers out of the match. Instead, he took 5–111 off 32 agonising overs in the tourists' second innings. His right leg was the one that bore the brunt of his weight every time he bowled, and on the morning of the first day of that Test, his knee had locked up and he was struggling to even walk. But he knew that Alderman had dropped out that same morning because of a groin strain, and was prepared to accept Errol's word that he probably wouldn't do any further damage to the joint if he had an injection and played.

Merv had the needle, passed a fitness test, and then went and bowled 18 overs on the first day, finishing with 2–63. He took 34 wickets that Australian summer, never at any stage stopping to tell anyone in the media about his ailments, while his admiring team-mates whistled through their teeth and reflected yet again what a giant he was.

Merv could also bat when the demand arose. His did so without any great grace or finesse, but with the same earthy conviction and courage that defined his bowling and made him an exceptional competitor. He used a bat so heavy no one else could lift it, didn't have a backswing, and deserves to be remembered for two outstanding innings: at the Adelaide Oval in early 1989, when he scored an unbeaten 72 against the Windies and shared a ninth-wicket partnership of 114 with Dean Jones, who made 216; and on the Ashes tour later that year when he made 71 in the First Test at Headingley, the game in which Steve Waugh scored 177 not out, his maiden Test century. Inevitably, there are stories from these innings—stories that seem almost designed to mask the fact that in both cases Merv did a wonderful, critically important job. It would not surprise me to know he invented these tales to preserve his larrikin image (though they and a hundred like them should be preserved!). Dean tells how Merv came down the track in Adelaide and said, 'Don't worry, mate, I'll stick it out and you'll get your 200. Go for it.' Merv was promptly hit inside the thigh, on the fingers, in the guts and finally on the back of the head. Dean raced down the pitch to make sure he was okay, to which Merv cocked an eyebrow and grimaced, 'Are you 200 yet?'

When Merv went out to bat at Headingley he joined Steve Waugh at a time when Steve was at the absolute peak of his form. Our reminders as Merv left the dressing room were simple: 'Don't do anything silly, just give Stephen a hand.' Merv seemed to take it all on board and promptly lifted Graham Gooch over the top for six! 'What was going on?' AB asked later.

'Sorry, skipper,' Merv replied, 'I was playing carefully, like you told me, and I just followed through a bit too strong.'

I guess in today's commercial world, Merv will be remembered more for his image than his 212 Test wickets. When he was appointed an Australian selector in 2005, the general reaction of the public seemed to be surprise, as if they were asking, 'What would Merv know?' It seemed they'd forgotten what a clever, street-smart fast bowler he'd been. Whenever they show footage of Merv in action, television producers usually run with the one of the big bloke with the bigger moustache doing warm-ups in front of the crowd at the MCG, rather than showing him dismiss Gordon Greenidge at the WACA, or David Gower at Lord's, or Javed Miandad in Adelaide, or Viv Richards in Port-of-Spain or Mike Gatting at Old Trafford.

I am happy that Merv the cricketer is remembered as a man who won affection from the public and warmed to them as readily as they warmed to him, and as an 'unstylist' who did the job with a ready wit and a larrikin approach to the game. I know he doesn't object to that. But it will be an injustice if his importance to the Australian cause of his time is downplayed.

If a young cricket fan asked me about Merv, I would reply, 'If you think of Merv as a great character, you're right. Ask him for his autograph, he won't refuse. If he goes on a bit, go with him, you'll have a laugh for sure. But please always remember that he was a superb Test-match bowler, in his unique way one of the very, very best.'

16

HOOTER

Until he finally called a halt in 2006, the longest-serving member of the Australian cricket team was also its least publicised. He had been saving or making careers for Australia since 1984. Compared with the men he helped and supported he is unknown, yet I could mount a strong case that he had been as valuable as any of them.

I am writing about Errol Alcott, for more than twenty years the Australian team's physiotherapist. Errol was first appointed to that role for the West Indies tour in 1984, when Kim Hughes was the Aussie skipper. He was virtually unknown in cricket circles at that time, although he was quickly gaining a reputation for his physio skills in Sydney rugby league.

A former league second-rower, Alcott—as the cricketers soon discovered—was tough, willing and very committed to excellence in his area of sports medicine. However, initially at least, he knew very little about cricket and seemed to like it even less. On his first full day at the ground he grew more and more bored, until in frustration he muttered, 'When the hell does the hooter go?' Cricket, of course, ends for the day when the umpire calls 'time'. It's rugby league that ends when the siren (known colloquially as the hooter) sounds. The 12th man heard the remark and Errol has been known as 'Hooter' ever since.

He was big, strong and tough, but Hooter was (and remains) a very compassionate man, who quickly earned a reputation not just for his skills, but also as something of a 'father confessor' for the players. His massage table became cricket's equivalent of the confession box, with players liable to reveal their fears and worries about their games and even their lives. Never once did he betray a confidence. The players quickly respected him and at the same time learnt that when it came to matters of fitness they could never assume that he'd simply take their word for it. He was as strong as any of them—something he proved over and over, especially when some young, fit punk came into the team and took him on in a physical contest. I can recall Craig McDermott, Merv Hughes and Matthew Hayden all failing to get on top of Hooter.

In those early days, Hooter and I, plus whoever had been appointed manager for the tour, were the 'support staff'. So Hooter was not just the physio, he was also the trainer, dietitian, doctor and my invaluable assistant in running practices. There was never any task that he couldn't do capably.

But it was as a physio that he was in a class of his own. On my first trip I had some problems with a shoulder and made the mistake of mentioning it to Hooter. Within seconds, I was on his massage table—or 'torture slab' as some cricketers over the years have called it—and he probed for the sore spot. Once he found it, he was unrelenting as his iron hands and fingers manipulated the tender area. 'It's deep, Simmo,' was all he said and he dug enthusiastically away.

I have always had a high pain tolerance, but I must admit I struggled to keep my mouth shut. I really wanted to yelp 'Enough!' These sessions went on for days until the problem was fixed, thankfully never to return, and when they concluded he slapped me on the shoulder and said, 'You're a tough old bastard, aren't you?' The respect went both ways, 100 per cent. Hooter was my right-hand man for the ten years I was Australian coach.

I considered him a genius for his ability to get a player fit and back on the field as quickly as possible. Of course, he could only do this if the player involved cooperated, and a story from the 1989 Ashes tour illustrates this perfectly. At the time, we were having trouble with the wicketkeeping position. Although Ian Healy had kept throughout the tour of Pakistan in 1988, and in both the Tests and one-dayers in Australia in 1988–89, in our minds he hadn't nailed the spot down. Tim Zoehrer was a genuine alternative. However, a week before the First Test, both men went down with similar knee injuries.

Hooter was confident he could get them fit, but only if they were prepared to be treated every four hours, day and night. Zoehrer wasn't; Healy was. The choice was made for us, and Heals went on to become one of the most accomplished of all Australian keepers.

There is no doubt in my mind that Hooter was as big a hero in that situation as the man who ended up receiving all the on-field plaudits, because of the way he drove Heals to recover his match fitness. It isn't easy being always on call 24 hours a day, but Hooter saw this as part of his job.

Geoff Marsh was always a very nervous character before a big match, and on countless occasions he would ring Hooter in the middle of the night to say, 'Feel like a cup of tea, Hoot?' No player to my knowledge was rebuffed by the big man if they had a problem.

Though he had no specific background in cricket, his judgement of cricketers was rarely astray. In 1991, he toured with an Australian under-25 team to Zimbabwe, at a time when the senior team was desperate for a good fast-medium bowler, someone who could bowl tight. Errol and I always used to discuss the merits of various players, often considering their 'inner soul', and this time I said to Errol, 'This bloke Paul Reiffel from Victoria, I just don't know him. What did you make of him?'

'He's a tough fella,' said Errol. 'For a while over there, his feet were so badly blistered that every day he came off the field and was almost wringing the blood out of his socks. But he never said a word, didn't talk to me about it for ages. Just got on with it and did a good job. You'd want to keep him in mind, he's got something special.'

Errol could be a hard marker when it came to toughness, so I made a mental note that this Reiffel was one to watch. In the years to come I used to call 'Pistol' a 'wingman' because he was always on the periphery; even when you went out at night that's where he was. It was a bit the same with the media and the public—he never quite received the recognition he should have. There was one point during his career when we were picking him for Australia at a time when the Victorian selectors wanted to drop him from their team. Between 1992 and 1997 he was a vital member of the Australian team, most notably in the West Indies in 1995.

Of all the wonderful things that came out of that series, the two I recall most fondly were the way the Waugh twins batted in the final Test at Kingston after I asked the batsmen to stop being satisfied with making reasonable scores (Steve made 200, Mark 126) and the manner in which our bowlers so religiously stuck to the game plan. Not even Errol's magic could prevent us losing our two leading opening bowlers, Craig McDermott and Damien Fleming, before the First Test, which left us with a relatively inexperienced pace attack of Pistol, Glenn McGrath and Brendon Julian. Our bowling strategy was to keep it tight and pitched up, and to not give the Windies batsmen room. The scheme worked brilliantly, with Reiffel and McGrath superb. They harried the West Indies batsmen into submission.

By my reckoning, as much as 65 per cent of the dismissals we obtained during the series were secured in the way we planned— easily the highest percentage of batsmen dismissed as planned I have seen in my many years of cricket. Brian Lara, for example, was caught in the area between wicketkeeper and gully four times out of seven completed innings, as we relentlessly targeted him on a good length and on (or just outside) his off stump. In that same Kingston Test in which Steve and Mark scored all their runs, Pistol took seven wickets, including Richie Richardson in both innings and Lara for a duck in the second. It might have been his best ever Test, and he sure deserved it. I wonder if he realised the role Hooter played in getting him started?

Errol was also a grand psychologist who was always quickly able to ascertain if a player's ailments were real or imaginary. I will never forget a physio who worked with the Pakistani team in the 1990s, who was always in our dressing room, picking Hooter's brain. One day at the Melbourne Cricket Ground, a Pakistani batsman went down after being struck in that painful and private area just below the belt, and Hooter's mate rushed into our room. 'What can I do?' he pleaded. 'You seem to get your men better much quicker than I can with mine.'

Quick as a flash, Hooter grabbed a tablet from his medicine chest, handed it to the Pakistani physio, and said with a wink, 'Get him onto his feet, give him this pill and he will be okay.'

Without stopping for breath, the physio raced to the centre of the field, grabbed the poor suffering batsman under his arm and hauled him painfully to his feet. Then he rammed the tablet down his throat. At this point, I looked at my trusted colleague, and raised my eyebrows.

'Don't worry, it's only a smartie,' Hooter said with a grin. 'I've done the same thing with our blokes from time to time.'

Hooter has all the answers. In 2006, his good mate Russell Crowe convinced him to leave the Australian team and take up a job with Crowe's beloved South Sydney rugby league team. Errol's career as a sports physio had gone full circle. For the cricketers, I don't think life will ever be quite the same again.

17

OPENING UP

Opening batsmen are the explorers of cricket. Virtually every time they go out to bat they are entering unknown and often unfriendly territory. While the unknown for them is only 22 yards, this terrain has proved on occasions to be almost as unpredictable as some of those confronted by great adventurers of the past. While there might not be hostile natives with threatening weapons to face, a five-and-a-half ounce red missile can inflict almost as much damage—but like all true adventurers, good openers know that successful forays into the unknown can bring enormous personal rewards, success for their comrades and, at Test level, glory for their country. Failure, on the other hand, carries with it personal disappointment and hardship for the side.

For most of the years from the unfortunate sacking of Bill Lawry and the retirement of Ian Redpath to the emergence of David Boon, Geoff Marsh and then Mark Taylor, Australian cricket suffered from a lack of successful openers, and it is no coincidence that this period proved to be one of Australia's least successful. In contrast, the efforts of openers such as Tubby Taylor, Michael Slater, Matthew Hayden and Justin Langer in the last decade is one of the primary reasons Australia has been so triumphant. I may be biased, but I feel the opening positions are the most important spots in the batting order. While facing high-speed bowling or cunning operators of the new ball may not be everyone's cup of tea, it can be immensely rewarding. Doing it well must be as satisfying a job as there is in cricket. And it is also not nearly as difficult as many would have you believe, providing the batsman desperately wants the job and has done his homework.

For all this, it is not necessarily enjoyable. After all, it would take a masochist to find pleasure in facing a tearaway bowler operating at 150 km/h or more with a 'drawn' cricket ball at 22 yards. No batsman of my experience has liked facing pure pace. Some may suggest they do, but I am yet to see a totally fearless batsman who has never flinched against this sort of speed. Even the great West Indian batting line-up of 1978 backed off against Jeff Thomson at Bridgetown during the Second Test, when he bowled the quickest spell I ever saw from first slip. To this day, the 'Bajans' will tell you it was the fastest bowling ever seen in the Caribbean.

I have seen some of the bravest batsmen I have known struggle with the mental and physical rigours of facing class express bowlers. Colin McDonald, my opening partner during the 1960–61 series against the West Indies, was acclaimed for his courage when he stood firm against Wes Hall and was repeatedly hit about the body. He took a tremendous battering and, while I admired his gallantry and tenacity, it was obvious at the end of the series that his game was suffering.

In modern cricket, even with all the armour the batsmen wear, it is still not easy against quick bowlers. Indeed, in some ways today's warriors are more vulnerable—if not to physical injury then definitely to mental scarring—as they attempt misguided hooks or to avoid the ball in a technically flawed way. At the last moment these batsmen turn their heads and rely on their helmet to save them from a potentially disastrous injury. By my estimate, batsmen

of the 'helmet era' (post-1978) are hit in the head around ten times
more often than those from pre-helmet days. Every hit will dent the
confidence of the batsman and reduce his run-making capacity. Yet
far fewer batsmen would be hit if they did not try to hook when
they were incapable of doing so properly, or if they just watched the
ball onto the bat or through to the keeper.

The old boxing adage of 'you never see the punch that hits you'
is also true of the fast bowler's missiles. While every batsman is
different—physically, physiologically and mentally—and no two
should necessarily adopt the same method, every batsman needs
to have a method of playing fast bowling. In the end, survival *and*
scoring runs is what it is all about, and it doesn't matter how you
do it to achieve this result, so long as you do.

•

As a coach, my most celebrated case of having to rework the method
of a batsman against fast bowling did not involve an opener, but
a man who went on to become one of Australia's greatest ever
middle-order batsmen: Steve Waugh. Still, it's a case study that
offers lessons for all budding opening bats. In the early 1990s, Steve
was in strife. He obviously did not like fast bowlers and was having
trouble scoring runs as the pacemen directed their deliveries at his
ribs and often got him caught down the leg-side. Further, he was
too side-on, with his toes pointing to point when he went back,
which meant he could not get inside the ball or glide it away on
the leg-side for singles to get off strike. This put a lot of pressure
on him.

At that stage of his cricketing life, Steve hadn't appreciated that
the best place to be against good pace bowlers was at the non-
striker's end (more on that in a moment). But he accepted this advice,

and learnt to open up his back-foot defensive shots and pushed the ball away for singles on the leg-side. In addition, he worked out how to let balls go that were aimed at his body by ducking under or swaying away from them. Not pretty, but effective and frustrating for pacemen, who hate to see a batsman easily dodging their fastest deliveries. They'd rather see a batsman trying to knock the steepling ball down or attempting to hook or pull, for they know such reactions are the ones that will most likely lead to a wicket. Steve also stopped focusing on the ball as it bounced off the pitch; instead, he taught himself to watch it right out of the bowler's hand.

Invariably, most batsmen who are having trouble with fast bowling are not watching the ball all the way; they have preconceived ideas about what might be coming and that too often leads to late or panicked shot selection. When Steve started watching the ball out of the bowler's hand, he suddenly had at least an extra metre to pick up the line and length of the ball, giving him extra time to get himself in the right position to play the appropriate stroke.

There is no doubt that what we did worked, because for a period from 1995 to 2001 Steve was, to my mind, the greatest batsman in the world. While my friends in the Subcontinent and in other parts of the world may disagree and push the claims of two great little men, Sachin Tendulkar and Brian Lara, I feel that during this time, day in and day out, in every part of the world, in varying conditions and match situations, Steve was the most consistent and successful. The knowledge that his technique was sound gave him confidence and this was never better demonstrated than in the West Indies in 1995, when despite being subjected to an illegal amount of the short stuff, he was clearly the batsman of the series. While his style may not have been that attractive—especially when bowlers such as Curtly Ambrose, Wasim Akram or Allan Donald were pitching short at him—if my life had depended on one innings he was the man I wanted to bat for me.

Another good batsman I remember suffering from watching the area around the bowler's hand and not the ball itself was India's Sourav Ganguly. I remember observing him in a preliminary game against Australia at the 2003 World Cup, when he opened up and was trying every weird way to overcome the pace bowlers, especially Brett Lee, who was at him unmercifully. Ganguly backed away, charged the bowling, but nothing was working. He just looked out of his depth, which was unfortunate because at his best he is a very fine player.

He was late or desperate with his shots, classic symptoms of a batsman not watching the ball. In the end, Lee pitched the ball up wide and Ganguly thrashed wildly at it. He'd worked himself into a state of mind—expecting another short one, no doubt—where a pitched-up wide one was always going to attract him like a magnet. The result was a thick edge and Adam Gilchrist did the rest.

Even if you do watch the ball correctly, you need to be wary of your concentration snapping. I can think of two classic instances of this. The first occurred when we played Barbados in 1965. Sam Trimble, a lovely man and the Queensland opener who was picked as cover for Bill Lawry and me, was always saying, 'Jeez, I wish I could get a chance.' Bill had the tour game off in Bridgetown and I said to Sam, 'Mate, this is a great chance for you to show us what you've got.' Wes Hall and Charlie Griffith must have bowled 40 bouncers in the first hour and Sam was ducking and weaving all over the place. Finally, after an hour, Richard Edwards came on as first change. Edwards was nicknamed 'The Professor' and he was reasonably quick, but after Wes and Charlie he was slow motion. Straight away, Sam wound up for a big cover drive and nicked a catch into the slips. After that, Norm O'Neill, Grahame Thomas and I all scored centuries, and Sam never suggested again that perhaps he should be in the Test side.

In the previous series against the Windies, in Australia, much the same thing happened to me. The scene was the Adelaide Oval, late on the fourth day, after Frank Worrell had delayed his declaration until 45 minutes before stumps, when he set us 460 to win in 395 minutes. We had no option but to play for a draw, especially after Les Favell was caught behind and Colin McDonald was run out to leave us 2–7. Norm O'Neill and I set out for stumps, and even took 19 from one Wes Hall over, but then with just one ball remaining—and me expecting a short ball from Wes to end the day—he offered me a well-pitched-up wide one, which I chased and edged through to the keeper Gerry Alexander. It was a terrible stroke that didn't do my reputation any good at a time when I was still establishing myself in the Australian team.

•

Given that courage is such an important prerequisite for an opening batsman, it is not surprising then that a successful opener must, first of all, have an appetite for the job. It is no good going in first if you would really rather be batting lower down the order. It is a given that an opening bat must not be afraid of fast bowling, but he must also possess quick reflexes, a good eye and a batting technique that can defend against pace, but also attack when the opportunity arises. He must not be overawed by the occasion, or unnerved by the heightened tension that normally accompanies the start of a match or a new innings. He must have a sense of responsibility. This, of course, can be said of any batsman, but the opening pair have the particular responsibility of trying to get the innings established by seeing off the new ball and giving their fellow batsmen something substantial to build on. An opener must be brave, but he can't let bravado get the better of him, because he isn't there to throw his wicket away by playing an irresponsible shot. He must have patience, determination and the ability to concentrate, all in good measure. These, along with the correct batting skills and a fair share of good luck, should get the team off to a good start.

Of all positions in the batting line-up, the opening berth is the one that most requires that the batsman knows his strengths and limitations and that he has a clear and concise view on how to play within both. It also requires that he understands the strong points of the opening bowlers, and that he is prepared to be adaptable to counter or control them, and also recognises their weaknesses, so he can take advantage of them.

Obviously it is vital for all budding openers to have a sound basic technique that can withstand the mental pressure exerted by a fast bowler hell-bent on knocking his opponent's head off or his wicket down. The more correct that technique is, and the better the understanding the opener has of his own game, the more likely will be his success. Further, all batsmen—and openers in particular— must assess, before each match, the opposition bowlers and the most likely way they can get you out. For instance, a left-hand swing bowler normally tries to get a right-hand batsman lbw playing back to an inswinger, or have him caught behind with one that leaves him. Armed with this information, a right-hand batsman should be trying to push forward whenever possible to nullify these tactics. Obviously, he won't push forward to everything, but if the 'computer between the ears' is alerted before the contest it will react quicker when called upon. All bowlers have a most likely way to get a batsman out and this knowledge, along with the best strategy to combat their tactics, must be fed into the computer before each match so that batting instincts are pre-fired.

But while technique and skills and courage are all necessary requirements of an opening batsman, it is almost impossible to succeed without a compatible partner. I argue that just about the most important characteristic a successful opener has is a total understanding with—and commitment to—his partner.

If I had to pass on just one tip about how to be a successful opener, it would be: get to the bowler's end as much as possible. If you are at the bowler's end you can't get out! But before you start thinking that this is a selfish philosophy, if both batsmen are working on the same principle and rotating the strike, the bowlers have less chance of exerting pressure or operating to their game plan. That's the key. That's what a *partnership* is all about and why it is so important to have a compatible mate. More excellent opening bowlers are seen off through strike rotation, which puts them under pressure and produces loose deliveries, than any other form of attack.

While opening the batting may not be fun, it is seldom dull. Those 22 yards of unexplored territory, and the new ball, see to that. Undoubtedly, a cricket pitch is the most discussed piece of real estate in the game. Inevitably, before play it is scrutinised and argued about, generally without much success. Even today, I still can't tell precisely how a pitch will play, and I doubt whether anyone else can either. What I do know, however, is that runs can be scored on almost any pitch, providing the batsmen treat every ball on its merits and don't go looking for a minefield. Similarly, new balls are always a challenge—no two play the same, not even when they're from the same box. They can be affected by manufacturing, atmospheric conditions or the pitch itself. So openers may as well

forget about what the ball and the pitch might do and get on with
the job.

•

During the 2004–05 season, I was invited by the News Limited
papers in Australia to select my 'best ever' Australian team. I was
asked to keep it to players I had seen, and the team I came up with
was Bill Lawry, Bob Simpson, Sir Donald Bradman, Neil Harvey,
Greg Chappell, Allan Border, Adam Gilchrist, Alan Davidson,
Shane Warne, Dennis Lillee and Jeff Thomson, with Norm O'Neill
12th man.

The toughest decisions were over the final batting spot, between
Border and Steve Waugh, and the opening bowlers. With both the
new-ball exponents and the opening batsmen, I decided to go for
partnerships, which in the case of the bowlers meant I had to choose
between Lillee and Thommo, Keith Miller and Ray Lindwall, and
Glenn McGrath and Jason Gillespie. My final decision came down
to instinct—who would I least like to bat against?—and I decided
that the searing pace of Thommo and the sheer determination and
talent of Lillee would give me the most trouble. I must stress this
was a very tough decision; leaving out Lindwall and Miller, two of
the heroes of my youth, seemed almost sacrilegious.

I was severely criticised in some quarters for picking myself, but
as I said I decided to select the best partnership and I'm prepared
to back Bill Lawry and myself against any other Australian opening
pair, even Matt Hayden and Justin Langer.

A lot of my peers agree with me that this current era is a good
time to be an opener. I also had to consider that Bill and I never
had the chance to play against New Zealand, Sri Lanka, Zimbabwe
or Bangladesh. At the time we opened, both South Africa and the

West Indies could lay claim to be the best team in the world, while neither Australia nor England were up to that standard. The West Indies had Wes Hall and Charlie Griffith taking the new ball, while Mike Procter and Peter Pollock spearheaded the Springbok attack. The Poms had to 'make do' with two fellows by the name of Fred Trueman and Brian Statham.

While Bill Lawry and I may have been a little unfashionable as an opening pair because of our style and method, we had that most important asset for opening batsmen: the ability to rotate the strike. This allowed us to be very consistent and score more quickly than many stroke players who were reputed to make their runs more quickly than we did but in fact rarely did.

The excellent cricket website <www.howstat.com.au> records that in cricket history as at 1 June 2006, only twelve opening pairs in cricket history have batted together on more than 50 occasions in Test cricket. Of those twelve, Bill and I have the best average (3596 runs at 58.95 runs per partnership). Of all pairs to score even 1000 runs, we rank sixth, and second of Australian duos, behind Jack Fingleton and Bill Brown, who averaged 63.75 in sixteen partnerships between 1935–36 and 1938. The best average of all time belongs to the great English pair, Jack Hobbs and Herbert Sutcliffe, who averaged an amazing 87.81 in 38 stands between 1924 and 1930. Hayden and Langer have averaged 51.07 in 104 innings.

I know it sounds big-headed to pick myself in such a team. My objective was twofold: one, to put the case for how effective our style was as an opening pair; and two, to try to give Bill some of the recognition he has been missing for many years. You never hear Bill's name mentioned when people start talking about the great Australian batsmen, and I think that's just dead wrong. Most of the credit for our record as an opening pair must go his way. Bill was undoubtedly the best opener of my time as a Test cricketer. Maybe he wasn't the most naturally talented of all Aussie batsmen, but he was definitely one of the most valuable.

Bill was at his best against pace, never wavering or shirking his responsibility. And he was as courageous as they come. Against Wes and Charlie in the West Indies in 1965, when more bouncers were bowled than I have ever seen in any one Test series—even more than in WSC—he showed both his physical and mental toughness. During a particularly torrid time against Charlie, in the Test where we added an Australian record of 382 for the first wicket in Barbados, he was struck on the face and the fieldsmen came towards him, to see if he was all right. Bill told them to buzz off, or words to that effect, saying to us later, 'They try to hit you all series and when they succeed they want to offer sympathy. I want none of their sympathy, I just want to score runs against them.' A peculiar sideshow to that incident was that around the time Bill was struck I asked the umpire what exactly Charlie had to do before he'd be warned for intimidatory bowling. The ump said he'd have a word to him, which he did, putting his arm around the bowler's shoulder as they walked back to Charlie's bowling mark. Unfortunately, that didn't do much good because five of the next six balls were bouncers. Only then did Charlie receive an official warning.

Bill was not always the slow player he was often labelled. On his first tour of England, in 1961, he was often dynamic and handed out the biggest hidings to Tony Lock I have ever seen. His first Test century was scored at Lord's in the Second Test, on a pitch that had an infamous ridge running across it, which made facing up to bowlers like Trueman, Statham, Davidson and McKenzie a very dangerous business. Only three batsmen got past 50 in an individual innings in the Test—Kenny Barrington, who scored 66 for the Poms, the redoubtable Slasher Mackay, who scored 54 in our first innings, and Bill, who made 130 in a tick over six hours. This was England's first Test defeat at home in five years. One great innings had made that possible.

In those days, Bill was a brilliant hooker and driver who was very hard to contain. Later on the responsibilities of captaining weak teams tempered his play, but when the circumstances were right he could still push the score along. At Adelaide in 1965–66, Graham McKenzie bowled out England on the first day for 241 and Bill and I resolved to be as assertive as possible in our reply. The result was an opening stand of 244 in 255 minutes, and we ran most of them. People who like to argue that cricket in the 1960s was slow and boring rarely mention partnerships like that one. As I remember it, Bill and I invariably scored at a good rate because our styles blended. We both liked working the ball about and rotating the strike through singles. This achieved all the advantages I referred to earlier.

Unfortunately, when I retired in 1968, Bill did not bat with partners who shared this skill, which meant he couldn't play as he liked. He would push a single but then not get back on strike for ages, and when he was in trouble he couldn't get away as his partners were not adept at stealing that crucial single to help their mate out. With his preferred pattern broken, Bill found it difficult to score as quickly as he once had. The result was a reputation for slow batting that he found impossible to shake off. It was used as the excuse to drop him in 1971, a decision which remains one of the most illogical and callous ever made by an Australian selection committee. It is such a pity Bill is remembered in this way, because when you study all the components of what makes for the perfect opening batsman, as I've listed them in this chapter, no one fitted the bill better than Bill Lawry. Most definitely, he was one of the greats.

18

TWO OF A KIND

I first met Steve and Mark Waugh after I was appointed coach of New South Wales in 1984. They were shy teenagers, but still I was immediately struck by their natural talent and fascinated by their contrasting personalities, build and style. Steve and Mark shared a huge talent for the game, but otherwise there was not too much identical about these Waugh twins.

They were highly successful at whatever sport they took on, but as cricketers, Steve at age nineteen was producing a little more than Mark, so it was he who made the state side first. Steve hit the ball amazingly hard in those days, but it was obvious that he had a few technical problems, particularly the fact that he batted with very stiff knees, which meant that he could not take a full step forward or get his eye-line right over the ball. He couldn't 'smell it out', as the old-timers used to say. This meant he tended to drive with his weight on the back foot, and consequently sometimes hit the ball in the air or edged catches into the slips. Yet he still made the Test team before his 21st birthday, in part because there were not too many accomplished Australian cricketers around at that time, but also because his huge potential was there for all to see. He was too gifted a player to waste and no sound judge doubted that he would eventually establish himself in a big way.

In fact, it took him three-and-a-half years to score his first Test century, and all of seven-and-a-half years before he cemented his place in the Australian side. This was because natural talent on its own was not enough, and he had to work hard to remedy technical flaws before he could set about making an extraordinary contribution to international cricket.

The first real glimpse of his class at the top level came at the 1987 World Cup, when he earned the nickname 'Ice Man'—so cool was he when he bowled the 'death overs' (the final overs of the required 50 in an innings), especially in crucial preliminary matches against India and New Zealand. For a period it was his bowling that kept him in the Australian side, as he impressed with the way he was prepared to think outside the square. Steve was always experimenting, always trying something new and unexpected. Indeed, both he and Simon O'Donnell became engrossed with innovations, which in Steve's case included the perfection of slower balls using a leg-break action. This was no mean feat for a man who bowled much quicker than most batsmen expected. He varied his pace, made the leggie drop suddenly, and was never afraid to use this surprise packet, even in a pressure situation. Batsmen who just wanted to hit everything out of sight got into all sorts of embarrassing difficulties, and nobody ever really worked out all of Steve's subtleties.

And he didn't restrict his repertoire to limited-over cricket. I remember the Test at the Gabba in 1988–89 when Viv Richards ducked under a slower ball which looked as though it had slipped out and would pass high and harmlessly over the stumps. Instead, it dropped sharply, hit Viv in the middle of the back, and the only bloke on the ground that day who thought it wasn't lbw was the umpire. Steve was naturally aggressive as a cricketer and his bowling often reflected this. He was quicker than he looked, so he could force batsmen onto the back foot and then surprise them with a yorker. I thought that for a period between the 1987 and 1992 World Cups he was just about the hardest bowler to tackle in international one-day cricket.

He did play some decent innings in his early years as a Test cricketer, as well as some exciting cameos with the bat in one-day cricket, but it was not until the 1989 Ashes tour that he put it all together as a batsman. He began that Test series with scores of 177 not out at Headingley and 152 not out at Lord's, playing some magnificent shots. My favourites were the wonderful pictures of him playing forward and driving with his back knee actually on the ground. Not the sort of stuff they put in a coaching manual, but remarkable for its flexibility.

However, Steve's success on that tour camouflaged the reality that he still had problems with his batting. I outlined in the previous chapter how we had to fix up his technique against short-pitched fast bowling; the key there was that he was prepared to listen and work hard to get things right. He is a classic example of an exceptional talent who needed the nuts and bolts of technique to put his God-given gifts to full use.

Steve played a lot of indoor cricket as a kid and that undoubtedly helped him to develop his exceptional fielding ability. The indoor game is played in restricted space, the need for run-outs is paramount, and its fieldsmen develop a quickness of mind and hand. You could see it when Steve flicked the ball through his legs or round his body, or attempted the impossible return to the stumps. He actually got a couple of run-outs at the non-striker's end by deliberately putting just one finger on the ball to deflect it back onto the stumps as it sped past on his follow-through.

I've seen very few players who would even think of that *after* the opportunity had gone, but Steve did it straightaway, as it happened, reflecting a very quick cricket brain. When you added together all of his qualities as a batsman, bowler, fielder and captain, the result was a unique, wonderful package.

•

Mark Waugh's retirement in 2002 left a huge hole in Australian cricket that in some ways has still not been filled. It wasn't only the runs he scored, the enjoyment he provided or the superb catches he took, it was the matches he won off his own bat. Since the Second World War, I reckon only Don Bradman, Doug Walters and Mark Waugh have had the necessary talent and intuition to change the fortunes of a game purely by their own batting genius. Sure, there have been a number of great Australian batsmen in this time— including Neil Harvey, Greg Chappell, Allan Border, Steve Waugh and Ricky Ponting—but Bradman, Walters and Mark Waugh were the three who had the capacity to single-handedly win the day.

Sir Donald and to a lesser extent Dougie brutalised opposition bowlers; Mark, in contrast, charmed them into submission. He dominated bowlers and was easily Australia's longest six-hitter of his time, but all the while he looked as if he had just caressed the ball when he sent it into the wide blue yonder.

Until Mark came along, I always said that if I was offered the opportunity to watch just one batsman for an hour, I would ask that the batsman be Norman O'Neill, for he was a joy to watch when he was in full cry. I long marvelled at Norm's grace and talent. He was so orthodox at his best and so technically correct, with the left elbow up, and he was the first bloke I'd ever seen who could drive genuine pace bowlers straight back past them off the back foot. I think that I'd still go for Norm as my first choice, but only just, for when I think of some of Mark's finest stands—such as Kingston in 1995 when he and Steve set up one of Australia's most important victories, or at the 1996 World Cup when he was simply magnificent in scoring a match-winning century against New Zealand in Madras—he was simply glorious.

Like Doug Walters and Mark Waugh, Norm O'Neill was supposed to be a little unreliable. Sometimes he did get out in unusual and spectacular ways, but like Dougie and Mark that made him even more exciting. All three averaged over 40 runs per Test innings during their careers.

Unlike his twin, who hated throwing his innings away, Mark was the supreme entertainer. Drawn-out, unfinished innings were not his scene, unless that was required by his team. And Mark had other strings in his cricketing bow besides batting so beautifully. As a bowler, he had the versatility to make himself adept at pace, swing or spin at different stages of his career. When I first saw him, he was something of a tearaway bowler. In his first season in first-class cricket, 1985–86, the season after Steve made his Shield debut, I had him opening the bowling. He could send them down as quickly as anyone in the side, loved to bowl bouncers, and would take on any batsman regardless of his reputation. He also had the knack of looking like a lucky bowler, but that was a mirage—like Ian Botham at his best, Mark bowled with a lot of imagination and variety, and often got batsmen out with an apparently innocuous delivery that was actually quite tricky and well executed.

As a fieldsman, Mark had the softest hands in the business—a cushion that gave with the ball and almost never allowed a chance to escape. Wherever he stood in the cordon, he had the old-fashioned virtue of letting the ball come to him rather than offering his hands to the ball—a trait that meant he could take the ball late and enabled him to hold on to chances very wide of his body, even a ball that had passed him. If he ever got a hand on half a chance at slip, he usually held the rebound because the ball never bounces far out of his grasp. When he was left out of the Australian Test team, after 128 Tests, the slip cordon suddenly had a vulnerability about it that has never been shaken off. In the outfield, Mark had a relaxed body, which meant that even on the roughest playing surface you seldom saw him fumble. He also moved very quickly for a big man, had a strong arm and rarely wasted a second getting rid of the ball.

Sadly, there was always a mistaken belief that Mark was too casual and lacked dedication. From my experience, this was utter rubbish. He was actually a tough cookie whose casual-looking style masked a considerable inner toughness. Playing more than 100 consecutive Tests meant that for nearly ten years he maintained his form, kept the selectors' faith, and never succumbed to injury— three considerable achievements. You can't last as long or attain the success he did unless you are dedicated and in love with the game.

As I said, he and Steve were different in so many ways. But in that last regard—their great love for the game—they were very much one and the same.

19

FOR THE LOVE OF THE GAME

For the first two to three years when I was Australian coach, I sensed that Allan Border didn't really want to be captain. He was unsure of himself, and didn't like the responsibility that came with the post. He was miserable in New Zealand in early 1986, and then in India, after doing a sterling job on the final day of the Tied Test, the tour lost impetus. It really wasn't until we started to win that he began to enjoy the captaincy. And he didn't become a more positive captain until after we started winning. You cannot be a good cricket leader if you haven't got the bowlers, so it wasn't until our Test attack got some venom that he found the confidence as a captain that he'd been lacking. He was actually a much better one-day captain than a Test captain, which is strange because one-day captaincy should be harder. The 50-over game, with its limited time frame, forces captains to be proactive, which I think is what happened with Allan. He did a great job and eventually became a good Test captain as well.

Allan was a cricketer who had a tendency to dwell on things and allow them to fester until a minor matter became traumatic. This meant there were times when his players were wary of him as they waited for an outburst, which wasn't always good for morale. The reason for this was that Allan just didn't like confrontation. A big deal had been made of the fact that in 1989 in England he stopped talking to the opposition, but I didn't think it was such a huge thing at the time. Looking back, maybe it was more important than I thought, but not so much because it meant the Australians were now going to be bastards on the field, like the teams of the 1970s, but rather because it meant that Allan was growing up as a captain, and that finally he was going to be decisive in his leadership because that was what it takes to win. Previously, he had wanted to be loved by colleagues and opponents alike. Allan is a very nice person and likes the companionship of cricketers, and for the first five years of his captaincy he wanted to be good mates with everyone, even when people were letting him down or getting the better of him. But from 1989, winning came first. Finally.

There is no question at all he was a special cricketer. In the tempestuous 1980s, when he was often the only class batsman in the Australian side, he had more chances than most to display his courage. There were a lot of fast bowlers around who targeted him as the chief threat, but he was so mentally tough. Being the one good batsman in a side is a heavy burden to carry because you know that if you get out, the team will be in trouble. That was why the West Indies fast bowlers of the 1980s always bore in at the opposition captain, because they knew that if the skipper cracked the whole team might crumble. Allan never cracked; it wasn't in his nature. If you are the best batsman in a mediocre side, you really have to concentrate, never avoiding the responsibility that comes with your rare skill, but also never forgetting the fundamentals. Allan was the classic example of the batsman who worried only about the ball he was about to receive. Nothing else mattered. None of the knocks he took or the wickets that fell at the other end ever blurred his focus. He was a very, very tough individual.

There is no way Allan was as gifted a batsman as the other great Australian left-hander of my experience, Neil Harvey, but he was as effective. It's almost unfair to compare them. Their batting styles were completely different—Neil was very elegant, a complete all-round batsman, whereas Allan knew his limitations and batted within them. Both were very brave. Allan was probably more determined than Neil, in part because he wasn't granted Neil's huge natural talent, but then Neil was never placed in as many back-against-the-wall situations as Allan found himself in.

One of the hardest jobs I had as coach was getting Allan to bowl more. I remember we were playing Sri Lanka in Hobart in 1989–90 and we needed to bowl them out on the last day. At lunch I said to him, 'Allan, you've got to bowl. You know that wicket out there is flat, it's a bit low. That's your sort of wicket.' I kept at him through the entire interval. As he was going back out I grabbed him one more time, and said, 'Allan, don't forget you said you were going to take the first over after lunch.'

'Okay, coach,' he replied flatly.

He didn't. He could never understand how batsmen got out to his bowling because he always used to say, 'I wish I could bat against myself.' In fact, he was a much better bowler than he gave himself credit for. Against the West Indies in Sydney in 1988–89, when he took 11 wickets in one Test, he came on fourth change, landed it on the spot straight away, and started to bounce and spin. He showed during that match that he could do it, but in the next Test he hardly bowled. He played another 55 Tests after that Sydney game and took only 12 more wickets.

One thing he did love was practice. Or maybe it was just that he loved cricket. At practice he had a ball or a bat in his hand and that was good enough for him. He was never much good at trying to run a fielding drill because he wanted to be in the middle of it all the time, engrossed in his own fun, which is one reason why he was happy to have me around—I could do all the fidgety things and take the pressure off him. All Allan then had to do was turn up, and he did that every time. Soon, our roles were etched in stone: I looked after everything off the field, he was in charge on the field. At breaks in play, we might have a chat, but only if he wanted one.

Allan was never keen on taking days off. I always tried to restrict a practice session to no more than two-and-a-half hours, because I wanted the time to be busy and energetic, and I wanted the boys to do it right. Halfway through a session, I'd leave and go 50 or 100 metres away to observe the activity from afar, and if I couldn't hear a lot of noise going on I knew I hadn't been doing my job. If that was the case I had to go back and reactivate the energy level. If things were going well, Allan was inevitably in the middle of it. If the session did need reviving, he'd happily do that.

I wanted the boys to enjoy practice and enjoy improving and Allan warmed to that philosophy. He also agreed with me that any practice involving an Australian cricket team needed to be competitive—it was a bowler's job to get the batsman out; it wasn't the bowler's job to give him practice. It was the batsman's job not to get out.

By 1993–94, I thought we needed a new captain and I sensed that the selection panel felt we needed a new captain, too. Finally, at the Sheraton Hotel in Hobart, we pinned Allan down and he indicated that he didn't want to go to Pakistan the following August. It was explained to Allan that if he dodged that tour it would be very difficult for him to remain captain. I think, deep down, even he knew the time was right, but being the competitor and the cricket lover he was, part of him still wanted to continue. The 'younger' blokes in the team—the Waughs, Healy, Taylor, McDermott—were now established Test cricketers and were looking for new leadership. Some loyal servants, such as Geoff Marsh and Merv Hughes, would play their entire Test careers under him.

Allan did retire, but grudgingly. If he had changed his mind and said he wanted to go to Pakistan he would have been judged on his recent form. He was still getting some runs, but his innings were taking longer and longer. I can't speak for the other selectors, of course, but I don't think I would have pushed for him. I thought it was in the interests of the team that he didn't go, so it was a bit of a relief when he eventually revealed he was calling it a day. I didn't enjoy one minute of the conjecture that had preceded that announcement, and will always remember the talks I had with him about his retirement as one of the least pleasant points of my time as a selector.

For me, the pure joy of coaching was seeing the players improve and aim for excellence. That and the winning; I always liked the winning. I always enjoy it when someone brings up an infamous quote from the former England batsman James Whitaker. 'The big problem with Bob,' Jim said when talking about my time as coach of Leicestershire, where he was a player, 'is that he wanted us all to be Test cricketers.' I couldn't see anything wrong with that. Still don't. His comment typified county cricket in the 1990s.

I remember when I was coaching at Leicester, at one point I had to go to Sharjah, where Allan and the boys were involved in a one-day tournament. It was in my contract that my role as Aussie coach had to take precedence. Early on our first day back together, I asked the boys to do the 'circle', a drill in which the stumps were put in the normal position, 22 yards apart, Errol (our physio) was the wicketkeeper, and I'd be at the bowler's end, he and I with baseball gloves on. The team would surround the 'pitch', at normal fielding depth, and the idea was that Errol and I would be throwing the ball out, trying to get it through the gaps and they would be dashing in, picking the ball up and throwing to the end we'd nominate. I always tried to make it competitive, never too easy, and they had to back up the throws and work together. They did the circle like geniuses that day and you could see when they walked away they were proud of what they'd done. I certainly loved being in the middle of such a brilliant effort. You could sense it in them afterwards, not least by the look in the captain's eye . . . it was as if they were saying, 'Simmo, you're back with the Aussies now.'

There wasn't a day when I was a coach that I didn't want to be back with the Aussies.

20

THE LATEST FAD

One of the great difficulties in trying to mimic other people's styles and tactics is that you must have the talent—and in many cases, the physical attributes—to do so, otherwise you will just become a very ordinary copy. But this has never stopped the latest fad, trend or theory from becoming a popular part of cricket, particularly at the international level. It's been happening for as long as I can remember. Let me give you a few examples . . .

When I first came into first-class cricket in the early 1950s, in Australia the bowling team was able to claim a new ball after every 40 eight-ball overs. Apparently, the officials straight after the Second World War felt bowlers needed help in a game that before the war had featured some hefty scores. Remember that in the last Ashes Test of 1938, England scored 7–903 declared and Len Hutton made 364. However, Sir Donald Bradman loved the idea of being able to throw a new ball at his champion fast bowlers every 40 overs, and with Ray Lindwall, Keith Miller and Bill Johnston in rousing form the spinners hardly got a look in. So effective were Lindwall, Miller and Johnston that many thought it was the end of slow bowling, and the popularity of this theory in Australia was part of the reason a string of wrist-spinners—including Colin McCool, Bruce Dooland, George Tribe and Cec Pepper—were lost to the Australian game when they went to England to play either league or county cricket.

The 'Benaud era' saw balance restored to bowling line-ups, with a blend of pace, swing and spin bowlers a feature of most teams. However, the success of Dennis Lillee and Jeff Thomson, then the imposing West Indian juggernauts, meant that in the late 1970s and throughout the 1980s fast bowling was king. The Windies' domination had a profound effect on the game in that time, but while having a four-man pace attack was great for the men from the Caribbean, it didn't always suit everyone else. Still, that small matter didn't stop other countries, including Australia, from often trying to slavishly follow the latest trend. In 1985, at Headingley, Australia went into the First Test with a bowling attack of Geoff Lawson, Craig McDermott, Jeff Thomson and Simon O'Donnell. Allan Border bowled three overs of spin, otherwise it was all quicker stuff, and England won by five wickets. Four years later at the same ground, the Poms left out off-spinner John Emburey, went into the First Test with an attack made up of Phil DeFreitas, Neil Foster, Phil Newport and Derek Pringle, and we declared at 7–601.

It wasn't until Shane Warne emerged in 1993 to show the world that there was a place for quality spin bowlers in top-level cricket that true parity was restored. Nowadays, teams need a really good reason before they'll go into a Test match without at least one spinner.

The 1950s really were quite a decade for the latest fad. My international career began eighteen months after Tony Lock and especially Jim Laker destroyed the Australian batting line-up in 1956 on jumping, turning minefields that some Englishmen described as first-class standard pitches. Six years earlier, the West Indian spinners, Sonny Ramadhin and Alf Valentine, had enjoyed considerable success in England, in the process putting to bed for a while the theory that you had to have pace bowlers to be successful.

Then Len Hutton retained the Ashes in Australia in 1954–55 on the back of his fast bowlers and people were thinking again that it might be pace and then more pace that was the go. Eighteen months later, it was Laker and Lock's turn, and the spinners were firmly back in vogue; but then, in 1957, Peter May and most notably Colin Cowdrey adopted a 'pad and bat' theory of playing spinners when they faced Ramadhin and Valentine again. When that strategy worked, the idea of pushing forward with the bat and pad locked together to counter the spin became the fashion of the day. I, along with all the other impressionable young cricketers, accepted this method without question, because our peers were recommending it.

I remember I got a couple of big scores for Western Australia against New South Wales in Sydney in 1959–60, facing many overs from Richie Benaud, and afterwards the renowned cricket writer Ray Robinson said to me that he had never before seen a player whose bat was completely covered in pad paint on the inside edge. I hadn't noticed that, but when I had a look at the bat he was right. My technique had become so tight—bat and pad close together— but I don't think this prevented me being aggressive when the game demanded positive play. However, while this style seemed to suit me, it didn't fit with many other batsmen; instead it restricted their natural flair. Peter Burge, who was always at his best when he was attacking the bowling, was one batsman who struggled a little in this manner. Peter was in and out of the Australian team for four years after the 1956 Ashes tour, playing in only eight of Australia's 23 Tests between 1957 and the 1961 trip to England. At Lord's in the Second Test of 1961, we crashed to 4–19 chasing just 69 to win, and stand-in skipper Neil Harvey said to Peter, 'Get out there and belt the thing.' He produced several fantastic pull shots off Brian Statham, finished 37 not out, and gave 'Harv' a perfect record as Australian captain. From this tour on, Peter went back to his attacking ways and was a key member of the side.

In the 1990s, a new fad developed—the idea of the opening bats in one-day cricket attacking from the very first ball. Now I'm all for aggression, providing it is channelled into constructive, thoughtful cricket, and the openers who were able to bat sensibly in this way— Adam Gilchrist, Sachin Tendulkar, Sanath Jayasuriya and Herschelle Gibbs—were often spectacularly successful. But what I found quite ironic was that what actually set off this trend—the success of the Sri Lankans in the 1996 World Cup—had little to do with the blazing batting of their opening bats. Yes, they definitely used these tactics, but if you really look at what happened, Sri Lanka won that World Cup *despite* their openers, not because of them.

The batting of Jayasuriya and Romesh Kaluwitharana at the top of the order first came to our attention in 1995–96, when Australia beat Sri Lanka 2–0 in the final of that year's World Series. They weren't used as an opening pair until halfway through the competition, but though each of them played a couple of exciting innings, as a partnership they averaged only 34.33. Still, Sri Lanka weren't expected to make the finals in front of the West Indies, according to general opinion, so they must have been doing something right. Again, at the World Cup, these two openers blazed away in the preliminary matches, but their stands in the quarter- final against England, semi-final against India and final against Australia were 12, 1 and 12 respectively. Little Kaluwitharana, who apparently encapsulated this new hitting policy better than anyone, scored 8, 0 and 6 in these games. But again, no one had expected Sri Lanka to win the Cup, so there had to be a reason for their newfound success.

NEW State cricket representative 16-year-old Bob Simpson shapes up confidently for his first practice with the NSW team at the SCG.

At the Sydney Cricket Ground nets at age sixteen, just prior to my Sheffield Shield debut.
Collection of Bob Simpson

In 1953, *Pix* magazine showed remarkable foresight in featuring these seven sporting teenagers. I'm far left, with future Grand Slam tennis champions Lew Hoad (second from left) and Ken Rosewall (third from right), Olympic swimming gold medallists Jon Henricks and Lorraine Crapp (third and fourth from left), the fifth man to win a million dollars on the USPGA golf tour, Bruce Crampton (second from right), and Australia's youngest Test cricket captain Ian Craig (far right). *Collection of Bob Simpson*

The NSW team that played Western Australia in 1953–54. Back (from left): Ron Briggs, Ian Craig, John O'Reilly, Arthur Fagan, Ted Cotton, Bob Simpson, Billy Watson; Front: Ray Lindwall, Jim de Courcy, Keith Miller, Richie Benaud, Geoff Trueman. *Collection of Bob Simpson*

The Australian side that toured South Africa in 1957–58. Back (from left): Les Favell, Wally Grout, Bob Simpson, Ian Meckiff, John Drennan, Ken Mackay, Lindsay Kline, Barry Jarman; Front: Jack Norton (manager), Peter Burge, Richie Benaud, Neil Harvey, Ian Craig, Colin McDonald, Alan Davidson, Jim Burke, Mitch McLennan (scorer). *Collection of Bob Simpson*

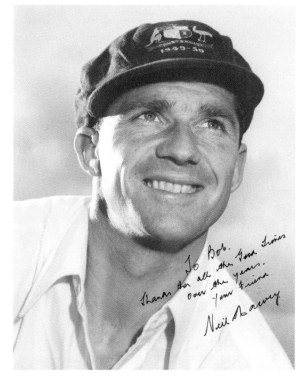

The great Neil Harvey, who played a vital role in my career, assisting me on the techniques of the game and advising me to open the batting, because that would give me the best chance of winning a place in the Australian team. *Ern McQuillan*

Ian Meckiff bowls to South Africa's Trevor Goddard at the Gabba in December 1963. Four times in this over, square-leg umpire Col Egar (far left) called Meckiff for throwing. The two fieldsmen out of the photograph were both on the offside, at cover point and extra cover.
Collection of Bob Simpson

The 'Grizzling Grunter', Wally Grout. When I was named Australian skipper, Wally stood up and said, 'I don't know what you think of Simmo, and I don't care. He has been appointed captain and as such he has my total loyalty and support.' I've never forgotten that.
Collection of Bob Simpson

Everyone's 'Little Favourite', Johnny Martin.
To play grade cricket in Sydney every
Saturday, Johnny would leave his home at
Burrell Creek on the NSW north coast at
9.15 p.m., catch the mail train from Taree at
10.20 p.m., arrive in Sydney at 5.18 a.m., play
from 1 p.m. to 6 p.m., catch the mail train
home at 8.20 p.m. and arrive back in Taree
at 4 a.m. *Collection of Bob Simpson*

Ron Roberts' 'International Cavaliers' team, which toured South Africa in 1960. Back (from left): Bob Simpson, Ray Illingworth, Mike Smith, Geoff Pullar, Alan Moss, Norm O'Neill, Ken Funston; Front: Ken Barrington, Len Maddocks, Tom Graveney, Richie Benaud, Brian Statham, Fred Trueman, Ron Roberts (manager). *Collection of Bob Simpson*

DINNER

IN HONOUR OF THE

AUSTRALIAN CRICKET TEAM

IN THE DINING ROOM OF

THE HOUSE OF LORDS

THURSDAY, 13th JULY, 1961

The front cover of the menu for a dinner held at the House of Lords during the 1961 Ashes tour. We used to love these functions, but I'm not sure the players of today look upon them with quite the same enthusiasm. *Collection of Bob Simpson*

Host   ·   ·   ·   ·   ·   -   THE LORD TENBY

Oops! I guessed that because Big Wes Hall had got his run-up wrong the ball would be pitched up. But it wasn't and I had to get my unprotected head out of the way fast. *Collection of Bob Simpson*

The end of my highest score in Test cricket: 311 at Old Trafford in 1964. I was looking for quick runs when I was dismissed, which is why I'm a couple of strides down the wicket as keeper Jim Parks throws up the ball. *Collection of Bob Simpson*

Three important figures from Australian cricket in the 1960s: Graham McKenzie, Neil Hawke and Bill Lawry. For some reason, all three have been somewhat underrated in the years since they retired, but as their captain I know how good they were. *Collection of Bob Simpson*

Australia has just won the third Ashes Test of 1964, and I greet Ian Redpath on the steps up to the dressing rooms at Headingley after he hit the winning runs. 'That was for you, skip,' he said. Vice-captain Brian Booth is behind 'Redders'. *Collection of Bob Simpson*

The Sri Lankans' style was well suited to the small grounds and benign pitches on which the World Cup matches were played. But it wasn't the blazing starts that were winning Sri Lanka their one-dayers, it was the simple fact that they were a very talented all-round team. Especially on the Subcontinent, their bowlers were superb and contained almost every team they faced. They also had an excellent fielding team—as good if not better than Australia's at the time—and their middle-order batting was terribly underrated. At the time their No. 4, Aravinda de Silva, was one of the best batsmen in the world, as he showed in the World Cup semi-final when he came in at 2–1 and scored 66, and in the final when he was in at 2–23 and scored 107 not out.

When I was Australian coach, we based our batting tactics on early consolidation, with the aim to accelerate in the final 20 overs. We wanted a high-order batsman such as Geoff Marsh, David Boon or Dean Jones to play a substantial innings, so that hitters such as Allan Border, Steve Waugh and Simon O'Donnell could lash out near the end of the innings. This strategy worked brilliantly at the 1987 World Cup, not least in the final against England at Eden Gardens in Calcutta when Boonie was named player of the match after scoring 75—and continued to work well right through to 1992; our winning percentage in one-day internationals from the start of the 1987 World Cup to the start of the 1992 Cup was 76 per cent. The Sri Lankans did thrash in the first 15 overs, but then they settled down to consolidate before quickening again in the final 10 overs. Interestingly enough, both these approaches tended to produce similar innings totals.

In the years that followed the Sri Lankans' 'golden' period, the Australian teams of Steve Waugh and Ricky Ponting won the 1999 and 2003 World Cups using a batting philosophy that involved trying to maintain the same tempo throughout the entire 50 overs. This has worked extremely well; however, I can't help but think that part of the reason for this success has been the blandness of opposition attacks. Just trying to contain the batsmen seldom works. There is nothing easier for a batsman than receiving similar deliveries almost every ball. When I coached the Australian team, we always felt that good bowling and fielding would put pressure on a batsman, but now that philosophy seems to have been reversed. Tough old-style hustling by the fielding team seems to have gone out of fashion. But clearly the best way to slow the scoring down is still to take some wickets.

Maybe the next development in cricket will be bowlers who can concentrate, mix their pace and maintain pressure on the batsmen, and fielding teams who get on with the game and play it with huge energy and verve. Then someone will have to come up with a new fad to try to counter this well-tested approach to the game. It will be interesting to see what that might be.

21

THE NATURAL

In the 50-plus years that I have been involved in first-class cricket I have never seen a bowler with as much natural talent as Shane Warne. He is the greatest leg-spinner of all time. What is most amazing about this is that he started his career at a time when there were plenty of people wondering if cricket would ever see another good—let alone great—practitioner of spin. It's when you put Shane's career in that context that you realise just how phenomenal and important he has been.

As Australian coach I was lucky enough to get a close-up view of Shane's first four years in international cricket. That was why, when Shane took his 500th Test wicket in Sri Lanka in March 2004, I was thinking how fitting it was that he reached that landmark in the country where, barely a dozen years earlier, he had come of age as a Test-match spinner in his first overseas tour with the full Australian team.

Prior to his 1992 tour of Sri Lanka, Shane had appeared in only two Tests, with somewhat disastrous results. In the first week of January 1992, he made his debut against India on a very flat Sydney wicket, and an 18-year-old Sachin Tendulkar and especially the more seasoned Ravi Shastri had thrashed him all around the old ground. Tendulkar made 148, Shastri hit a brilliant 206, and Shane finished his first innings in Test cricket with figures of 1–150. In the next Test in Adelaide, he took 0–18 and 0–60, and was left out of the final Test in Perth, where we went in with four quicks and won by 300 runs.

Bringing Shane into the Test team at that time had been a huge gamble, a tribute in a roundabout way to his great natural talent, which we had been aware of for a couple of years, and also an admission that our spin-bowling stocks were not too good. Peter Taylor, an excellent off-spinner in one-day cricket who struggled to break through at Test level, had played in the first two Tests of the series and taken one wicket. In our previous series in the Caribbean, our first-choice spinner Greg Matthews had been totally dominated by the Windies top order. When we first picked him, Shane was unfit and, quite frankly, knew little about leg-spinning except that he could spin the ball like a top and he had a great flipper. Training was something that other people did. His natural gifts were all that he needed, or so he thought.

Fortunately, Shane was a young man who readily took advice. In the winter before the Sri Lankan tour he realised he had a fantastic opportunity, and he lost nearly ten kilos and looked trim and fit when we began an intensive ten-day preparation in Colombo prior to our first game of the tour. It was in that 'camp' that his real career began. Prior to that tour, he bowled more with hope than with thought or planning. His length was erratic and he bowled the wrong line. It wasn't until he accepted the idea that bowling outside off stump was wrong, and that his big spinning leg-break would be more dangerous if it pitched on leg stump—or even just outside leg stump—that the genius hidden within his raw talent began to emerge.

Once he followed our suggestion to bowl this leg-stump line, his action and accuracy improved as he got his left shoulder pointing more at the batsman, which meant he no longer pitched the ball short too much, and it also accentuated his right-hip drive, thus allowing his full body to be in the correct position as he delivered the ball. His action could then be completed in the correct order— arm, wrist and fingers flowing with the body—and he was now a real chance of getting lbws with his top-spinners and even some leg-breaks, something that was not possible with the old tactics. He was transformed from a bowler who beat the bat too often with his big leg-breaks into an artist who gave little away and always put enormous pressure on the batsmen.

I'd first become aware of his huge potential when I was coaching at Leicestershire in 1990. The Australian Under-19 team was travelling to the West Indies via London that year and the ACB asked me if I would look after them in Leicester after their travel arrangements were thrown into disarray and they had to spend a few days in the United Kingdom. That's when I first saw how far he spun the ball. Eighteen months later, I gave him a particularly torrid time in Hobart when he was part of an Australian XI team that played the touring West Indians. I knew he was on the brink of Test selection, so I wanted to measure his fitness. After the team completed a typical high-catching drill, I said, 'Shane, please stay back for a bit, will you?' He tried bloody hard to make all the extra catches I hit at him, but afterwards both he and I realised he wasn't really fit enough. In the following August, we were practising fielding at the Sinhalese Sports Club in Colombo, on a ground that had just been top-dressed with ashes. I didn't realise the damage these abrasive ashes could do, until I saw that the now much slimmer Shane, who had been diving around and doing very well, had blood all over his arms and legs. 'For God's sake, don't dive anymore,' I cried out, but he still did. He needed to prove a point to me, and I admired and respected that.

With the work he did before and at the start of that Sri Lankan tour, Shane was ready to hit the big-time, though it would not be until mid-1993 that he truly exploded onto the world cricket stage. He did bowl reasonably well during the First Test against the Sri Lankans in Colombo, responding best when Allan Border risked him at the death of what was a remarkable game. With Sri Lanka seven down and 30 runs from victory, Allan put his faith in his young leggie, and Shane came up with the three wickets. But even so, he wasn't picked for the Second Test and failed to take a wicket in the Third. Back home, Shane had one great day at the MCG when he took 7–52 to spin Australia to its one Test win of the summer, but his impact on the rest of the series was minimal. Then he had a terrific tour of New Zealand—the poor Kiwis never had that much of a clue against good leg-spin bowling—before knocking over Mike Gatting with his celebrated first delivery in Ashes cricket. The rest of the England tour was a triumph for him and he's been an extraordinary bowler ever since.

Why did this evolution happen so quickly? Obviously, Shane has been blessed not just with vast natural talent but also with a rare nous for wrist-spin bowling and a unique instinct for slow-bowling strategies. And from just about day one with the Australian squad he saw what good advice and a good work ethic could do. From that moment—because he was already quite an accurate bowler, with good flight and tremendous confidence—he was on his way to greatness.

While Shane's commonsense can sometimes wander off the field, when it comes to bowling he is the master of not just commonsense, but also patience, bluff and mystery. When we first saw him, he bowled those big-spinning leg-breaks and he had a great flipper. Once he got his line right, that was enough to make him a highly effective bowler. He hardly bowled a wrong 'un, and when he did it was hardly special. His conventional top-spinners were fair, but he had never heard of a top-spinner delivered through the fingers. When I showed him how to bowl it, I thought he'd take at least twelve months to get it right, but he grabbed the concept, understood the method and within three weeks was bowling it in first-class cricket. A little while later, he was using it effectively in Test matches. For a while, he called it his 'zooter', but these days, it's his 'slider'. Throughout his career, he has remained extremely 'coachable'; as recently as during the first Ashes Test of 2005, when I reminded him about the need to use his body and not just his arm, and to make sure he *really* followed through, I found him to be a superb listener when it came to cricket matters.

In his very early days with the Australian team, Shane wouldn't go around the wicket in a game. He didn't see it as attacking bowling. However, at practice, if he wasn't going well, he'd be happy to follow my advice to try this new angle, the idea being to get him more side-on when he delivered the ball. For Shane, this was about technique, not tactics, so it was okay. But I knew that a leggie could be dangerous bowling around the wicket—I'd done it myself in the final Test of my 'first' Test career, in early 1968, when I took eight Indian wickets at the SCG. So in Perth in 1992–93, when Shane was not in the Test XI but was with the squad, I took him down to the nets and bowled leg-breaks at him from around the wicket. I had him in a fair bit of trouble, but that was okay because he came away from that session not just appreciating that going around the wicket can be an attacking option, but now determined to master it. Which he did, and some of his best wickets in the 1993 Ashes series—and in the years that followed—came when he was bowling this way.

A terrible irony of his life is that the media have sometimes come down hard on him, exploiting occasional moments when he's let himself down off the field. I say 'irony' because as well as being a clever bluffer on the field, he didn't mind using the media to his advantage, especially at the start of each new season when he'd announce the discovery of his latest 'mystery ball'. His opponents would see all the headlines and read the column pieces and stress out about something that didn't exist. In reality there was never any new ball.

What there was, though, was a further improvement in his accuracy and flight, and always further finetuning of his existing arsenal. Then, perhaps as the number of overs he bowled caught up with him, we saw less variety (these days he hardly bowls the flipper at all), but even more guile. Always, he has possessed an extraordinary ability to seize the moment.

Over the years I have seen countless examples of his unique ability to play mind games with opponents, and to home in on a weakness that perhaps only he has spotted. He is brilliant at knowing when to go around the wicket, and which batsman is susceptible to being bowled around his pads. The way he taunted South Africa's Daryll Cullinan was almost unprecedented, reducing a good player against every other team to a cheap wicket for Australia. If I had to nominate one example above all others, perhaps I'd go again to Sri Lanka in 2004, to the First Test in Galle.

Australia had been bowled out for 220. At stumps on the second day, Sri Lanka in reply were 6–352 and Australia looked down and out. In his first Test back after serving a twelve-month suspension, Shane's bowling had been okay, but nothing out of the ordinary.

For some inexplicable reason, when Sri Lanka resumed on the third morning they seemed content to survive, hoping that runs would come and their lead would grow. Unfortunately for them, Shane read the situation immediately. I'm sure he benefited from the fact that the batsmen weren't game to put him under pressure, so he lifted his tempo, energy and aggression, bowled like his old self, and the whole game changed. The last four wickets fell for 29 runs in 21.4 overs, three of them to Shane, and Australia was back in with a chance. Matthew Hayden, Darren Lehmann and Damien Martyn all scored centuries as the tourists totalled 512 in their second innings, and then Shane and Stuart MacGill spun the Aussies to a stunning 197-run victory.

As well as being Shane's first Test back from suspension, this was also Ricky Ponting's first Test as Australian captain. For both men, the revival that won this game was important, as it provided a momentum they rarely lost in the following two years.

I thought at the time and still think now that Shane's enforced twelve-month break might have been the best thing that could have happened to his career. This was not because it gave him time to rest, but because the lay-off allowed him time to appreciate just how much he loves the game. I bet the longer the suspension went, the more he missed cricket. There were times during his career when, though he never shirked responsibility at the bowling crease, he did neglect his physical conditioning. I doubt that will happen again before he retires, because he'll remember that enforced absence. I reckon, injuries permitting, he'll still be outsmarting Test batsmen when he's 40.

Those times in the past when his dedication to fitness slipped were always revealed by variations in his bowling action. At his best, Shane exploded at the crease with a tremendous hip and body movement that saw his follow-through end four or five metres beyond the stumps at the non-striker's end. So powerful was that hip movement, his right foot would swing to stump-high after he drove his body and shoulder into a powerful position that allowed his arm and fingers to get the most out of each delivery. When this happened, he dipped and dropped the ball into the right-handers with colossal spin, and his wicketkeeper was taking the ball at waist height, sometimes even higher.

It did take Shane a while to learn that leg-spin bowling is in many ways as physically tough as fast bowling, and whenever his physical conditioning wavered his hip and body action was less obvious, and he relied more on his fingers and shoulder to generate spin. I believe that was why first his spinning finger required an operation and then his right shoulder gave him trouble. Those two ailments reduced not only his spin but also his sharp dip and swerve. I remember during the 1999 World Cup, when he was not long back from major shoulder surgery, it was not until the semi-final that he really got that shoulder working. After looking ordinary and disheartened in the preliminary games, in both the semi-final and the final he was player of the match. He might not have been quite as explosive as he had been before the operation, but still he was clearly the best bowler in the game.

Shane has big and exceptionally strong hands and fingers, and a powerful body. At his peak, it was really amazing to be able to stand in the nets at the bowler's end and hear the ball fizzing out of his hands and displacing the air as it spiralled down the pitch. I have seen and played against many fine spinners in my time, but I have never heard the ball hum out of the hand as it did when Shane got it right.

Perhaps in the mind of his public, the most lasting memory of Shane will be the delivery that bowled Gatting at Old Trafford in 1993. People marvelled at the width of turn he generated, as the ball turned from just outside leg stump to hit off stump, but the beauty of the ball was that it deceived, opened up and beat Gatting *before* it hit the pitch. This was achieved by swerve through the air, which is only possible when a leg-spinner really rips the ball and imparts side-spin.

In my view, Shane was at his very best between 1993 and 1998. He was a very fine bowler afterwards, and since his return from suspension he has been relentless, but in those six years he was almost freakish. Which brings me to the thing that I admire most about him. It is not the sheer natural ability that was so often on show during those early years of his career, but the way he handled himself during the 'tougher times', when his body couldn't always do what it had done. Once, he had been the roguish gambler who spun the ball a mile, dropped it on a ten-cent piece time after time, and extracted more bounce from any pitch than anyone could expect. From 1999, he became more calculating and conservative as he bowled within limitations, but he still applied a pressure that few batsmen could withstand. Throughout, his influence on the game was as great as any Australian player since Sir Donald Bradman. When he finally retires, there will be plenty of records and mountains of good memories in his pocket, all of them deserved, but what he has given to cricket is worth so much more. The game is lucky he came along when he did.

22

THIS ISN'T CRICKET

Bowlers who throw the ball have actions that are against the law, and they obtain an unfair advantage over bowlers who comply with the Laws of Cricket. These two facts are why our game needs to be diligent when it comes to judging the legality of bowlers' actions. Once you play outside the rules of the game, the game changes. The sooner we get away from the second-guessing and media frenzy that stirs whenever a bowler's action is questioned the better.

To my mind, if an umpire judges that a bowler's action does not conform to the laws of the game, he should call, 'No ball'. Simple as that. And the people who appointed that umpire to do his job should back him 100 per cent. I do not sit in judgement on the morality of the umpire or bowler, and I view the 'no ball' call in the same way as I would a call for overstepping the popping crease or going wide on the return crease. That ball is an illegal delivery, and the bowler needs to correct the flaw in his method or else his next ball should be similarly judged. Unfortunately, in today's cricket world, this is not what happens. Instead, allegations against high-profile bowlers generate hysteria and massive media coverage. Convicted throwers are tagged as 'cheats' of the worst kind. It is as if the reputations of entire countries are at stake. And because of that, cricket politics being what it is, getting these stars who stray outside the rules to fix their actions—so they can play on the same level as everyone else—has become almost impossible.

Throwers, or 'illegal-action bowlers' as I prefer to call them, have been in the game since bowlers were first allowed to deliver the ball with the arm above the shoulder in the 1860s. By the 1890s they reached plague proportions. Australian fast bowler Ernie Jones became the first man to be no-balled for throwing in a Test when he was called by umpire Jim Phillips during the 1897–98 Ashes series. The crisis was so bad that in January 1897 'Demon' Spofforth, arguably the greatest Test bowler to that time, wrote a letter to the editor of London's *Sporting Life* suggesting— tongue firmly in cheek—that throwing should be legalised. First, referring to English cricket, Spofforth stated that there was 'scarcely a first-class county which does not include a "thrower" amongst its cricketers', and then he continued:

> This practice of throwing is growing rapidly, and many young cricketers are now adopting it who a year or so back were quite above suspicion. Australia has now taken it up, and with the last eleven [the 1896 Australian team that toured England] there was one who hardly ever delivered a 'fair' ball, and although I am quite aware I may raise a 'hornet's nest' above my head by mentioning names, I allude to McKibbin who, I shall always maintain, should never be allowed to play under the existing rule . . .
>
> The remedy for this unfair play is rather hard to find, especially as there is no umpire in England who dare no-ball a cricketer, while should a fair bowler even touch the bowler's crease when delivering a ball he is at once 'called'.
>
> I am of the opinion the best way to put down throwing is to form a committee of all the captains of the first-class counties

with Lord Harris as chairman, and on anyone being reported for throwing, a vote be taken, and if unfavourable the cricketer should be suspended for a week, if brought up a second time fined and suspended, a third time he should be disqualified for the season. Both jockeys and footballers are suspended and fined for unfairness, and why should cricketers be exempt.

In conclusion, if nothing is done in the matter, the best way is to legalise throwing, and in one season it would bring about its own cure.

Fortunately, instead of giving the chuckers free rein, the umpires went to work, and crucially the administrators and the media backed them. First, umpire Phillips no-balled Jones, and then in the following three English seasons a number of high-profile bowlers, including the leading amateur C.B. Fry and the Lancashire express Arthur Mold, were called. There were threats about that suspected throwers would be banned completely, or at least for a season, and then in 1901 Mold was called sixteen times in one match against Somerset and never played for his county again. By 1902, this first major throwing storm had just about been settled.

It wasn't until the late 1950s that public attention was drawn to the problem once again. By this time, it seemed as if every Australian state had a suspected 'chucker' in its squad. Throwing was again in the headlines in the mid-1960s when the West Indies' Charlie Griffith and many others were on the rampage. In the mid-1990s, the issue surfaced again.

While I have never categorised throwing as evil, I have always been a strong advocate of determined action to rid the game of a dangerous threat. I have never felt anger at someone called for throwing. Rather, my wrath has been directed at the coaches, team-mates, captains and club officials who have allowed the problem to fester, due to their selfishness or lack of courage.

Not clearing up bowlers with unfair actions today is even more worrying than in the past because of television and the vast coverage the game now receives. As Spofforth alluded to in his letter to *Sporting Life*, youngsters see throwers taking wickets and try to be just like them, just as Australian kids wanted to bowl fast like Lillee and Thommo and then leg-breaks like Warney. Today, children from all over the world can view their heroes in action and copy them. International players are reporting that they are facing rookie cricketers in the nets who are bowling like the wicket-takers they've seen on television. Some kids today have never seen their heroes live, but can still duplicate their every movement.

What advantage does a bowler with an illegal action gain over others who abide by the laws? For a fast bowler, the main benefit of an illegal action emerges when they change their pace by accelerating or slowing down the straightening of the elbow. When they do that there are none of the giveaways that legal-action bowlers reveal as they accelerate into the crease or use more or less body action to change the pace of their delivery. Over the years, this ability to change speed with little apparent change in the action has allowed illegal-action bowlers to hit and maim more batsmen than legal bowlers. Further, throwers use virtually only their elbow and arm when 'bowling' and this takes less energy than full-body-action bowlers.

Finger-spinners get another huge advantage from a bent-arm action. When an off-spinner bends and then straightens his arm at the point of delivery he can make the ball jump and spin a great deal and at good pace. The straightening of the arm holds the key for this and, with the aid of the wrist, allows greater flexibility and rotation.

The wave of sympathy for bowlers who are no-balled for throwing is something I struggle to understand. What about the batsmen who have been dismissed by someone with an illegal action? In some cases, batsmen have been struck frightening blows in the head and never played again, or have lost their nerve, which has cost them their place in the team. It is also unfair to the bowling team-mates of the thrower, who battle to get wickets with a fair action while their mate reaps the rewards and benefits of his illegal action.

The laws relating to throwing have always been simple and adequate. If you asked a young boy—as I once or twice did with my grandson Ashley as he was growing up—to identify illegal and legal actions he would have no difficulty doing so. If kids know what is right and wrong, why shouldn't we adults?

•

In 1996–97 an International Cricket Council Advisory Panel on Illegal Deliveries was constituted to handle bowlers with doubtful actions. The panel consisted of a representative from most of the Test-playing teams—Brian Basson (South Africa), Andy Pycroft (Zimbabwe), Javed Burki (Pakistan), Kapil Dev (India), Michael Holding (West Indies), Doug Insole (England), Ranjan Madugalle (Sri Lanka), John Reid (New Zealand) and myself—plus the chairman, Sir Clyde Walcott, and Nigel Plews, a former Test umpire from England.

At this time, the umpires retained—and rightly so—the authority and responsibility to no-ball bowlers whose action they felt did not conform to the Laws of Cricket. But if they, for any reason, did not want to call the bowler on the field, they could report their concerns to the match referee, who was then required to pass the matter on to the ICC Advisory Panel for examination. After each of the panel members viewed footage of the cricketer in question, a telephone hook-up was arranged and the bowler's action discussed. If the action was deemed doubtful, remedial coaching was recommended. No bowler was ever given a permanent clearance, and his action could be queried the next time he bowled if the umpires or match referee felt this was warranted.

Until the middle of 1999, the only power held by the panel was to recommend that a bowler whose action they believed infringed the law should seek remedial coaching. Some countries accepted this advice. Others did not.

In May 1999 a recommendation was accepted by the ICC that the panel should be empowered to suspend bowlers who in their view infringed the law. Following this decision, two of Pakistan's fast bowlers, Shabbir Ahmed and Shoaib Akhtar, were reported, and the panel decided their actions were not acceptable and suspended them until they fixed their problems. Quickly, Pakistan complained to the then ICC President Jagmohan Dalmiya about the legality of the decision against Shoaib, and Dalmiya, in consultation with Sir Clyde Walcott (the chairman of both the ICC Cricket Committee and the Advisory Panel on Illegal Deliveries) then allowed him to play in the one-day series against Australia and India. The dubious logic behind this decision was that because only Shoaib's bouncer had been deemed questionable, and under the rules of the time bouncers were no-balls in limited-over cricket, he could continue to play that form of the game. His suspension in Test cricket was sustained, though not for very long.

In 2000, the full ICC Executive met in Singapore and, while supporting the existence and decision of the ICC Advisory Panel on Illegal Deliveries, decided that Shoaib's suspension had thrown up a number of legal procedural issues. They withdrew the power of the panel to suspend any bowler whose action they believed did not conform to the law. While unhappy with this decision, members of the panel decided to continue their role in the belief that these legal problems could be sorted out. The driving force in reaching this decision was the panel's concern at the increase in illegal-action bowling and the need for strong action to stop it. But we persevered, even knowing that while some countries would be very cooperative with the directions issued by the panel, others were more likely to ignore them, and the ICC would not be able to do anything about it.

•

Until the early 1990s, whenever chucking reared its ugly head, it was solved (albeit temporarily) with commonsense and a desire to do the right thing *for cricket*. This usually occurred only after parochialism and misguided loyalty initially clouded judgements when bowlers first came under suspicion, as friends and supporters passionately defended their team-mates and heroes. This was clearly evident in the late 1950s during an Ashes series in Australia, when we reacted with much indignation when some of our bowlers were tagged as chuckers by the English players and press. But we needed to remove the blinkers and start to appreciate just how quickly other bowlers would copy these guys if they continued to take wickets at the highest level.

By 1960, it seemed as if every state in Australia had at least one 'suspect action' bowler. South Australia's new-ball bowlers, Peter Trethewey and Allan Hitchcock, were dubbed 'Throwewey' and 'Pitchcock' by the English press because they felt their actions were dubious. It wasn't until Sir Donald Bradman produced his documentary evidence—showing past and present bowlers whose actions were suspect on film—that the illegal actions were put under genuine scrutiny. Quite a few bowlers accepted that their actions didn't conform with the rules and tried to change, while others were eased out of the game by umpires and selectors. As the next step, prior to the 1961 tour of England, a secret agreement was reached that no player with a suspect action would tour with the Australian team and England would also not pick any bowler who fell in the same category. The Australian team hierarchy was also asked to confidentially report any bowler whose action, it believed, didn't conform to the rules. Seven county bowlers were subsequently reported.

Two years later, word spread across Australia about the controversial bowling action of Charlie Griffith, the West Indies' new fast-bowling star. Griffith had made his Test debut against England at home in early 1960, but missed the West Indies' 1960–61 tour of Australia and didn't play Test cricket again until after he was something of a surprise selection for the Windies' tour of England in 1963. After a disappointing opening Test of that series, Griffith made a huge impact through his wickets, his extreme pace and his startling bowling action. Despite only ambling to the crease, he could lean back and fire down a bumper or yorker that was yards quicker than his normal delivery. Tony Cozier, the respected West Indian broadcaster and writer, still considers him to be the most dangerous and lethal 'bowler' to have come out of the Caribbean.

Without the advantage of cable television none of the Australian team had sighted Griffith before we arrived in the West Indies in 1965. But once we saw him we had no doubt his action was contentious, a fact well and truly confirmed for us when Richie Benaud, who covered the series as a journalist, published photographs he had taken during the First Test that showed Griffith's action appeared to be outside the law. However, Griffith was never called;

instead, we began noticing that youngsters were copying his style. When we faced a Barbados Colts team, four of their quick bowlers threw. As we drove around Trinidad, we took bets among ourselves as to how many crooked actions we'd see in local park matches. Eventually, we had to change the wager to how many legal actions we'd see, because there were fewer to count!

How quick and dangerous was Griffith? The fact that in 1965 the Australian batsmen preferred to face Wes Hall sums it up best. Afterwards, following all the negative publicity, Griffith modified his action and became only half the bowler he had been. He took 48 wickets in his first eleven Tests (up to the end of that series against Australia), including five wickets in an innings four times, but just 46 wickets in his last 17, with one five-for. At the same time, there was an increase in public demand to eliminate illegal actions throughout the Caribbean. Significantly, as Charlie Griffith faded from the scene there were few opening bowlers with legitimate actions to take his place, and from 1968 to 1973 the West Indies pace attack was often sub-standard.

From the late 1960s to the early 1990s, world cricket had a quiet time as far as chucking was concerned. Some queries were raised about some of the West Indies bowlers as their feared pace attack dominated cricket for two decades, and I remember Ted Dexter questioning the action of Australia's Len Pascoe during the 1977 Ashes series, but that was just about it. Now, though, the chuckers are back. In the past ten years, I reckon every country in Test and one-day international cricket has used bowlers with illegal actions.

•

I desperately fear that we are becoming too scientific about the throwing problem and not applying enough commonsense. Rather than cracking down on the throwers, they have been given approved degrees of bend. The great risk is that the game is being changed forever.

I may not be a scientist or a biomechanic, but five decades of involvement in cricket at the top level has given me a fair knowledge of technique and movement when it relates to our beloved game. Perhaps this is why I was so bewildered that it took *so long* for Muttiah Muralitharan's *doosra* to be examined by the experts. When 'Murali' first came into Test cricket, his action so confused Allan Border that on first sight AB thought the Sri Lankan was a leggie. At that time, Murali bowled a top-spinner that was very much like his *doosra*, with the back of his hand pointing at the batsman. We tried to mimic him, but the only way we could find the flexibility needed to do so was to bend our elbow to get the back of the hand facing the batsman, and then straightening the elbow to propel the ball at good pace to the other end of the wicket.

In December 1997, while I was acting as a match referee for a series between Sri Lanka and India, I questioned the bowling action of two cricketers—India's Rajesh Chauhan and Sri Lanka's Kumar Dharmasena. My report went to the ICC, along with videos of the two bowlers' actions, and these were then forwarded to all members of the ICC Advisory Panel on Illegal Deliveries, with the exception of myself, and Kapil Dev and Ranjan Madugalle, the representatives from the two countries involved. After a telephone hook-up, the panel concluded that both bowlers had problems with their actions and remedial work was recommended so in future their actions complied with the law. India's response was to state that I was wrong to report the players, because in effect I was saying that I knew more than the umpires. What I thought the Indians were doing was neatly capturing one of the major problems in the game today—the fact that people are keener to support their countrymen than recognise that cricket has a problem that desperately needs fixing. There is a consensus among players that there are quite a few bowlers around whose actions are suspect, and they'll openly name players from other teams who are transgressing, but in the same breath they'll passionately deny any suggestion that one of their own might be doing anything illegal.

This is just what we did in Australia with our illegal-action bowlers in the late 1950s. My good friend Everton Weekes was the same in 1965 when he said to me over a rum or two in Barbados, after I queried the action of quite a few of the local bowlers: 'Well, Bobby man, what you must understand is that people walk differently.' I thought about that, had another rum or two, and decided that I didn't mind bowlers looking different as long as their actions were legal.

It has been suggested that any bowler who doesn't straighten his arm once it is bent has an acceptable action. But I have never seen a decent bowler who delivers a ball with the elbow bent from start to finish. The fact is that it is the very straightening of the arm that gives bowlers the ability to deliver the ball quicker, change their pace better, and in the case of spinners also spin the ball further and make it drop more. The bent elbow must straighten for the bowler to gain power. If it doesn't, the illegal-action bowler would be lucky to get the ball to the other end. Try it yourself.

If we are to overcome today's throwing problem, every different ball bowled by doubtful bowlers must be examined under match conditions. We need to let the umpires do their jobs and support them when they do it. However, unlike the late 1950s and 1960s, today's officials and supporters don't appear as if they want to accept the verdict of umpires. The problem is not going to go away. If the ICC and cricketing boards across the world don't step in immediately, more and more youngsters will continue to copy the stars, and the throwing plague—and I use the word 'plague' advisedly—will only get worse and worse.

•

During 1999–2000 I was a member of an MCC committee whose aim was to redraft the Laws of Cricket. This committee featured a number of former Test cricketers, Test umpires, experienced cricket officials and one lone woman Sheila Hill, who was a long-serving administrator in women's cricket in England. It was interesting how, while we ex-internationals haggled over how we thought the various laws should be framed, Sheila often brought us back to reality by quietly saying, 'Don't forget that the laws of cricket apply to all who play the game, not just first-class players.' Quickly, we became more than happy to be guided by this extraordinarily talented lady, who was an absolute whiz in expressing our thoughts in the clearest possible way.

Given the publicity the question of throwing had been getting at the time, it was inevitable that the old Law 24.2—the definition of a throw—was high on the agenda. Most of the committee felt that the existing law was satisfactory, but wasn't being interpreted or enacted firmly enough by the umpires.

To clarify and simplify, and to assist the umpires, a new Law 24.3 was added, which read:

Definition of a fair delivery—the arm
A ball is fairly delivered in respect of the arm if, once the bowler's arm has reached the level of the shoulder in the delivery swing, the elbow joint is not straightened partially or completely from

that point until the ball has left the hand. This definition shall not debar a bowler from flexing or rotating the wrist in the delivery swing.

This amendment had actually been proposed by the ICC Advisory Panel on Illegal Deliveries, on the basis that if it was applied diligently it would assist umpires and cricket in general. It didn't alter the fact that even a child could quickly recognise an illegal-action bowler in a line-up. Unfortunately, not long after the new law was introduced, the ICC totally changed the way its Advisory Panel operated, effectively turning it into a lame duck.

Under the new arrangements, if a bowler's action was questioned in a match referee's report, the player's home board's bowling advisers were required to review the referee's report and then work with the bowler to correct his action. After six weeks, they were required to submit an assessment to the ICC, which would be circulated to umpires and match referees. During this period, the bowler was permitted to continue playing. If the bowler was reported again by a match referee within twelve months of the first report, the ICC would then appoint one of its own advisers, who would work with the reported player on his action. Within three months, an assessment would be submitted to the ICC, which would be circulated to umpires and match referees. During this period, the bowler was permitted to continue playing. A third adverse report from a match referee within twelve months of that second report would finally see the Advisory Panel involved. Members would meet with the bowler and his representative to consider the reports, discuss the problem and study video footage and any other evidence provided. At the end of this hearing, the panel would vote to decide if the bowler did have an illegal action. If it ruled he did, he would be banned from bowling in international cricket for twelve months.

What a marathon! Under these procedures it could take as long as two years for an independent body to officially examine a suspect action. Of course, the countries that had selected the 'doubtful' bowlers in the first place had a vested interest in retaining them in international cricket for as long as they could. As I have already explained, the members of the Advisory Panel were keen to stay involved because we knew that the problem of illegal-action bowling was growing. But we also knew strong action was required to stop it. When I realised we were wasting our time, I resigned from the Advisory Panel.

•

By the start of 2005, the ICC was reminding me of the United Nations— it appeared to want to be all things to all people. Unfortunately, this philosophy seldom solves true quandaries. After mounting criticism that the system of 'self-regulation' was not working, the ICC had reclaimed responsibility for testing and reviewing problem bowlers, rather than leaving the onus on individual boards, and had reduced the review period to just 21 days (during which time the reported bowler would be banned). They had also decided that if a reported bowler was reported again within two years he would be put out of the game for twelve months to sort out the problem, and also determined that birth defects would no longer be an excuse for chucking. (It always seemed weird to me that almost every bowler who came under suspicion had either a childhood injury or a congenital defect that prevented him from straightening his arm properly, or had a looseness of the joints that somehow allowed him to hyperextend the elbow and give the *illusion* that he was throwing.)

This was a giant stride in the right direction, but what I could not agree with was the decision to allow bowlers to bend their arms up to *15 degrees* before they straightened their arm during delivery. In 2001, the ICC had introduced three 'tolerance limits' on the degree of bending of the arm: five degrees for spinners, seven-and-a-half degrees for medium-pacers and 10 degrees for quick bowlers. Three years later, another advisory panel recommended that the limit be increased to 15 degrees for all bowlers. The panel had been convinced by biomechanics that when bowlers' arms were bent less than 15 degrees, the naked eye couldn't always pick up any bend at all, and that under the old rules some bowlers who we'd all regarded as having classic actions were actually breaking the law. I knew this was bunkum—any batsman, watcher or child can recognise an illegal action well before it reaches this arbitrary 15-degrees mark.

What really troubled me was how these biomechanics explained that they couldn't actually work out if a bowler was legal or not until they got him into the laboratory, where they could undertake their complicated but apparently necessary procedures to complete their analysis. This, of course, is a process fraught with danger, simply because a bowler could change his action in the lab to pass his test. If you'd sent a fast man with a sometimes suspect action to the lab he just might not bowl his most fearsome yorkers and bouncers, at least not in the way he would in Test matches. Surely the only way a fair-dinkum judgement can be made is under match conditions. If the 'experts' cannot make their assessments from live analysis and videos of actual matches, the system is flawed and their conclusions doubtful.

I am of the view that an umpire standing back two metres from the stumps at the non-striker's end is in a better position to identify illegal-action bowlers than a bloke wearing a white coat in a laboratory. From that on-field vantage point, I believe it is relatively easy for an umpire to pick up the signs of a bent elbow in a bowler.

But instead of backing our umpires by telling them that they are the best people to judge, we have instead reached the point where we are accommodating bowlers who break the laws of the game. Is it a good thing that we now have a system that will lead to coaches around the world teaching their bowlers to throw? Umpires have to be intimidated by the idea that their on-field judgements will be second-guessed by analysts armed with protractors and science degrees who sit well beyond the boundary. Umpires have been forced to turn a blind eye; instead they hope that the match referee and the ICC will sort everything out. How long before 15 per cent becomes 17 per cent, or 20 per cent? When will it end? Perish the thought, but what if some unfortunate batsman is hit and maimed by a very quick bowler with a suspect action? Don't say it can't happen. In 1962, India's opening batsman, Nari Contractor, was hit in the head by Charlie Griffith in a match between Barbados and the touring Indians. For some days after he was struck, Nari hovered between life and death in a Bridgetown hospital. To this day, he carries a steel plate in his head. If something similar happened today, perhaps cricket would end up in a court of law, and then we could get the judges and lawyers to decide what is and isn't a throw.

The Laws of Cricket were originally drawn up to be fair to both bowlers and batsmen, but the new system for identifying chuckers does not consider the batsmen at all. The old law as written was sound, but umpires, match referees and especially administrators didn't have the stomach to enforce it strictly. Instead, the game so many cricket lovers have cherished for so many years has been

changed for the worse. I say again, bowlers whose actions are illegal
are breaking the law. To allow illegal-action bowlers to prevail,
when all other laws have to be obeyed, might be politically correct
but it just isn't cricket.

•

When I think about cricketers who don't abide by the laws of the
game, my mind sometimes goes back to my youth, to the Sundays
when I was carrying a large golf bag around Bonnie Doon golf
course in Sydney for a caddy's fee of four shillings per round. Today,
a 'foot mashie', a 'practice niblick', a 'hand iron', a 'hand-and-sand
iron' and a 'pocket drop' are not well-known terms in golf. But back
then, not long after the Second World War, they were very much
part of our language.

To get to the course, I had to run for a couple of miles along the
Cooks River and cross over at what we called 'the old stink pipes'.
Then it was four or five hours on the fairways and in the rough
without getting a solitary hit. Four shillings, around 40 cents in
today's language, might not seem much of a return for all this, but
if nothing else the examples of gamesmanship I saw and the way
we ignored them laughed at them or responded to them, stood me
in good stead to handle life in general, and certainly the antics of
some Australian cricketers when we found ourselves on the golf
course in years to come.

Those terms such as foot mashie, hand iron and so on were
the caddies' way of describing some of the forms of cheating we
saw from our masters. A conventional 'mashie' was a five iron; a
foot mashie was used by a golfer to better the lie of his ball in
the rough. Some players had an uncanny ability and flexibility to
surreptitiously manoeuvre the ball while blocking out what they

were doing from their fellow players, and their ball usually ended up lying well enough for them to play a low iron at the ball instead of hacking it out with a sand wedge. The best exponents of the foot mashie could get their ball to shift yards without anyone noticing, so that the damn tree that had been blocking the path to the green was now no longer a concern. We rated one particular doctor as the world champion, for he always appeared to have amazing luck with the lie of the ball if he was the first to locate it in the rough. Occasionally, we caddies would even the score a little by stamping on the doc's ball to grind it further into the grass and then standing nearby so he wouldn't be game to move it. That was the caddies' way of making life fair.

Over the years, I found that the best users of the foot mashie were the caddies in South Africa. They used to bet like the dickens on our games, always confident they could help their man to victory, so if your caddie found your ball—even if the scrub all around you was several feet high—when you caught up you would be greeted with a wide grin, a three wood, and the words, 'Gee, you were lucky boss, the lie is perfect.'

The hand iron was a very sophisticated 'club', used by the golfer who would bend over to move a leaf or a loose branch that was nestled near their ball, and lift not just the vegetation but the ball as well. Another miraculous lie! The best exponent of the hand-and-sand iron in my time as a caddy at Bonnie Doon was one of Sydney's leading solicitors, who was a member of the club. There was a particularly deep bunker on one hole not far from the clubhouse, and whenever an unfortunate golfer was entombed in there all you could see from around the green was the head of the club at the top of the backswing and during the follow-through. This adroit legal expert had tangled with the bunker in the past without success, so he devised his own method of getting out. From the green it all looked perfect. There was a big swing, a flurry of sand, and the ball gently popping out onto the green. Two putts and he'd escaped with a bogey.

It all looked a bit too good, however, because on every other hole this bloke clearly demonstrated that he was no great bunker player. So one day, when the opportunity presented itself, we caddies resolved to find out exactly what was going on. Sure enough, the solicitor found the bunker, but rather than head for the green, one of the caddies took off for the next tee, where he had a clear view of the man and his sand. With perfect timing, the solicitor held his club with both the ball and some sand in his right hand, and at the bottom of the downswing he would lob the ball and the sand up and over the front lip of the bunker onto the green. It was almost a shame to spoil the ruse, but that was the caddies' code, so in future, whenever this fellow found himself in the sand, one of us would position himself in close proximity.

Back in the early 1950s, 'niblick' was the popular term for a nine iron. The practice niblick was employed when a golfer found his ball lying deep in the rough, with the prospect of the long grass impeding his backswing and likely stopping him making clean contact on the downswing. The practice niblick aces would take a couple of what looked like legal practice swings that in reality were clearing away that troublesome grass, and then the real shot was played with relative ease.

Few 'shots' needed more skill and daring than the pocket drop. Just when it seemed that a player would have to declare his ball lost, and with the other members of his group—and, of course, we caddies—all feverishly searching for it, the sneaky golfer would suddenly cry, 'Here it is!' What he had done was put an identically marked ball in his pocket, and then when he arrived in the area where the 'lost' ball had gone he transferred the ball to his other pocket, which just happened to have a substantial hole in it. The really outstanding pocket-drop exponents might even set it up so another person found the ball. We had a real 'pro' at Bonnie Doon and his skill and stealth were amazing. The caddies eventually stopped this cheating, however—not by ratting on him, for that would have cost them their jobs, but by carrying more identically marked balls. Seconds after he proclaimed his good fortune, they also loudly announced they had found the elusive ball.

After this happened a couple of times, the man's partners started to comment on the coincidence of identical balls being found in such numbers. The game was up and we caddies didn't see the pocket drop again, at least not from that particular golfer. It wasn't so much that we caddies saw ourselves as soldiers of virtue, rather that it was very hard to admire these blokes who were reverting to such devious means. And there was always a certain impish joy in exposing them, or at least making them play by the rules.

Golf, of course, is a sport that prides itself on its integrity. The vast majority of the men I caddied for were totally honest, which only made these few cheats stand out even more. The etiquette of golf is superb; I think you're a better person if you can stick to it. The thing I found most revealing about these episodes was the way we young caddies so quickly lost respect for men—some of them very successful and wealthy people away from the golf course—who couldn't play the game by the rules. The thing about golf is that, like cricket, the rules are there for a reason. Both sports are much too good to let a few odd people spoil them.

23

ANOTHER BRADMAN?

Ricky Ponting's extraordinary batting performances in Test cricket since the start of 2002 have raised comparisons between him and Sir Donald Bradman. From the start of 2002 to the end of Australia's series against Bangladesh in 2006, Ricky played in 53 Tests, scoring 5610 runs at an average of 71.01. He scored 22 centuries in that time, going past 150 eight times, past 200 four times, and past 250 once. One of the television channels even asked its viewers to answer yes or no to the question: 'Can Ricky Ponting be compared to the great Don?' Sixty-seven per cent of the viewers—most of them, I imagine, either very young or very parochial towards today's generation—said yes.

During his twenty years of Test cricket between 1928 and 1948, Bradman scored 6996 runs at an average of 99.94. He scored 29 Test hundreds, passing 200 on twelve occasions, and 300 twice. Ricky's good, but he's not *that* good.

My view is that it is an impossible task to compare players from different eras. If you try to do so, you have to take into account any number of questions, including the quality of the teams the players faced, the strength of their own teams, changes to the laws of the game, and variations in batting conditions and the quality of wickets. Many of these questions are simply unanswerable. How might Bradman have gone against the West Indies fast bowlers of the 1980s? The Don went all right against Harold Larwood, except when the Poms bowled Bodyline (which restricted his series to a 'measly' 56.57), but how might he have fared against three or four Larwoods, all at once? How would Ponting handle a nagging medium-pacer like Alec Bedser on an uncovered wicket? There isn't a bowler like Bedser in the game today, with the ability to pitch a persistent line and length and swing the ball away from the right-handers.

I suppose you could rely on statistics as a common factor in comparing champions of different eras, but stats can be dramatically inflated or contained by considerations such as those listed in the previous paragraphs. A few not-outs can add some points to a batting average, but do they reflect a batsman's true worth? A few low scores on rain-affected wickets will drag a batting average down, but that should not necessarily detract from a batsman's high rating. I've often wondered what would have happened to the career batting averages of cricketers such as Bill Lawry, Norm O'Neill and me if we had played, say, twelve Tests against New Zealand in the 1960s. Kenny Barrington averaged 99 in five Tests against the Kiwis, while Ted Dexter averaged nearly 60 in eight Tests; we never played even one Test against them, because the Australian Cricket Board of Control arrogantly decided New Zealand wasn't up to Test-match standard until 1973. For all this, while statistics alone from one era to another do not usually provide a true comparison of cricketers, in the case of Bradman I think they do, simply because he is so far ahead of his rivals. Even Ricky Ponting.

Knowing Ricky, he would be embarrassed by the comparisons between Bradman and himself. Indeed, in an interview conducted after his 102nd Test, when he matched Bradman's record of 29 Test-match hundreds, Ricky quickly and wryly noted that it had taken him 'twice as many Tests' to reach the landmark. An honest reply from a very realistic cricketer.

So just how good a player is Ricky? In my view, he is right up there with the other wonderful players of world cricket history (apart from Bradman)—South Africa's Graeme Pollock, the West Indies' George Headley and Everton Weekes, and England's Herbert Sutcliffe, Ken Barrington and Wally Hammond—who have scored more than 2000 Test runs and averaged more than 58 during their Test careers. Undoubtedly, he is the finest all-round batsman in the world today. He has demonstrated this in all the countries in which he has played, even when he has also carried the added responsibility of captaincy. Of those six batsmen apart from Bradman who averaged more than 58 over their entire careers, only Hammond ever captained his country.

The demands of captaincy and the strain that it imposes has seen the decline of many a fine batsman. The latest victim of the pressures of captaincy appears to be South Africa's Graeme Smith, who has had a dreadful run in recent Tests against Australia, both in Australia and at home.

I first saw Ricky when I was coaching Australia and visited the Australian Cricket Academy as a guest coach. He was sixteen at the time and hit the ball with a fluency that I had never seen in a batsman of that age. Even at that point of his career he struck the ball with portentous timing and surprising power. He was a natural athlete and it seemed all ball sports came easily to him. His dad was a professional golfer. Ponting himself is a superb golfer who currently plays off a three handicap.

I didn't get to know Ricky well until a few years later, when he was selected in the Australian XI team that played against the English tourists at Hobart in 1994–95. He had made his debut for Tasmania in late 1992, a month before his 18th birthday, and made an immediate impact, scoring 781 runs in 10 Sheffield Shield matches, including two centuries, and finishing fifth in the season's Shield averages (minimum aggregate of 600 runs), behind batsmen of the quality of Damien Martyn, Jamie Siddons, Michael Slater and Matthew Hayden. The Australian XI game in 1994–95 was the first such match since Ricky made his first-class debut. In those days, these contests were viewed as an ideal opportunity to assess the young, up-and-coming players in a tougher environment than the Shield. They were approached as though they were a Test match and the Australian support team, as small as it was in those days, was in charge.

I put the team through the same procedures as I would the Test squad. We found these games invaluable as they quickly identified the exceptional players with the heart and mind for higher honours and those who were happy to be Sheffield Shield cricketers. Ricky, to say the least, made an inauspicious beginning, as it needed a call from our manager to wake him up and get him to the ground barely 30 minutes before the match. Fortunately, once he got to the ground he was all concentration and commitment. He was a superb all-round fielder. While he had spent time during the previous two seasons at the Australian Cricket Academy, he still needed some finetuning. He tended to over-balance occasionally when pushing forward and gave the impression that he was trying to hit the ball on the run, which made him vulnerable to the ball moving away. It has always been my view that any technical problem with your batting that you sort out early in your career will lie dormant and can return to haunt you. Ricky is a magnificent player today, but early in his innings there are still times when he could be in trouble when he plays forward 'on the run'. But in the last five years, if you don't get him out early by capitalising on this flaw, he's made you pay big time.

I also think Ricky works the ball too much on the onside, but like some other great players of the past (Viv Richards immediately comes to mind), he does it so well that it is his main scoring shot. Against Pakistan in Australia in 2004–05, when he averaged 100.75 for the three-Test series, there was one innings of 62 when he scored 59 of his runs into, through or over the leg field. This says much for Ricky's phenomenal ability in this area, but surely also something about the line the Pakistanis bowled.

When I think back to those first impressions I formed of Ricky back in the early 1990s, some have only been enhanced. Kilo for kilo, he is up there with Johnny Martin as the biggest hitter of a cricket ball I have seen. His timing, placement and power are, as they say so often these days, awesome. His fielding, too, is a joy to watch. He is undoubtedly the best all-round fieldsman in the game. When South Africa's Jonty Rhodes was playing some suggested he was better than Ricky, and Jonty was certainly a wonderful exponent of the art, but whenever there is a chance of a run-out, Ricky hit the stumps with greater regularity than Jonty ever did.

Ricky's amazing run of centuries—36 international tons between August 2001 and August 2006 if you count Test matches and one-dayers—has been well deserved and a joy to watch, but I don't think there is any fantastic secret to his success. He has displayed wonderful concentration and is judging the length of the ball perfectly, which gives him the extra time and security to get into the right position as quickly as any other batsman I have seen. And some of his hooking reminds me of film I have seen of the great Bradman.

There is no higher praise than that.

24

A CHALLENGE THAT'S CATCHING

It should come as no real surprise that all the great teams have featured many brilliant fieldsmen and an especially classy slip cordon. I think of some of the great teams that I have seen, and arguably their five best fieldsmen (most of whom were excellent in the slips). I will leave it to you to decide who were the finest:

Australia, 1960–61: Neil Harvey, Alan Davidson, Richie Benaud, Norm O'Neill, Bob Simpson.

Australia, 1974–75: Greg Chappell, Ian Chappell, Ashley Mallett, Ian Redpath, Doug Walters.

West Indies, 1984–85: Roger Harper, Viv Richards, Clive Lloyd, Gordon Greenidge, Richie Richardson.

Australia, 1998–99: Mark Waugh, Mark Taylor, Ricky Ponting, Steve Waugh, Shane Warne.

In a way, it is surprising that so many great slips fieldsmen have been produced over the years, because I know that most youngsters see the slips as a part of the field to be avoided at all costs. I certainly did. When I was a kid, there just wasn't enough action in there;

I aspired to be a boundary rider or a cover specialist. The only real appeal of the slips was that Colin McCool, my hero in the Australian team straight after the war, fielded there. I'd seen him take a blinder there one day at the SCG. So I drifted, rather than ran, into the slips when I first went to the Petersham–Marrickville grade club as a 15-year-old. A couple of seasons later, as I have already recounted, I was in my second season in first-class cricket and 12th man for New South Wales when captain Keith Miller stationed me at first slip because he had nowhere else to put me. An hour later, I had taken two catches and it seemed my reputation as a capable slips man was assured.

I have thought long and hard over the years as to why I may have had some talent in the slips. I honestly believe it can be tracked down to when I was about nine or ten, when I accompanied my family on our annual holiday to Blue Bay on the New South Wales Central Coast, just north of Sydney. My two brothers were older than me and also cricket mad, and they had assigned to me the job in the weeks leading up to our holidays of collecting the tennis balls and even cricket balls we would need for our time away. This was no problem, for I was already a keen golfer and spent many weekends scouting for lost balls at the Marrickville Golf Course. The Cooks River, which ran through the course, was lined with reeds, while opposite the course and indeed all along the banks of the river were cricket grounds and tennis courts. Many errant balls that landed in the water were destined to end up lodged in my reeds. It was a must for me to be first to the reeds every Sunday morning, always in the hope that a near-new six-stitcher with only a few overs of wear would be waiting for me. The certainty was that there would be at least a few tennis balls there.

Suitably stocked up, our holidays were largely spent on the beach where I believe my skills and technique were honed. I wasn't aware of this at the time, of course; nor could I have known that catching wet tennis balls is ideal training for catching cricket balls. In both instances, unless you have soft hands and perfect coordination, the ball won't stick. We hurled balls at each other for hours, often bouncing them off the water or the wet sand to make it even more competitive. The soft sand was for diving, but even then we always insisted on two hands whenever possible. As we didn't have a cricket bat, we found a suitable branch and shaped it to our requirements and used this to edge catches.

When I read about the childhoods of the Chappell brothers and the Waugh twins I wonder if their catching was also shaped in the backyard or on holidays. Most likely, it was. For the Simpson boys growing up in Marrickville in the 1940s, the streets and the parks were ours in a way they probably aren't for most kids today. The main thoroughfare, Illawarra Road, had a tram line running down the middle of it and there wasn't any curbing and guttering, which for the development of our throwing arms proved pretty handy. There were also plenty of loose stones around to throw at the nearest pole.

It has always been my contention that you can make just about anyone into a good fieldsman—perhaps not great, but definitely adequate. This applies just as equally to the slips, though I should stress that I think the elite slips fieldsmen are born with a special talent.

•

One thing's for sure, there is nothing more galling for a bowler than to see a fieldsman in the slips put down a catch after he has forced a batsman into error.

Matches are certainly won by first-class fielding and can be lost by sub-standard efforts. Since 2002, the Australian team has been dropping too many catches—a number in the slips—but has been able to mask the problem because the strength of their bowling and the weakness of the opposition allowed them to create more opportunities after the misses. But this wasn't possible against England in 2005, who batted and bowled with more consistency than Australia and rightly deserved to reclaim the Ashes.

What has gone wrong with the slips fieldsmen? In my view, there have been a few factors involved, such as wicketkeeper Adam Gilchrist standing too deep and thus upsetting the alignment of the cordon. This said, it is not a problem that is confined to the Aussies. There has been a dramatic drop in the technique of most of the slips fieldsmen in world cricket.

Catching a cricket ball in the slips is a challenging experience. It requires 'soft' hands, good arm and body movement and the patience to watch the ball right into the hands. There is only a tiny margin for error and unless you do the basics right you increase the chances of dropping a catch. Good slips fielders are always judged on how many catches they drop, not necessarily how many they take, and I think this is a fair measure. I know when I was in the slips I had a very aggressive attitude. I wanted that ball to come to me, no matter what, and I was prepared to do anything to get it. And I got as much pleasure out of taking a really good catch as I did scoring runs. This must have helped me, because I didn't drop many, whereas the current Australian cordon is hardly infallible, which is why I don't think it can be compared favourably with the great cordons of the past. Right now, I believe only Shane Warne has the technique and skills to be considered alongside the outstanding slips fieldsmen of earlier decades.

Don't let anyone tell you that today's Australian slip cordon ranks up with the best of previous eras. The thing that sets great slips fieldsmen apart from the good ones is the ability to consistently take catches when other men would only get a hand to the ball or not even touch it. Right now, not even Shane is in this category of the very best, but is close to getting there. In my view, the only present-day slips fieldsman who you might possibly rank with the best of all time is England's Andrew Flintoff. A huge man, Flintoff is quick and amazingly soft in his movements and techniques. He invariably gets two hands to almost everything and can cover good distance in any direction to 'make' a catch.

Unfortunately, as I look around the slip cordons of the cricket world, I am concerned with what I see, especially the fact that many of our slips fielders are restricting their talents with faulty methods. Graeme Smith of South Africa and Marcus Trescothick of England are cases in point. Both stand with their feet too far apart, which tenses the body and makes it nearly impossible to move with speed and control to either side of the body. They are forced to dive—or is it fall over?—to anything outside of their body, thus creating a huge margin for error and restricting the area they can cover.

For some reason many fieldsmen today are using a technique usually used by soccer goalkeepers when they dive. Some clubs in English county cricket are employing goalies to teach this technique to their cricketers, which I find quite appalling. A diving goalkeeper's main aim is to push his hands at the ball and force it around the posts or tip the ball over the bar. Technically, that is completely wrong, for a fieldsman needs soft hands when he tries to catch a cricket ball and must increase the chances of catches being spilt.

I have always believed that Australia's long-running reputation as having the best slips fieldsmen in cricket was due to our aggressive attitude. For many years, our mantra was that it was better to miss a catch than not get to it. As a player and then coach, I always wanted the slips to stand as close as possible to the batsman, to cut down on the chance of a nick falling short. This might have meant we dropped a couple, especially when the batsmen slashed at a wide one, but we earned a few dismissals that would otherwise not have come our way.

In addition, we fielded wider and more staggered than any other nation. By staggering, I mean that first slip stands about a metre behind the wicketkeeper, second slip is about level with the man with the gloves, and the rest of the cordon is staggered in the same configuration in a straight line to the man at gully. During my career, if I ever wandered even remotely too close to our great wicketkeeper Wally Grout, he invariably hissed out of the corner of his mouth something like, 'Buzz off, Simmo, I still prefer girls to boys, you know.' Some people don't like being too far from the man next to them, for fear of a catch going untouched between them, but let me assure you that more catches are let go in this area by fieldsmen being too close together than wide apart. If you're too close, it can be hard to fight the urge to leave the chance to the other man. If both men do that, someone's got to go down to the third-man boundary to retrieve the ball that's gone for four.

In regards to who goes for what, my philosophy has always been . . . first in best dressed. If the man 'in front' thinks he can catch the nick then he goes for it and the man behind covers him. If you are focusing properly on the ball you shouldn't ever see what the man next to you is doing.

And what about the old chestnut: do you watch the ball or the bat when you're in the slips? The accepted theory seems to be that the wicketkeeper, first slip and perhaps second slip should watch the ball, with the wider slips and the gully focusing on the edge of the bat. But if this is right, a couple of questions need to be asked. What part of the edge: the top, middle or bottom? What happens when the batsman is flashing the blade around like a demented swordsman? The truth is that fieldsmen who are watching the edge are looking at an imprecise area around the bat. In my view, all the fieldsmen from keeper to gully should watch the ball out of the bowler's hand, because this will give them a more precise appreciation of just how hard the ball is coming to them from the bat if it is hit in their direction. I always felt that the best way for me to take a catch was to watch the ball from the moment it was delivered and then react when I knew it was coming my way. Usually, my concentration, reflexes, quick body movement and soft hands got me in the right position to complete the catch.

•

Very good slips fieldsmen of the past came in all shapes and sizes. England's Colin Cowdrey had as soft a pair of hands as I have ever seen. He never pushed his hands at the ball but allowed it to come to him. He was a class act, but not a genuinely *great* catcher because he seldom made the distance to take a 'blinder'. I must stress that I am setting a very high bar here. Two of Australia's highest-rated catchers, Ian Chappell and Mark Taylor, were similarly excellent but not great. Both had wonderful hands, but in my opinion they didn't cover enough territory to satisfy the criterion I have set for the absolute best. Taylor was a 'faller' rather than an effective mover to wide balls and while he took some very good catches, I felt he took too many one-handed when he could have used both hands to ensure the chance was taken. I did admire his ability to take catches off the spinners, which is a crucial test to assess the quality of a slips fieldsman.

One thing I did like about Taylor was that he took my pet theory about watching the ball into your hands to the extreme. His head and eyes were still locked onto the ball in an exaggerated manner long after the ball had been safely caught.

Interestingly, unless they have been taught to do so, only about five or maybe ten per cent of cricketers watch the ball right into their hands. If you want to check this out, throw a few balls to youngsters and you will find that when the ball reaches them they will be still looking ahead to where they last saw the ball. It is only those who 'nod' the ball into their hands who are watching it all the way until it reaches its proper final resting place. 'Nodding' the ball into the hands means that you not only catch the ball more safely but also give yourself more time. Invariably, if you don't watch the ball correctly you will take your hands to the ball, and two moving objects—hands and ball—colliding often leads to a dropped catch or a broken finger. I was lucky during my career in that I never missed a match with a broken finger.

Ian Chappell was more adept against the quicker men than Taylor, which was understandable given that his teams relied so much on pace, with only Ashley Mallett providing any high-class spin. Ian had great hands 'standing back', but the Australian slip cordons of the 1970s seemed to be too close together and didn't cover the ground that I would have liked. Ian took his stance with his weight on the inside of his feet and his knees a little knock-kneed, a position I advocated and Taylor later used as well, which allowed him to be well balanced and able to push off quickly and smoothly in any direction. This was one of the reasons his percentage of catches taken was high, a fact that entitles him to be on the second tier of outstanding slips fieldsmen, just below the very best.

Neil Harvey, who was the best all-round fieldsman I ever saw, was a magnificent cover fieldsman who gravitated into the slips later in his career. He was so good that in his very last Test match, against England in Sydney in 1962–63, he took six catches—from second slip to leg-slip to short leg to cover, and even a running one on the long-off boundary. After the Test, England captain Ted Dexter described the effort at leg-slip that dismissed Tom Graveney, which ended with Neil completing a somersault after he grabbed the chance, as the best catch he had ever seen. Graveney had leg-glanced Graham McKenzie off the full face of the bat; Neil moved brilliantly to his left and dived to catch the ball one-handed, giving us a key wicket just before stumps. At other times, they used to say that if you were running a tight single and Harv was throwing at the stumps, you may as well slow down. He rarely missed.

Two other Australians of my experience, Keith Miller and Allan Border, were fine fielders who took some good catches in the slips, but they both worried me with the number of chances they missed.

The West Indies have had some great fielders, but none greater than Clive Lloyd, Viv Richards and Garry Sobers. Lloyd and Richards started as superb cover fieldsmen before gravitating to the slips. They were both competent in that position, but it is difficult to assess just how great they were as they stood so far back to the steepling deliveries of their intimidating pace attack. It is not that hard to take catches in the slips when you are *that* deep. Sobers was Sobers; his fielding, whether in the slips, at short leg, leg-slip or any other position for that matter, was always pure quality. Perhaps, as with Harvey, if he'd spent his whole career in the slips, I'd be obliged to rate him as one of the very best.

The slower pitches in India and Pakistan in many ways offer the hardest conditions for slips fielders, because so often they have to stand too close for comfort against the fast bowlers to ensure the ball carries to them. Only the very best slips fieldsmen have even a chance of taking the opportunity when the batsman flashes hard at the ball and they are standing 'up close'. This is why, I'm sure, India have had many wonderful short-leg fielders but not many outstanding slips fieldsmen. Similarly, though Pakistan have had pacemen of the calibre of Imran Khan, Wasim Akram and Waqar Younis in the past 30 years, it is hard to think of one truly outstanding slips fieldsman who has consistently been able to support them.

So who do I rank at the very top of this elite list? I know I am probably biased, but to me only Greg Chappell and Mark Waugh were in the super class. They seldom dropped a catch, and both had the ability to turn a half-chance into a certainty, and the impossible into a probable.

How did they do it? Through immaculate technique, and smooth, quick, concise movement. Chappell and Waugh always attempted—and generally succeeded—in taking every catch two-handed, and when they went for the impossible one-handed, they still retained their form and technique to make it look relatively easy. If they had to dive, then in all likelihood it meant that no one else would have even got a finger on the chance. They let the ball come to them and invariably were side-on to the catch, and thus were *able* to let it come to them. That gave them maybe even a metre more to see the ball than the mere mortals.

Nothing gives me more pleasure in cricket than watching a great slip fieldsman moving with precision, style and grace to make it all look easy. Greg Chappell and Mark Waugh were all class and always a joy to watch.

•

The old saying 'catches win matches' applies today as much as it ever has. Of all the arts in cricket, I would argue that catching requires the most finesse. The only way you can obtain the very highest level and precision with fielding is to practise under the same pressure that is applied in a match.

A couple of years back I was shown some figures that detailed the large number of catches the Australians were dropping and also the number of run-out attempts they were missing. Separately, I was advised by a source close to the team that the team were only devoting between one-third and half the time on fielding that they did when I was coach. Since then I have watched with great interest and concern the continued declining standard of Australia's fielding.

It has gone practically unnoticed by the media because Australia is still winning most of its games easily, and also because occasionally an athlete such as Ricky Ponting, Andrew Symonds or Michael Clarke pulls off a spectacular grab which has commentators rushing for the superlatives and provides the mirage that the team is fielding well. It was only during the 2005 Ashes series, when a number of catches were spilt, highlighted by Shane Warne's crucial miss of Kevin Pietersen on the final day of the Fifth Test at The Oval, that people started to come around to my way of thinking. But then Australia went on another winning run in 2005–06, always managing to compensate for missed catches through the skill of their great players or the failings of their opponents, and the questions over the quality of their catching were able to be left unanswered.

When I took over as coach back in 1986 the Australian team was far from the talented group that represents the nation today. What I did was concentrate on small improvements in all aspects of their game, with a pronounced emphasis on their fielding. I knew from personal experience that fielding can be improved quite dramatically and quickly if the right type of practice and the correct fielding techniques are introduced. In addition, I also set out to make all fielding sessions enjoyable and competitive.

While some players—the lazy ones—may not have embraced this training, the majority did. I could see that they were especially enjoying the competitive atmosphere and the quick improvement in their skills once they started implementing the correct technique.

As a coach, I am quite liberal when it comes to batting or bowling. I am definitely not from the 'left elbow up and all that, old chap' school. Instead, I believe in enhancing and developing the naturalness of the talent available and am very reluctant to change natural instincts unless they are hindering the development and performance of the players. But never with fielding. When it comes to fielding, I am a great stickler for getting the players to adhere to tried-and-proven techniques.

The margin of error in dropping a catch or fumbling a ground ball is so high that it is essential to reduce it to the bare minimum by adopting the safest methods. Most of the catches I have seen dropped by the Australians in recent times can be attributed to hard hands, poor movement, little relaxation and very poor balance.

I will use Michael Clarke as an example. Michael has the attributes of a very fine all-round fielder and, as I said, he is capable of taking some sensational catches. Unfortunately, in the slips he tends to dive at the ball instead of letting the ball come to him, which not only reduces the amount of time he has to get into position, it also means that he is not as relaxed as he should be when the ball arrives. Relaxation, coupled with good concentration, is the key to movement and implementing the correct technique.

One of the points I hammered home to all players, including the very young, is that when they take up position in the slips they should be so relaxed that they feel as though their hands and arms are almost falling off.

Stress, strain, stillness and late reactions can all be attributed to either over-concentration or this inability to relax. Like almost everything in life, both of these traits can be learnt. I have always believed that you must learn to reduce concentration to the shortest possible time. My method, both as a batsman and a slip fieldsman, was to observe the bowler running up but to only switch into full-concentration mode as the bowler's arm came over for the final downswing before the delivery. This reduced concentration to the minimum; if I batted or fielded all day, I would still only be at peak concentration level for about 30 minutes. I was sharp when I had to be sharp. I think that helped me score big runs and undoubtedly it helped me be a better slip fieldsman. There weren't too many times when I was embarrassed because I lost concentration in the slips. The other point about this method was that when I said to myself, 'Now!' or, 'Concentrate now!' to switch on, it also triggered my 'initial movement' and the subconscious instruction to watch the ball out of the bowler's hand rather than the area around the arm and hand, which so many players at all levels of the game do.

Initial movement is as vital in the slips as it is for a batsman. It is impossible to move quickly into position without the right initial movement. Everyone's initial movement might be different (think about the different ways people get out of lounge chairs), but they all have one. When I batted, my initial movement was to push my front foot a little forward—without altering my balance. The idea was to move just enough to get my body ready for whatever the bowler delivered. In the slips, I developed the habit of squatting on my haunches as the bowler ran up and only moved into a relaxed position as I said, 'Now!' as the bowler was about to let go of the ball. This habit certainly allowed me to move quickly and safely into position (though I am sure it was also a contributor to the knee problems I now have).

All my fielding—and especially catching—exercises were based on using two hands. In the Australian team set-up when I was coach, we had catching competitions where I was the sole arbitrator, and if a fielder took a catch one-handed when I thought he could have got two hands to it, I disallowed the catch. Rough justice, maybe, but they quickly learnt that two hands were best and safest, particularly if 'the old bugger', as Merv Hughes liked to call me, was judge and jury. On the occasions that I have made a point of watching the current Australian team complete their fielding drills, I have been disappointed at the lack of intensity they show.

During the Fourth Test between Australia and India at the SCG in 2003–04 I arrived at the ground each day very early because it was Steve Waugh's last Test and record crowds were expected. This meant I had plenty of time to watch the Aussies practise and was amazed that in those five mornings I did not see the team involved in one full-scale fielding session. The only time I saw a special fielding exercise of any kind was when I noticed Justin Langer and Matthew Hayden trying fairly unsuccessfully to hit a stump from about ten metres. Their method was to rush in, pick the ball up, and take it over their shoulder before flinging it at the stumps, when they should have known that the quickest and most accurate way to do this is to move in quickly, stay low and balanced, pick the ball up with two hands, take one stride and then let the ball go underarm. The time saved doing it this way is highly significant, because taking the ball above your shoulder allows the batsmen to run at least a metre more—often the difference between being run out or safely reaching the crease. Supervising all this was Australia's only fielding adviser, the American baseball coach Mike Young. I have played baseball at a reasonable level and know there are few similarities in the techniques that cross over both sports.

In baseball, however, around 90 per cent of the time you know what your play will be if the ball is hit to you. For instance, if you are the shortstop and there is a runner on first base, if the ball is hit your way, you have to get the ball to second base to stop the runner at first advancing. All pretty simple. But the catching techniques in the two games are totally different. With the huge baseball glove you push your glove to the ball to catch it. With bare hands, you let the ball come to you.

In my view, if the Australian team wants to get back to the high fielding standards it once set, it must adopt a different attitude to fielding practice and take someone on board who knows a little about the specific principles and techniques of fielding in cricket. To me, practice should be 'bread and butter' for the players. It is here that you hone your skills for the matches ahead. Cricketers must work towards the same goals at practice that they wish to reach in a match. To do this they must treat all practices as though they are in a match, and must apply the techniques they'll need in the game whenever they practise. In no area of the game is this more important than in fielding.

And always remember practice doesn't make you perfect. Perfect practice does!

25

THE ETERNAL SEARCH FOR
A GENUINE ALL-ROUNDER

All-rounders, for so long the 'boiler room' of the Australian cricket team, have now reached the stage where they are in danger of being placed on the endangered species list. By 'all-rounder', I don't necessarily mean a true champion with the ball and bat, in the style of Keith Miller or Garry Sobers. I just mean a player who is good enough to hold a position in the Test XI through his individual talent as a batsman or a bowler, and as a bonus can also, if he's a bowler, score runs or, if he's a batsman, take some wickets.

For many years, Australian cricket was rich with players with the skill to either bat excellently and snare a few important wickets, or bowl superbly and also play some crucial innings. For example, in the Australian team straight after the Second World War, not only was Miller, the king of Australian all-rounders, in the side, but there were also frontline bowlers such as Ray Lindwall and Colin McCool who were capable of scoring Test-match centuries. Richie Benaud's side of the late 1950s and early 1960s featured accomplished bowling all-rounders such as Richie, Alan Davidson and Ken Mackay, while batsmen such as Norm O'Neill, Brian Booth and myself could take key wickets. Further, had it not been for a major injury, another fine all-rounder, Ron Archer, might have captained Australia before Ian Craig and Richie. Instead, on the way home from the 1956 Ashes tour, Ronnie ripped his knee on the mat in Pakistan. It was his last Test, a week before his 23rd birthday. He came back to play briefly as a batsman for Queensland, but eventually he retired from first-class cricket when he was 26, which was such a pity, because there is little doubt in my mind that but for that injury he would have gone on to greatness.

Colin McCool holds a special place in my cricketing heart because he was my first hero, I think at least in part because he was the type of cricketer I wanted to be. He was a good batsman, bowled leg-spinners and was sensational in the slip cordon. People like to talk about how great a slips fieldsman Keith Miller was, but my memory is of Colin McCool often backing him up, and taking catches that to my teenage eye Miller should have gone for. Colin was a little bloke who hit the ball hard and he came across as something of a battler, which appealed to my working-class roots, but he was also a star of the first Ashes series after the war, scoring 272 runs at 54.40 and taking 18 wickets at 27.27 (equal with Ray Lindwall as the most by any Australian). Unfortunately, he only played fourteen Tests before heading to England, a victim of the new-ball rule then in operation that restricted opportunities for spinners, and he starred in the Lancashire League and later with Somerset in county cricket. Colin's one Test hundred was obviously a beauty —104 not out against England at the MCG in 1946–47, made batting from the No. 7 spot after a star-studded batting order featuring Sid Barnes, Arthur Morris, Don Bradman, Lindsay Hassett and Keith Miller had stumbled to 6–192. He took five wickets in a Test innings three times, and actually took more Test wickets through stumpings (10 of 36) than any other mode of dismissal.

The first time I ever met Colin was on the flight down to Melbourne for the Centenary Test in 1977. I was walking down the aisle, looking for my seat, when I realised Colin McCool was in the seat next to mine.

Straightaway I said to him, 'You're my hero!'

Not surprisingly, I guess, he was embarrassed. 'I know who *you* are,' he responded. 'Why am I your hero?' That flight went way too quickly for me, but we were able to catch up again during the celebrations at the Melbourne Hilton and the MCG.

A short while later, I found myself playing in a 'veterans' match at the Kings School Ground at Parramatta, in the western suburbs of Sydney, and who should be a team-mate but one Colin McCool. Finally, I was actually fielding to his bowling, a scenario I'd probably dreamt about when I was just a boy. And then it happened . . . the batsman pushed forward at a well-flighted leg-break . . . it took the edge . . . and I snared the chance. No way was I dropping that one.

Ian Chappell's team of the 1970s featured specialist batsmen such as Dougie Walters, and the Chappells were also genuine partnership breakers, while for a couple of seasons Gary Gilmour opened the bowling and also played some important and exciting innings. However, as I write this book, it's been nearly 30 years since 'Gus' Gilmour played his last Test, and since then the closest thing we have seen to a genuine all-rounder in the Australian team for an extended period of time has been the Waugh twins.

Sure, players such as Greg Matthews, Simon O'Donnell, Andrew Symonds and Shane Watson have been picked as all-rounders in the Aussie team in the past two decades, but none has made a major impact with both their batting and their bowling. The only consistently effective 'all-rounder' has been Adam Gilchrist, but I don't see a batsman/wicketkeeper—even one as outrageously talented as Gilchrist—as an all-rounder in the true cricket sense of the word. Otherwise, does this mean we should also call someone such as Neil Harvey an all-rounder because he was such a superb fieldsman, or Ian Healy an all-rounder because he averaged nearly 30 with the bat? The true weakness of relying on Gilchrist as the all-rounder was exposed in the 2005 Ashes series, when Australia went into all five Tests without one man in the top six who could even tie up an end for a few overs. Ricky Ponting was left to either keep bowlers on, even though they were being belted, or keep over-using Shane Warne, which he often did. I believe this imbalance in the Australian attack was one of the reasons the Ashes changed hands.

The selectors seemed to recognise this by picking Watson and then Symonds for Australia's home Tests in 2005–06. But my fear with both these players, like some others before them, is that they have been chosen because of their collective skills, without being worthy of a position in the team as either a batsman or a bowler. I believe this strategy is wrong, and is why in the years since the 1970s we in Australia have been so disappointed with the performances of our all-rounders.

•

By my reckoning, during the time I have been involved in first-class cricket, there have probably only been five men who have consistently and genuinely been worth their place in the Test side as both a bowler and a batsman. The only Australian I include in this elite group is the mercurial Miller, a hero to his generation. The others would be the West Indies' Garry Sobers, England's Ian Botham, New Zealand's Richard Hadlee, India's Kapil Dev and Pakistan's Imran Khan. Interestingly, only Sobers of this five could be classified as a batsman who bowled; the other four were more bowlers who batted well, sometimes brilliantly. They were all naturally fine fieldsmen, which strongly suggests they were made for the game.

Of course, there have been some cricketers who should be placed on the tier just below this 'famous five'. If Richie Benaud had played every series like the one in South Africa in 1957–58, he'd be remembered as maybe the greatest all-rounder of them all. In the Fourth Test at Johannesburg, which we won to clinch a series few had expected us to win, Richie scored 100 batting four and then took nine wickets. For the series, he scored 329 runs at 54.83 and took 30 wickets at 21.93. During his career, he became the first man to score 2000 runs and take 200 wickets, but his final career batting average of 24.46 is not enough to suggest he was always going to make the side purely as a batsman. Similarly, Alan Davidson was the bloke, if I needed a wicket to save my life, who I'd have turned to. But though he scored two of Australian cricket's most famous innings—the 80 that almost won us the first Tied Test and the 77 at Old Trafford in 1961 that gave Richie the chance to spin us to victory on the final day—he made only five 50s and no hundreds in 44 Tests, so I couldn't rate Davo as a specialist Test batsman.

One overseas player I immediately think of when listing these 'second tier' all-rounders is South Africa's Trevor Goddard. A left-handed opening batsman and a left-arm bowler who could deliver both swing and spin, Goddard was a wonderful contributor to South Africa's great team of the 1960s. He scored 2516 runs at an average of 34.46 in 41 Tests and took 123 wickets at 26.22. Two others are the Indians, Ravi Shastri and Vinoo Mankad, who both scored more than 2000 Test runs and took more than 150 Test wickets, while one of the most underrated all-rounders I ever saw was England's Tony Greig. In the brutal era of Thomson, Lillee and the West Indies tearaways, Greig scored 3599 runs and took 141 wickets. He could bowl medium-pace and once won a Test at Port-of-Spain bowling off-breaks, while he also captained England to a series win in India, which is never easy to do.

One current player not far behind my top five is England's Andrew Flintoff, especially after all that he did against Australia in 2005; perhaps his performances in the 2006–07 Ashes series will see him rated among the all-time greats. Another modern-day cricketer, Jacques Kallis of South Africa, has impressive statistics, having recently become, after Sobers, only the second man to score 8000 Test runs and take 200 Test wickets, but while I rate him a wonderful batsman, I would describe him as a handy rather than frontline swing bowler, who would struggle to make too many Test teams on his bowling alone.

•

I have been asked many times—usually by Australian fans who fondly remember cricketers such as Benaud, Davidson and, most of all, Miller—why the player with genuine all-round skills has disappeared. I wonder whether it goes back to the time around 30 years ago, when children were told that they needed to specialise. To survive in that school of hard knocks out there, they needed to focus on one skill, one profession, one sport, even one facet of one sport. It was said that dual sportsmen were a thing of the past, and because of this they were made to choose early what role they were going to play.

In cricket, this meant batsmen were suddenly reluctant to bowl in the nets, while tailenders stopped working on their batting. One of my strongest memories of my early days as Australian coach was having to force Merv Hughes to have a bat in the nets. I felt he was underrating his batting and had discovered that he was an opening batsman but when he was younger with the bravado of youth, Merv told me that he didn't want a hit. I think he was worried he would look foolish if he did have a hit. 'That's okay,' I said to him. 'If you don't want to bat at practice, then you can run around the oval with your pads on for your batting time.' That did the trick, and over the next couple of years Merv worked on his batting to the point that, while he was never a genuine all-rounder, he was also never an easy bloke for the opposition to get out. Steve Waugh's work with Glenn McGrath has become legendary, and the Australian 'tail' these days is as hard to shift as any late order in cricket history. But at the same time, the batsmen have not been working on their bowling, and there are consequently too many blokes around today who virtually can't roll their arms over and would never be considered for a bowl in first-class cricket.

These days, we have organised schools for batsmen, spinners and fast bowlers. There are batting, bowling and fielding coaches, and players are shuffled into one of the groups. But has there been any consideration for the potential all-rounders? They were once a strength of Australian cricket, and can be again, but only if the natural individual skills that Australia breeds in abundance are fully nurtured.

26

A FEARLESS GENTLE GIANT

England all-rounder Andrew Flintoff's brilliant performances with the bat and ball in the past three years has seen the English media upgrade him to the status of a true hero. Time will tell, of course, whether the publicity is fully justified, but what I can tell you now is that he is one hell of a cricketer. Furthermore, I also know that whether or not he ever reaches the same pedestal as, say, Ian Botham, he will remain the same easygoing giant whom I first met when I coached Lancashire in 2000 and 2001. He was then a respectful, gentle colossus; I'd be surprised if superstardom has changed him.

The greatest joy I get out of coaching at any level is to help my charges improve. I don't expect them to wave a magic wand and turn into instant champions, but I enjoy working with players who want to do better. I have been luckier than most coaches, for I have had the opportunity to work with many gifted players and watch their talents blossom. Undoubtedly, the most gifted of them all have been the Waugh twins and the genius leg-spinner Shane Warne.

There is a special challenge and excitement when you recognise an exceptionally gifted player. I got that adrenaline rush one freezing north-of-England day when I viewed 'Freddie' Flintoff during my initial session as Lancashire coach. I had put on all the training clothing

I could muster and as I walked onto Old Trafford I felt and must have looked like a 'Michelin man'. But though I might have been a little embarrassed by my size, I was still dwarfed by the towering height and width of a broad 22-year-old lad named Flintoff.

I saw nothing impressive as I watched this huge and slightly awkward youngster go through the warm-ups. But once he put his pads on and strode into the nets it was different. The awkwardness was gone, replaced with graceful fluid movements and enormous power. What impressed me most, though, was his ability to judge the length of the ball and his near-perfect technique. Sure, he sometimes pre-empted shots and his concentration wasn't all that flash, but I knew immediately that his potential was enormous.

Six weeks later, in the second match of the season, we played Kent, who were then coached by John Wright, at Canterbury. It was a game ruined by the weather, but Andrew still managed to score 77 in our first innings under difficult conditions. Afterwards, John came around to see me and said, 'You have a good one there. He makes it all look so easy.' Freddie had made his international debut against South Africa in 1998, but to this point had enjoyed little success at the highest level, at a time when England was craving for a star in the Botham mould. John Wright could see the talent and admire the easy style, but unfortunately the English selectors and management perceived a different picture. They saw Freddie's bulk as fat and leaked these views, apparently hoping to goad him into getting fitter and improving his attitude. The English press joyfully jumped onto the bandwagon and for weeks they harassed the young man.

I quickly realised that one thing Freddie Flintoff didn't have was an attitude problem. Nothing could have been further from the truth. In fact, the big man was just a different character to the many dull personalities who exist in county cricket; the people then in charge of English cricket just didn't know how to handle him. I couldn't understand why they seldom bothered to contact him, or to sit down with him so they could explain their position. Instead, they seemed happier to drip-feed the media with erroneous information.

Not surprisingly, Freddie's mindset became confused, and it says much for his personality, courage and determination as a young man that he came through this period.

What annoyed me most was the nitpicking about his weight. He may have been carrying the odd pound or two, but he was still fast in the field, had tremendous stamina and was going harder at the end of the day than most of his team-mates. Personality wise, even at such an early age, there was a lot of the Merv Hughes about him. He was always the life of the party, a man who kept the spirit of the dressing room high. But where he was most like Big Merv was in his work ethic.

He loved cricket practice and the more competitive it was the better. His size made him look more ferocious than he really was, but still he was never shy to bowl a bouncer or two or three . . . or even four. Again like Merv, and quite amazingly really, although he peppered the batsmen he was immensely popular with both team-mates and opponents. Their similarities ended with the bat, however, for while Merv was a bowling all-rounder, Big Fred's greatest strength was his batting. Never was this better demonstrated than in England's Test matches of 2004, when even though his 43 wickets for the year at 25.77 were impressive, it was his 898 runs at 52.82, with two centuries and seven 50s that really caught the attention. England played seven Tests at home that year, and Freddie scored at least one half-century in each of those games.

His efforts in the 2005 Ashes series were not quite so impressive from a purely statistical point of view, even though he scored a brilliant century at Trent Bridge and hit a match-winning double of 68 and 73 at Edgbaston (a Test in which he also took seven wickets and England won by two runs). But the manner in which he took the fight up to the Australians, especially to the legendary Warne, captured the attention of the entire nation in a way perhaps even Botham never quite managed.

Undoubtedly, Freddie's greatest strengths are his astounding power combined with the correctness of his technique. While he hits the ball as hard as anyone I have seen, he is also very clever in picking up singles and is very quick between the wickets. As a fielder, he has huge hands, is an exceptionally quick mover and has the ability and softness of hands so necessary to be a good catcher. He also once had a fantastic throwing arm—in the Norm O'Neill class, which is as good as it gets—but after getting advice from a local trainer linked to a rugby league club based near Manchester he built up the muscles in his shoulder to the point that he could no longer throw. That football man might have been a weights expert, but he didn't understand cricket mechanics. It took Freddie nearly twelve months before he could throw well again.

Often, though, when assessing big aggressive men, the critics— whether they know the subjects they're judging or not—tend to label them as being not too bright. No one should categorise Freddie Flintoff this way. He does have a very sharp brain, befitting a man who was once, amazingly, a Lancashire schoolboy chess champion. In 2001, I recommended him as a future Lancashire captain, but that didn't go down well with the chairman of the club or the committee. Now, of course, Freddie is a captain of England. One of his most attractive traits is that he is a good listener who will consider advice and accept it if it is sound and to his advantage. He has done this in all aspects of cricket. As an example, for a period his bowling action led to injury. He was proactive in seeking advice, and once he worked out the way to go he spent a long time in the nets sorting things out. Similarly, there was a time when he couldn't square- or back-cut and was prone to being caught behind as he tried to whip balls through the covers off the back foot. We spent many hours in the indoor nets at Lancashire fixing that problem, and nowadays he is even late-cutting the spinners.

While Big Fred is a tough competitor on the field, he is a softie off it, particularly with his family and at home. He is a great dog lover and a boxer fancier. While I was at Lancashire he bought a boxer, but loved it so much that he went back the next day and bought the last of the litter so his dog would have a brother. Not long after, the breeder rang him to enquire whether he could handle another one. As the breeder explained, a client's marriage had broken up and consequently the estranged wife could no longer keep a two-year-old white boxer. Old softie could not say no and suddenly he had three dogs. Unfortunately, this latest addition didn't get on with the two pups, but Freddie loved him, too, so rather than return the dog to the breeder he convinced his father, no great dog lover apparently, into taking the two-year-old. I can well imagine the look on Freddie's face as he implored his dad to help him out. As it happened, Mr Flintoff senior, who is as big as Freddie, is also just as soft and within three months he had dropped 12 kilos by exercising the dog and himself.

Back in 2000, there was a point where Freddie had me very frustrated, because he wasn't getting the wickets or scoring the runs that he should have been. The effort was there, but sometimes his judgement wasn't right. He was his own worst enemy. 'Andrew, you've got everything it takes to be great,' I said to him, 'but at present you're not showing it or using it.'

Actually, I was a lot blunter than that, but the message was the same. It was up to him whether he got all that he could out of his cricket. The thing was, he was terrific. I knew he was a man I had to talk straight to. If I'd tried to fool around with him, tried to con him into being a better cricketer, he would have lost all respect for me. And that's the last thing I would have wanted. I like the bloke too much.

Two catches, one among my favourites, the other not so good. Top: England captain Ted Dexter is caught off Alan Davidson's bowling at the SCG in 1962–63. I took the catch with both hands, and always felt perfectly balanced. Below: India's Gundappa Viswanath is caught off Wayne Clark's bowling in Adelaide in 1977–78. This time, my concentration was poor and I was on my heels, surprised when the ball came to me. I was lucky to hang on. *Collection of Bob Simpson*

With cricket's greatest ever all-rounder,
Garry Sobers, in the West Indies in 1965.
Collection of Bob Simpson

Another landmark for Simpson and
Lawry. We opened the batting 62 times
for Australia and averaged 58.95 runs per
partnership. *Collection of Bob Simpson*

Our series against India in 1977–78 proved hugely popular despite being up against World Series
Cricket. One of the reasons was the good relationship between the two sides, a rapport captured in
this photograph of me with India's captain Bishan Bedi. *Collection of Bob Simpson*

I might look happy enough, but I never enjoyed leaving my family to go on a long tour, in this case to the Caribbean in 1978. My wife Meg is kissing me on the cheek, with Debbie (left) and Kim behind me. *Collection of Bob Simpson*

After my grandson Ashley, then aged seven, met Sir Donald Bradman, he told his mum, 'I met the best golfer in the world yesterday!' It was true that The Don and I had spent a good deal of time talking about putts and fairways, so Ashley was entitled to be mistaken. *Collection of Bob Simpson*

Allan Border's young side in Calcutta after winning the 1987 World Cup. Standing (from left): Bob Simpson (coach), Simon O'Donnell, Tim May, Tom Moody, Greg Dyer, Bruce Reid, David Boon, Peter Taylor, Andrew Zesers, Errol Alcott (physio), Alan Crompton (manager); Front: Mike Veletta, Dean Jones, Allan Border, Geoff Marsh, Steve Waugh, Craig McDermott. *Adrian Murrell/Getty Images*

The men who retained the Ashes in 1989, photographed at Lord's. Back (from left): Errol Alcott (physio), Trevor Hohns, Tim May, Geoff Lawson, Carl Rackemann, Tom Moody, Merv Hughes, Terry Alderman, Greg Campbell, Mike Walsh (scorer); Front: Bob Simpson (coach), Tim Zoehrer, Mark Taylor, Dean Jones, Allan Border, Laurie Sawle (manager), Geoff Marsh, David Boon, Steve Waugh, Mike Veletta, Ian Healy. *Collection of Bob Simpson*

Contrasting images from the Caribbean. Top: Peter Toohey has just been hit by an Andy Roberts bouncer at Port-of-Spain in 1978. I am on the left, Trevor Laughlin is holding a towel to Toohey's face, and Gary Cosier and Desmond Haynes follow behind. *Collection of Bob Simpson* Below: Seventeen years later, the Australian mood is much brighter as Paul Reiffel bowls Brian Lara for a duck in the series-deciding Test at Kingston. *Shaun Botterill/Getty Images*

I have never seen a bowler with as much natural talent as Shane Warne, photographed here with me in 1993. *APL*

With Mark Waugh at the 1996 World Cup. Of all the players who contacted me when I was sacked as coach after this tournament, it is Mark's call that I remember the most. *Shaun Botterill/Getty Images*

I'm not sure my eyes are quite as focused on the ball as I would have liked, but I do like this photograph, if for no other reason than it reminds me of the joy I always feel when I'm in the middle of a training session. *Collection of Bob Simpson*

England's 'Freddie' Flintoff attacks Shane Warne during the 2005 Ashes series, with Australian captain Ricky Ponting in the background. *Stu Forster/Getty Images*

I was inducted into the Australian Cricket Hall of Fame on Allan Border Medal night in 2006. This was one of my proudest moments, not least because I was able to share the experience with my family. *Kristian Dowling/Getty Images*

27

WHERE HAVE ALL THE SWING BOWLERS GONE?

Only five Australians have taken more than 250 Test wickets. Three of them have played Test cricket in the 21st century: Shane Warne, Glenn McGrath and Jason Gillespie (the other two are Dennis Lillee and Craig McDermott). One other Australian bowler of the 21st century, Brett Lee, has taken more than 200 Test wickets, while two more, Stuart MacGill and Michael Kasprowicz, have taken more than 100.

Partly this is a reflection of the amount of international cricket that is played these days, but what having this number of frontline bowlers available for the past six years also means is that the Australian bowling attack of the last few years has seen very few changes. Sure, at times we have seen men such as Andy Bichel, Nathan Bracken, Shane Watson, Shaun Tait and Stuart Clark bowling for Australia, but until Clark had a terrific series in South Africa in early 2006 no bowler outside of the 'magnificent six'— Warne, McGrath, Gillespie, Lee, MacGill and Kasprowicz—had contributed in a major way to the Australian Test team's fortunes for anything more than the odd match here or there.

Having high-class bowlers of the calibre of Warne, McGrath and company constantly available is, of course, very exciting and has led to many Test-match victories. However, it has also camouflaged the fact that very few Test-quality young bowlers have come through in the past four or five years. Part of the reason for this has been that some potentially high-class young fast bowlers have been getting injured at a worrying rate. Just as concerning, the art of swing bowling appears to have virtually disappeared from all standards of cricket in Australia. Only Lee of the magnificent six is not well past his 30th birthday (and Lee will turn 30 a couple of weeks before the start of the 2006–07 Ashes series); if there is not a group of younger bowlers ready to step into their places, the next few years might not be as productive as Australian fans expect.

To me, it seems that the injury problems date back to when the Australian Cricket Academy became so influential in the development of our young cricketers. Many states, even in the early years of the Academy, were baulking at sending their promising new-ball bowlers over because others had returned either with injuries or newfangled bowling actions. While the Academy has access to experts on fitness, biomechanics, sports medicine and physiotherapy looking at the problem, the injuries haven't stopped. Almost everything has been blamed—bowlers were delivering too many overs, or bowling too fast, bowling for too long, overusing the gym, changing their actions too often. At the same time, there has been this almost total decline in the art of swing bowling in Australia.

My strong view is that the demise of swing bowling is really not that surprising, since pace and pace alone was the consideration for many years. It got to the ridiculous stage when Jeff Hammond, the Australian fast-medium bowler of the early 1970s and then the coach of South Australia, placed an advertisement in the papers offering an open trial for any pace bowler. Medium-pacers need not apply! That was the fad of the time, in part brought on by the success of Lillee and Thommo for Australia, and Andy Roberts,

Malcolm Marshall, Michael Holding and company for the West Indies. The influence Dennis enjoyed through his fast bowling academies furthered the spread of this philosophy, in the process destroying the proud and successful history of swing bowling in Australia.

Throughout my very long time in Sydney club cricket, from the early 1950s to the late 1970s, almost every team had at least two swing bowlers in every grade. Now, as I visit the clubs each season to try to help them best run their practice sessions, I very rarely, almost never, see a bowler swing the ball. It's not that they can't, for once they are shown how it is done they start moving the ball. The problem, of course, is that very few coaches know how to do it.

Every cricketer, whether a batsman or a bowler, should follow what is natural for him. Unfortunately, fashion, fads and theories often impinge on this principle. Dennis Lillee had his own wonderful way of bowling, and he was a magnificent competitor and one of the all-time great wicket-takers. It is not surprising then that he coaches the way he bowled, but unfortunately, as I often argue, what may be right for a champion such as D.K. Lillee is not always the best for everyone else. Dennis held the ball with his fingers close together on the seam, banged it into the pitch, was amazingly astute in reading batsmen, and had wonderful control and the heart of a lion, but he didn't swing the ball. For 100 years, all new-ball bowlers were encouraged to hold their pointer and second finger on either side of the seam about three-quarters of an inch apart, with the seam pointing either to first slip or leg-slip depending on which way you wanted to swing the ball. With the fingers spread, bowlers could hold the ball in a relaxed manner and thus found it easier to get the flexible wrist needed for the bowler to keep his wrist behind the ball and the seam more upright. By doing this it is possible to avoid the trap of rolling the wrist at the point of delivery, which leads to a 'scrambled' seam and the ball keeping its line rather than swinging through the air.

McGrath, Gillespie and Kasprowicz have demonstrated over the last decade that new-ball bowlers can obtain wickets in ways other than just sheer pace. However, all three have relied in the main on movement off the pitch to get their wickets. They have rarely bowled the length that the superb swing bowlers of the past focused on. In reality, Damien Fleming was the last genuine swing bowler selected for Australia, but sadly injuries cut short his career before he could have the impact he might have had.

•

To be honest, I feel a little like a voice in the wilderness when it comes to swing bowling. I think I know how Bill 'Tiger' O'Reilly felt in the years before Shane Warne, when he kept saying leg-spin would make a triumphant return at a time when all the experts had pronounced it dead and buried. I know that one day I will rejoice again at the sight of pace bowlers moving the ball in the air during the opening overs of a Test match, because all the things that do work in cricket never go totally out of fashion. I have become very bored with bowlers pitching too short to be truly effective; if the ball seams, it has done too much by the time it reaches the batsman and doesn't claim an edge. Only the great ones such as Lillee and McGrath can rely on movement off the pitch to get their wickets. The decline of swing bowling across the cricket world is one of the reasons, in my view, why world cricket has very few genuinely outstanding fast or fast-medium bowlers at the moment.

But still I have never known a period in cricket when so many batsmen play and miss. Commentators continually claim the bowler is unlucky, but those with experience know it is not a matter of luck but poor bowling. If the bowler tried a fuller length they would pick up the edge. Unfortunately, the routine length of most new-ball bowlers for the last couple of decades has been between one and two metres shorter than what was considered a 'good' length in previous eras.

At Headingley in 1989, England captain David Gower was heavily criticised for sending us in, especially after we then went out and scored more than 600 in our first innings. Mark Taylor and Steve Waugh both got big hundreds. But the fact was Gower was let down badly by his bowlers. *We* would have sent *them* in if Allan Border had won the toss, even though at first glance the pitch was white, which suggested it was dry. In fact, there was plenty of grass on it and there was moisture about, too. Before we bowled, I took our bowlers out to the pitch, to show them how the Englishmen had got it wrong. Because the wicket was so white, there were pitch marks all over it, and these showed that the home team had consistently pitched the ball too short. 'We're going to land it up there,' I said, pointing at an area around two metres closer to the stumps than where the Poms had been pitching. On the last day, our men—especially Terry Alderman—were brilliant, England capitulated, and the tone was set for the rest of the series.

Sixteen years later, Australia lost those Ashes. The team that went to England in 2005 was accompanied by a large support staff, yet problems which to me seemed obvious were either ignored or deemed unimportant. Two obvious ones which contributed to the loss were that the Aussie bowlers sent down too many no-balls and the batsmen were unable to handle swing bowling, which led to a number of middle-order collapses.

Coach John Buchanan's admission that he had left it to the bowlers to sort out among themselves their no-ball problems was a clear sign that attention to detail regarding technical difficulties had been given a low priority. The situation appeared to be rectified during the following Australian season, but I have been left with the sneaking suspicion that little has been done to redress the batsmen's susceptibility against high-quality swing bowling. Most certainly, they saw very little of that kind of bowling against the West Indies, South Africa and Bangladesh, and it could well be that England will find them out again when the Ashes comes to Australia in 2006–07.

I must confess to having a quiet chuckle when the critics said it was *reverse* swing (the practice of swinging the old ball) that worried the Australians in England. It wasn't just reverse swing that worried them, but swing in general. The English camp studied Australia's helter-skelter approach to batting and came up with a simple plan—because such out-and-out aggression only works if the bowling is poor, they aimed to put enough balls in the right spot and waited for the errors brought about by failures in the batsmen's techniques.

During the series, Justin Langer was caught at short leg off bat and pad more than once, as his front leg pushed to point, rather than in the direction he wanted to hit the ball. The result was that his bat didn't have a clear passage to the ball, his balance wasn't right, and the inside edge ballooned up to Ian Bell. Matt Hayden was going too hard at the ball and offering catching practice to the slip cordon. Damien Martyn's indecisive footwork meant he was troubled by good-length balls outside the off stump and often trapped lbw. Adam Gilchrist was stranded when Andrew Flintoff went round the wicket and aimed consistently at short of a good length in at his ribs. Many times, the reverse swing applied the coup de grâce. Of this quartet—all of them fantastic players for Australia over the years—only Hayden seemed to make any adjustment during the series, and he did so by batting in a very circumspect manner when he made his first-innings century in the final Test, at The Oval.

Because the true art of swing bowling has been dying, many modern batsmen haven't got a clue how to handle this form of bowling. They have been programmed to face bowlers who keep banging the ball in short of a length, and are coached by former cricketers who faced the same thing. Today's batsmen seem to have lost the ability to judge the length of the ball and end up straddling the crease, neither forward nor back. Far more batsmen are dismissed lbw these days than they were 40 years ago, and that's not just because of the pressure television replays put on umpires. These batsmen are ripe for swing bowlers to create havoc, because if they play across the crease they are suckers for any ball that moves in the air.

So why did it take a new concept of swing—this 'reverse' swing—to bring swing bowling back into vogue? Because the old ball doesn't bounce as much, some bowlers tried pitching it up more, and they found that not only did it swing if they gripped it right, it also confused batsmen not used to the combination of swing and a full length. Of course, when bowlers pitched at that fuller length without the ball swinging it was being constantly hit away for four, but when it did swing it caused some havoc. The next step in this 'innovation', I confidently predicted in early 2006, would be that a new-ball bowler would start swinging the ball in the manner of Alec Bedser, Ray Lindwall, Fred Trueman or Alan Davidson. I was sure that when that bowler came along he would make, as Warne did in the early 1990s, an immediate impact.

•

Now I am not suggesting that Stuart Clark is another Bedser, Lindwall, Trueman or Davidson, but on what we saw during the Australia versus South Africa Test series in South Africa in early 2006, he could be close to that new-ball swing bowler I've been searching for. In the first three Tests of his career, at the age of 30, he took 20 South African wickets at 15.85 and was named player of the series.

It is very rare now for a cricketer to slip through the radar of the game's 'grapevine'. Now this in itself is no mean feat, because that grapevine—which involves the passing of messages and news within the cricket community and has been in existence forever— is a very effective way of letting cricket aficionados know exactly what is going on. In the very early days, news of the rise of gifted players was passed on purely through word of mouth and newspaper reports, then came newsreels, radio, local television and now satellite television. These days, you can go to a place such as Nepal, as I did in late 1999, and watch Test matches or one-day internationals that are being played in various parts of the world. The grapevine allows batsmen, in particular, to gain early knowledge of a new bowling talent and how best to cope with him. Not many have escaped such attention, but somehow Stuart Clark did, even though he had played 15 one-day internationals before his Test debut, and had been called up as cover for the injured Glenn McGrath during the 2005 Ashes series.

Part of the reason he slipped through the radar was because of his age. He had made his first-class debut way back in 1997–98, when he was touted as something of a Glenn McGrath. He was never explosive in pace, which made him a 'sleeper' in a cricket community obsessed with the search for the next express bowler. He also, I imagine, had to overcome those 'experts' who were telling him that, because he was 198 centimetres tall, lift from the pitch would be the key to his success. Gradually, he built his own bowling style and developed the tactical nous he'd need to be successful at the top level.

Today, I don't think as bowlers you can compare Clark to McGrath. Though they're both tall, one is a swinger and the other is a cutter. McGrath's normal length is shorter than Clark's, which is why he doesn't swing the ball very much. That doesn't diminish the great McGrath as a bowler at all, but just don't call him a swing bowler.

In South Africa, Clark gained his wickets in exactly the way that you would expect a fine swing bowler to do so. Six of his 20 wickets were out caught behind and five more were caught in the cordon between first slip and gully, which suggests his outswinger was moving nicely. A couple of caught-and-bowleds and a catch to mid-off suggest he had his slower ball working, while in the Second Test, Ashwell Prince was surprised by the lift of one delivery as he played across his crease, and popped up a catch to Mike Hussey on the onside. Jacques Kallis, South Africa's best batsman, was dismissed by Clark four times in six innings, and in four different ways—caught in the gully, caught behind, caught and bowled, and lbw. Undoubtedly, the major reason for the new man's success was his adherence to the old-fashioned principles of line and length. He has a wonderful pure action to swing the ball, and uses his wrist well (which, as I wrote, is the key to swing bowling), but what sets him apart from most of the other new-ball bowlers of today is that he aims at that fuller length, which allows the ball to swing.

I am sure that Clark will continue to confuse and dismiss batsmen if he continues to focus on his ability to swing the ball. The advent of reverse swing means, of course, that he can be a major strike weapon with both the old ball and the new. Shortly, the magnificent six might become seven. And further from this, we must all hope that present-day coaches—who still seem to have a one-bullet-point agenda of turning pace-bowling prospects into tearaways—will take a good look at what Stuart Clark is doing and absorb the lesson that high-quality swing bowling can undo even the best batsmen in the world.

28

THE ONE-DAY GAME

If you are a cricket historian, you would know that the game has been dying ever since it was invented. That is, if you are to believe the press coverage over such a long period.

Nowadays, with the advent of Twenty20 cricket, some people seem to have decided that one-day cricket has had its time. They base their contention on what to them has been a boring season or a one-sided tournament. Something radical must be done, they argue rather hysterically, to regain the public's interest. Unfortunately, these critics have listened to the adverse comment in the media but forgotten to check attendance figures or television ratings, which have always been a critical reason for the proliferation of one-day games. In recent years, television audiences have been increasing for Test matches *and* one-day internationals.

In many countries, Test attendances have slipped in recent years, which might be partly due to Australia's domination of everything except the 2005 Ashes series (when the level of interest, of course, was phenomenal). Many Tests involving the Australians have been completed in less than five days. But even in series where there have been empty seats while the Test matches were being played, in the one-day tournaments that preceded or followed the five-day games, the grounds have been vibrant, colourful and packed. The fans want one-day cricket, so the administrators' job should not be to do away with it, rather to make sure it retains its appeal.

This is not to say that one-day cricket doesn't have its problems. While I'm proud to say that I have long been a fan of the one-day game, I know that it has always been flawed. The coaching side of me loves the way the game tests certain skills of the players in ways no other form of the game can do so specifically; for everyone, the appeal of one-day cricket is the expectation of a close finish, and then the adrenaline rush and tension that comes with a thrilling climax. At the same time matches can be tedious for coaches, spectators and players alike if it becomes apparent early on that there won't be any nail-biting.

It's not just slow games that can be monotonous. I'm sure I am not the only person who finds over after over of big hitting by one team as repetitive and dull as a match where one team is bowled out for a low score, or crawls to a total that you know the opposition will obtain with many overs to spare.

Many critics described the game in Johannesburg in 2006 where Australia scored 4–434 but still lost to be the greatest one-day game ever. Certainly more runs were scored in this match than ever before, but is batting alone the final arbiter in deciding these matters? I hope not, for surely the thrilling ups and downs of a match in which batsmen and then bowlers have the ascendancy are the most fascinating. During that Johannesburg game—much to the amusement of my wife because I am usually quite a passive watcher of sport—I found myself yelling at the television screen. This was not because of the excitement, but because so many fundamentals of the game were being ignored. I was embarrassed that international bowlers could go for so many runs without trying to change their tactics, and distressed that those same bowlers seemed unable to direct the ball close to where they were aiming at. Full tosses, short and wide deliveries, and 'freebies' pitched on the leg stump were the fare of the day, while the only variety came when the bowling went from bad to worse. There is nothing easier for a batsman than receiving similar deliveries almost every ball.

I hope every coach in the world obtains a video of that game, looks at the bowling tactics of both sides, and sees how *not* to bowl in a one-day game. But I'm not sure if the right lessons will be learned, because the focus will be on the constant big hitting. Not long before I watched that run-fest, I read a magazine article in which a prominent international coach explained that he was asking his pace bowlers to 'concentrate on hitting top of off stump' when they bowled. Four paragraphs later, this same coach was quoted as saying, 'I think in the future someone will score 400 in a one-day cricket innings.' Of course, he was proved right in that prediction, but it is also true that if the bowlers had been constantly bowling an off-stump line and a length that would have knocked the bails off, there was no way either Australia or South Africa would have totalled anywhere near 400. Were the bowlers unprepared, out of form, or not good enough?

While batting strategies in one-day cricket have changed over the years, there has been a sameness about the bowling, which only geniuses such as Shane Warne have risen above. To most bowlers these days, one-day cricket is a negative game. They aim at leg stump, with as many fieldsmen as they are allowed in defensive positions, often trying to prevent boundaries rather than getting batsmen out. When any game concentrates solely on defence, much of its charm is lost.

I have always viewed limited-over cricket as the promotional arm of the game. Consequently, I am not too concerned with alterations to its format, providing those changes allow the one-day game to remain a serious challenge and don't impair the standards seen in Test matches. If the overall quality of the sport drops, however, this could be disastrous. And that's my fear at the moment. If that it is happening, a sudden plethora of Twenty20 games will hasten that trend.

If one-day cricket is responsible for the decline in international bowling standards in recent years, it would be a fact filled with irony given that for many years there were concerns that one-day cricket was ruining batting, not bowling. I always felt that many batsmen in the 1980s and 1990s used the so-called difficulties of batting in one-day cricket as a cop-out, an excuse to hide their inability to come to terms with the demands of what was then a new game. I had believed, from when I first came into contact with limited-overs cricket in the 1960s, that a disciplined Test batsman with a good cricketing brain and the right temperament could be successful in one-day games without resorting to 'slather and whack'.

To illustrate this point, I always use the example of Bill Lawry— the 'corpse with pads' as one unkind English cricket writer called him—who was actually one of the most efficient one-day players I have seen. I'll never forget the day in 1964, at the end of the Ashes tour, when we played Sussex in a 50-over game at Hove, and Bill and I put on 48 for the first wicket in no time. I think Sussex quite fancied themselves—they'd won the inaugural Gillette Cup one-day knockout competition the previous year—but we beat them easily without ever having to resort to slogging. Though Bill was not known for fast scoring in Test cricket, he was able to introduce a greater urgency into his one-day game plan without resorting to the unorthodox and risky shots that many less capable batsmen thought were compulsory. His aggressive running between wickets was as tailor-made for one-day cricket as it was for any other form of the game. The sloggers, I knew, might play the odd spectacular innings, but it is the men who stick to relatively orthodox methods who would always be the most valuable in the long run. The premier one-day batsmen of today—men such as Adam Gilchrist, Ricky Ponting and Sachin Tendulkar—are still technically sound when they score at better than a run a ball, even when they go over the top.

•

One-day cricket was designed from day one for television. In 1964, BBC2 was launched in England. The men in charge wanted cricket on the small screens, but only for a two-hour spot on Sunday afternoons. At that stage Ron Roberts, a respected Fleet Street journalist, was successfully staging first-class matches in various countries, including India, Pakistan, Rhodesia (now Zimbabwe), New Zealand and South Africa. He had taken a 'Commonwealth XI' team to South Africa in late 1959; a year later his team that toured South Africa and Rhodesia was sponsored by a tobacco company and known as the 'Rothmans International Cavaliers'. I was a member of both these teams and they, and others that Roberts similarly organised, were immensely popular wherever they went. The secret of this success was that the matches they played were genuine contests involving top cricketers from almost every country in the world.

The Cavaliers teams I was part of contained a number of recently retired greats, such as Denis Compton, Godfrey Evans and Frank Tyson, plus many established Test players including Richie Benaud, Fred Trueman, Ken Barrington, Brian Statham, Tom Graveney, Bert Sutcliffe and Hanif Mohammed, plus up-and-coming youngsters such as Norman O'Neill, Peter Philpott and me. It was a wonderful mix and so popular, in fact, that soon there were requests for the Cavaliers to play matches on Sundays against the counties in England. Ron Roberts died tragically of cancer in 1965, but Bagenal Harvey, Denis Compton's manager, became involved in the negotiations with BBC2. With some help from the senior players, they came up with a format: the innings would be limited to 40 six-ball overs, and the length of bowlers' run-ups would be restricted, with the idea being to get the games completed in a single afternoon. BBC2 would cover just the innings of the team batting second, in effect focusing on the hopefully exciting finish. The games proved to be an immediate hit, attracting big crowds through the gate and huge television audiences. The Gillette Cup, a one-day knockout competition involving the counties and featuring 65 overs and then 60 overs per side, had been staged since 1963, but it was the Sunday afternoon matches involving the Cavaliers and BBC2 that first truly popularised limited-overs cricket.

The proceeds of the Cavaliers matches were usually given to charity, or to county players who were enjoying benefit years. After two or three seasons, the games were the talk of cricket and often more than 10,000 people attended them. It was not surprising then that the MCC, who had given the matches their blessing, decided to start their own Sunday league. They didn't ban the Cavaliers outright, but did the next best thing by ruling that no current first-class player could play for them. But you always sensed that the MCC never really took to limited-overs cricket.

International one-day cricket began by accident. In 1970–71, the Melbourne Ashes Test was abandoned without a ball being bowled due to torrential rain. In a bid to recoup some money out of the Christmas–New Year holidays, a one-day international was played, involving 40 eight-ball overs per side. It was won by Australia by five wickets, provided some of the most entertaining cricket of the summer, and was watched by over 46,000 people at the MCG. However, another one-day international was not played anywhere until the end of Australia's 1972 tour of England, when a three-game series for the Prudential Trophy was staged. The first World Cup in 1975 seemed to be a great success, but it really wasn't until the advent of night cricket that the format really took off with cricket enthusiasts. Prior to WSC, there had been 44 one-day internationals, 15 of them in the 1975 World Cup. Since then, nearly 2500 more have been played; more than 100 one-day internationals were played in 2005 alone. A trickle became a flood.

•

For the past ten years, probably longer, I've not been able to recall the results of too many one-day games. The World Cup has real prestige, but if you'd asked me to remember what happened in last year's World, VB or Carlton & United Series, I'd struggle. The impression I get is that many other people have the same problem, and that this situation is not confined to Australia. Unless something very special has happened, a one-dayer quickly becomes yet another mere statistic. However, with the crowds still flocking to the games, and consequently with so much money to be made, the number of limited-overs games is hardly going to be reduced, so the onus on all involved is to find a way to make the games as interesting as possible. Twenty20 isn't the answer, a couple of shrewd rule changes might help, but I believe the solution is actually quite simple. I think the competitors have to display more imagination, and the bowlers especially have to go back to using some good old-fashioned cricket skills.

What should lead the way is more emphasis being put on winning matches by bowling the opposition out. Every strategy at present seems only concerned with restricting the scoring rate. Dismissing batsmen has become almost secondary, a bonus rather than a planned outcome, in contrast to the 'old days' when it used to be an accepted fact that the best way to reduce the scoring rate was to take wickets. Nowadays, even if the bowlers are on top after 15 overs, the captains automatically drop the field back and go on the defensive. In such circumstances, it is almost inevitable that a recovery will take place. Equilibrium is restored. If only the captains had the courage to attack a little longer. Cricket fans have always appreciated players who 'have a go'. In one-day cricket, that mantra should apply to more than just batsmen trying to clear the boundary rope.

Modern bowlers in one-day cricket seem to have lost faith in variety and seem driven by a desire to bowl yorkers. Frankly, I am sick to death of hearing commentators rattle on about the need to get the ball into the 'blockhole'. Surely they must know that any ball delivered there is actually an easy full toss, provided the batsman is on the ball. The yorker can only produce results if the batsman makes a mistake.

Oh, for a Steve Waugh or a Simon O'Donnell and their range of confusing slower balls in the 'death overs'.

Perhaps to encourage the return of more imaginative bowling, the game needs to think seriously about the way the size of the field has been reduced in recent years. Some of the sixes of today were once mishits that were easily caught on the boundary. It is often claimed that modern batsmen hit the ball harder than in the past and I won't dispute this. So they should be able to clear longer boundaries. These are the sorts of rule changes I think administrators need to consider if they want to help the game, rather than introducing power plays and substitutes that move the sport further away from its traditions.

Twenty20 cricket will not replace the one-dayers, but like limited-overs matches it can be a useful vehicle for the promotion of cricket. If the public want it and are prepared to turn up to watch, I think they must be given the opportunity to do so. It is already introducing new people to cricket in England, and the response so far in Australia has been excellent. What we must ensure, however, is that the quality of the game, from Twenty20 to Test matches, remains high. And please, we can't have too much of it. Whatever decisions are made, it is essential that everyone involved—players, fans, coaches and the media—is able to appreciate that they are watching something special. And the genuine skills of the game must always be encouraged and allowed to prosper.

Cricket followers will always respond positively to that.

29

SLEDGING IS NOT VERY APPEALING

As an opening batsman in a previous era, I was subjected to plenty of bouncers. I played in an era when there was no limitation on the number of short ones a bowler could send down, and that was under the old back-foot no-ball rule, which allowed bowlers to deliver the ball after a long last stride and 'drag' up to a metre closer to the batsman than they are today before they let it go.

Bouncers have been a part of the game since the days when Warwick Armstrong had Jack Gregory and Ted McDonald as his opening bowlers straight after the First World War. Bodyline in the early 1930s demonstrated just how effective a shock attack could be, and taught Sir Donald Bradman a lesson he never forgot. As soon as The Don had Ray Lindwall and Keith Miller under his control, his opponents felt the fear of whistling bouncers, setting a standard that continued through to the 1950s. I can well remember the manner in which Lindwall and Miller bounced the West Indies, and especially the famous 'Three Ws'—Everton Weekes, Clyde Walcott and Frank Worrell—in 1951–52, to the point that the Windies batsmen were battered into oblivion. The men from the Caribbean took the message home, and were still remembering it in the 1960s when they had Wes Hall and Charlie Griffith opening the bowling.

During the 1960s, when Hall and Griffith were the most feared bowling attack in world cricket, there were as many bouncers bowled as in any era of cricket. But while there was plenty of short-pitched bowling, I don't think the bumpers were delivered with the same animosity that they seem to be delivered with today. This said, I must say that the most vicious over I have ever seen was delivered by Keith Miller in a Sheffield Shield match for New South Wales against Victoria at the SCG in 1954–55. For some reason, Keith lost all control against an opening batsman named Jeff Hallebone. Now Jeff was a reasonable batsman, certainly no world beater, but this day he really riled Keith, who went around the wicket to him and let him have seven bouncers in the same eight-ball over. I was at first slip quaking and was nearly as relieved as the batsman when he was caught behind off Pat Crawford in the following over.

That kind of cruel assault was very much a rarity in cricket in those days. More often than not, encounters between batsmen and bowlers were short, sharp verbal exchanges that occurred in the heat of the moment. By the end of the day—even the session—the animosity had been forgotten.

Fred Trueman often doubted the legality of my parents' marriage, but his anger and frustration as Bill Lawry and I pushed him around for singles gave me enough satisfaction to ignore his outbursts. In fact, more often than not, the odd on-field 'discussion' between me and an opposition fast bowler tended, if anything, to cement friendships I built with the fast bowlers I encountered. Today, some of my best mates are fast bowlers who tried their hardest to knock my block off.

In those days, there was almost no baiting of the opposition. I can remember a bloke like Sam Loxton being pretty vocal on the field, but half of that was aimed at his own team. Sam did have a go at me one day when I hooked one of his bumpers; he seemed to think I was lucky to get away with the shot, and pointed that fact out to me! Another time, after I whacked Ian Johnson for six over 'cow corner' at mid-wicket, he applauded in a sarcastic sort of way, as if to say, 'You little bugger, I'll get you out now.' But I don't think sledging, as it is now known, came into vogue until the 1970s, and I am ashamed to admit that it was used more often by Australian players than by others. It was this sledging, I believe, that brought much of the ill will and the unpleasant behaviour that has now become part of cricket. Continuous sledging, particularly from the fieldsman at short leg or the men in the slips, is a little like water torture. The drip . . . drip . . . drip . . . of this abuse gradually wears away at the patience of the batsmen. Suddenly the game erupts and grudges develop.

As players got away with abusing each other, it was natural that soon they'd be having a go at the officials as well. Displays of displeasure at an umpire's decision became more and more prevalent, and in these days of mass television coverage, there are now more and more impressionable youngsters keen to mimic their idols. If it's good enough for my hero to shout at an umpire or appeal when he knew a batsman wasn't out, kids must think, then it's good enough for me.

Indeed, some officials involved in school and park cricket in Australia have told me that sledging has now reached epidemic proportions and that barely a match goes by without an incident. I went recently to watch my 16-year-old grandson play in a school match. He attends a well-known private school in Sydney, renowned for turning out well-mannered young men.

That may well be the case and I certainly like the way his school is implementing discipline at all levels. However, one Saturday, my grandson's school team played against an equally well-known and respected school. The match was conducted in a competitive manner, with perhaps too much meaningless on-field chatter. Suddenly, a batsman of the other school team was given out by his own coach. It looked close, but the student, as he walked very slowly off the ground, continually turned around and hurled expletives at his teacher. This tirade continued even after he reached the boundary, as several of his team-mates tried to calm him down. It was an astonishing and unprovoked display of rank bad manners and sportsmanship. On my scale of discipline, it should have brought a four-week suspension. After the match, I spoke to the teachers and was dismayed to hear that outbursts such as this are not rare at this level.

•

Even the very best umpires make mistakes. What everyone in the game—players, administrators and the umpires themselves—must do in my view is endeavour to create an environment where the umps can do their best. If they don't measure up in those circumstances, then I reckon we have to be brutal and replace them with men or women who might be good enough. But first, we have to give them a fair go, which I don't think they are getting at the moment.

One of the curses of the modern game is over-appealing, which has helped lead to a spate of very poor umpiring decisions in international matches. An appeal should be a request to the umpires to consider whether a batsman is out or not out, but unfortunately the appealing these days is more an aggressive demand than a request. Worse still, the frequency of these appeals appears in many cases to be orchestrated and designed to force, by sheer weight of numbers, a favourable decision for the bowling side.

In 2005, Australia's Brett Lee was fined after he demanded a reason from an umpire as to why he hadn't been given a favourable decision to one of his numerous appeals. I was glad that this disciplinary action was instigated, not because I have anything against Brett, but rather because I know that bowlers asking for, or in some cases demanding, a reason why the umpire hasn't given a batsman out can only lead to confusion, anger, discontent . . . and poor umpiring. I have always believed it is wise for umpires to be very careful in conveying their reasons for knocking back an appeal. Take, for example, the case of David Shepherd, one of the best umpires I have seen, during the 1999 World Cup match between India and Sri Lanka at Taunton.

During Sri Lanka's innings, Aravinda de Silva flayed at a wide, overpitched ball and was caught behind. However, 'Shep' thought otherwise and India's appeal was rejected. It was an obvious mistake but Shep made it worse for himself by signalling that the ball had clipped Aravinda's pad. Television replays quickly showed that when the ball clipped the edge it was a number of centimetres from the pad. This series of events could only diminish the players' respect for the umpires. In my view, appeals should only be answered with a 'Yes' or a 'No'.

If the bowler wants more information and if the umpire is inclined to answer, he should only say, 'In my view, the batsman wasn't out.' End of argument, for the power lies with the umpire. Funny, isn't it, that when an obviously wrong decision goes a bowler's way, he never strides up to the umpire to ask why the batsman was given out. He's just very happy to accept the bonus wicket.

When I was coaching Australia, the players would often come off the field after a session of play and ask, 'What did you think of that umpiring decision?' They knew I'd had the benefit of seeing the television replays in the dressing room. I always tried to answer honestly—agreeing that the umpire had made a blue or explaining that he'd actually been right—but sometimes I'd first ask, 'Would you have been happy to be given out in that situation?' Most times, I got a very non-committal reply. Poor decisions that went against them were outrageous; ones in their favour were all part of the game.

It was hoped that the so-called 'neutral umpires' would improve the standard of umpiring in international cricket. I have always felt that, with a few exceptions, all umpires did their best and as such were neutral. But even so, I think the move to use umpires from countries not involved in the particular international match was a good thing, and not just because, when it comes to fairness in sport, perceptions are almost as important as reality. The fact is that umpires today have it tougher than ever before, not just because of the constant appealing, but also because the commentators seem very happy to express their views, and not just immediately after an incident but also after they've watched a seemingly never-ending submission of replays from every conceivable angle. Quite often, I am still in doubt after viewing these replays, but not some of the commentators. Interestingly, the occasional embarrassing, wrong or silly gaffe made by a commentator is never mentioned again, while an umpiring mistake is often replayed at every opportunity.

Further, I wonder if bowlers who are verbally happy to chirp at umpires with a crack such as, 'Are you blind?', or 'How could you make that decision?' would enjoy it if the umpires, after a bad ball, said, 'How on earth did you get into the Test side?' I bet the players' association would be up in arms if that occurred, claiming that the umpire had no right to say such a thing, and that such a comment was 'unprofessional'. So why can't I argue that the players, when they over-appeal and run down the pitch after an appeal without looking at the umpire, are being less professional than they should be?

If we could get them to behave in a more professional manner, then I'm sure the umpiring will improve. No one can perform at their best when they are being harassed. The game will be no less of a spectacle (in fact, I think most fair-minded people would agree that it would be all the better for less 'aggro'), and commentators will start talking about all the fantastic things our sport has to offer. What have we got to lose?

30

SEVENTEEN QUESTIONS

Throughout my career, I have always been careful to respect the skills displayed by players of the past and present. I was lucky, in the seasons after I was first selected to play for New South Wales at the age of sixteen, to be part of an era when the Blues team was good enough to win the Sheffield Shield twelve times in fourteen years, including one run of nine titles in a row. I had the honour of playing with some of my heroes—men such as Keith Miller, Neil Harvey, Ray Lindwall and Arthur Morris—and cherished the experience. These champions were immensely helpful and kind to me.

In the 1980s, I became a national-team coach and gained a new respect for many of the players of that era. I never suffered from 'old-timer syndrome' and still don't. One of the great joys of my career was seeing young talent evolve and flourish, and as I had as a player I treasured my time as a coach. In the last decade, as I had for the previous 40-plus years, I have respected and admired the talents of the current and emerging players.

Of course, there are always some former cricketers who want to argue that their time was the best. This was happening when I was a boy, straight after the war, and it is still happening today. For me, when it comes to comparing the talents of players from different eras, everyone is entitled to an opinion, but what I won't cop are statements I have heard in the past few years from recently retired players who seem to believe that present-day international cricketers are 'more professional' than the players of the past.

Early in the England season of 2006, former England captain Nasser Hussain wrote that cricket was 'much more professional and multi-dimensional' these days. To be honest, I am not quite sure what he meant. Sure, if you relate professionalism to monetary rewards then current players are certainly ahead of the greats of yesteryear, and I am delighted that they are. Cricketers with matching skills from days gone by were poorly rewarded.

However, if Nasser is suggesting that the players of today are superior technically, mentally or physically, or are better prepared, I strongly disagree with him. Cricketers of the 21st century do have access to computers, science and so-called experts in a variety of fields, some of which are only loosely related to the game. But are these extra resources creating a better product than we have seen in the past?

There are few sports that have seen more technological developments in recent times than golf. Huge changes have been made to clubs and balls to enable players to hit the ball further and straighter, and to spin it more. Some courses have been lengthened and toughened a little, I know, but still, for all this scientific and technological assistance, the average score per round in professional golf has barely gone down a stroke from that achieved by Arnold Palmer, Gary Player, Jack Nicklaus and their contemporaries back in the 1960s.

If a time machine could get Palmer, Player and Nicklaus on the fairways of today, they would match it with Tiger Woods and company. Similarly, the 'average' golfers from the 1960s would keep up with the run-of-the-mill players of today. So it is with cricket. A 'middle-of-the-road' Test batsman still averages around 35, 'good' Test players average in the low to mid-40s, and the 'greats' have an average of more than 50. Bowling is the same. The 'champions' are averaging between 20 and 25, the 'good' bowlers in the high 20s and low 30s, and the trundlers' wickets cost them around 35 to 40 runs each.

Part of my coaching philosophy involves throwing questions at players, on the basis that if they think about what I am asking, their answers will help their cricket. So now I'd like to pose a few questions, the answers to which will at least challenge Nasser's claims that the game is so much more professional today.

1 Why do so many more players today get out without playing a shot than cricketers of earlier times? It seems at least one or two batsmen are out this way every Test.

2 Why are so many no-balls bowled in this 'more professional' era?

3 Why is it that more batsmen get hit on the head now than in any other era?

4 Why haven't helmets made today's batsmen better players of fast bowling?

5 Why do the top cricketers of today practise the skills of their game less than their counterparts in other professional sports?

6 Why do captains rarely use a third man for pace bowling despite the fact that 25 per cent of runs are scored in this unprotected area?

7 Why has conventional swing bowling with the new ball virtually gone out of the game, even though reverse swing with the old ball is so much in vogue?

8 What is the value of bowlers operating to a 'seven-two' field to both the new and old balls?

9 Why is it that almost every fast bowler is given two fieldsmen on the boundary behind square leg and only one man to guard the huge area remaining on the onside? Any reasonable batsman will milk this field all day.

10 Why are so many catches being dropped in Test cricket? (Nasser's article appeared a day or so after England dropped nine catches in Sri Lanka's second innings of a Test at Lord's.)

11 Why do wicketkeepers stand so deep these days? In the past, most keepers liked to position themselves so that the bowlers' stock deliveries came to them at about hip high. The modern keeper takes the same ball below his knees, which means he is so deep that too many nicks fall short of him. His poor positioning also forces the slip fieldsmen to be stationed too deep, which not only leads to potential catches falling short, it also mucks up the angles for the slip cordon and denies them the opportunity to cover as wide an area as possible.

12 Why do fielders slide or fall over almost every time they pick up the ball, when this method actually makes it harder for them to pick up the ball cleanly? Inevitably, batsmen can take an extra run when a player trying to field the ball is on the ground.

13 Why do fielders dive for catches or try to stop balls wide of them in the same manner used by football goalkeepers to push the ball over or around the posts?

14 Today, international teams employ a bevy of specialists to look

after the bodies, minds, fitness and strength of their players. Why then are so many cricketers getting injured?

15 Why are bowlers less accurate these days? They certainly must be, because opponents are scoring at four runs an over in Test cricket and ridiculous totals are being easily obtained in one-day internationals.

16 Why has the overall standard of Test cricket dropped so much? The West Indies, Pakistan and South Africa are nowhere near as good as they have been in the past, while in recent times India and England have also struggled on occasions.

17 Finally, just why does the average ball of 'good' length for fast bowlers now pitch at least one metre shorter than it once did? By bowling this length, new-ball bowlers are not giving the ball time to swing, yet they don't seem to be aware of the disadvantage they are creating for themselves. Secondly, the shorter length reduces 'the area of uncertainty'—the length where it is hard for the batsman to decide whether to play forward or back.

Let me quote from Nasser's article:

> One of the misconceptions that has arisen in the wake of Lord's is that England actually practise dropping the ball so they can work on taking rebounds. What they actually do, occasionally, is take the catches, but then throw them down at an angle to see if the guy next to them can take the rebound, but they certainly didn't do that before Lord's . . .

I can't get my mind around that one. It seems to me that this might be yet another example of a fad or half-baked theory, the kind of which cricket, quite frankly, has had far too many in recent times. One thing I am convinced about is that doing such a drill does not make the fieldsmen any more 'professional'. More likely, I reckon, it does the reverse.

31

THOUGHTS FOR THE FUTURE

One problem with being an ex-player turned columnist in modern cricket is that no matter how positive you are in your comments, as soon as you dare to criticise you're tagged a nark. It doesn't matter how constructive or how well argued your opinion might be, or that surrounding one criticism in an article you've written are paragraphs of positive thoughts, in some people's eyes you cannot be too friendly. This fact doesn't scare me, but let me tell you it does make me think my comments through before I put them down on paper.

Of course, there is plenty right about 21st-century cricket. We are in the middle of one of the great periods of Test-match batting, with players of the quality of Ponting, Hayden, Gilchrist, Dravid, Tendulkar, Sehwag, Lara, Inzamam, Kallis and Vaughan gracing the world stage. The bowling stocks are much thinner, though we still have the game's greatest spinner in our midst, plus McGrath, Muralitharan and Kumble, and a genuine world-class all-rounder in Andrew Flintoff. The Test cricket of today is as thrilling and pulsating as it has ever been in the game's history, while the efforts of the Australian team in the past decade, as it won Test after Test and one-dayer after one-dayer, have been remarkable. The win rates of Steve Waugh (41 Test wins from 57 matches) and Ricky Ponting (22 from his first 30) as Australian captains are super impressive, and make me (12 from 39) super envious.

The only thing I can say in my defence is also one of the great truisms of cricket and often forgotten—a captain is only as good as his team. I mention this not as a knock on my team (or on Steve or Ricky) but to highlight that both Steve and Ricky led fantastic combinations.

It can't be just a coincidence that the most successful captains have always been lucky enough to be around when their countries had great players and teams. It was said that when the West Indies were demolishing their opponents, all Clive Lloyd had to do was throw the ball in the air and whichever of his superb bowlers caught it would bowl the team to victory. This might be an exaggeration, but maybe not that much, especially with batsmen such as Desmond Haynes, Gordon Greenidge, Viv Richards, Richie Richardson, Larry Gomes and Lloyd himself all scoring plenty of runs, and the fielding usually being of a very high quality. As Ricky found out in England in 2005, if the bowlers can't consistently bowl the ball in the right spot it is impossible to set a field or bowl out the opposition for a reasonable score. That was the main reason Australia lost the Ashes, not because their leader was a poor captain.

Retirements of past champions, the loss of form of key players, injuries at the wrong times or an absence of high-class youngsters coming through are also hardly the fault of the captain. It's also usually a bit rich to blame the skipper if his players become complacent, or perhaps distracted by the off-field opportunities that come with success. The selectors might pull the wrong rein, or in the modern era, the coach or support staff might give the wrong advice. Yet if a team loses, it's still the captain's fault.

When you think about it, Australia's great run of success since 1989 is a remarkable tribute to Border, Taylor, Waugh and Ponting. Because the team has kept winning, all four captains have received much-deserved praise for their work. But after the 2005 Ashes series, when some experts, Dennis Lillee among them, started suggesting a change in the captaincy might be necessary to fix failings in the Australian team's performance, I think we got a glimpse of how the skipper will be treated when the side eventually loses its place at the top of the cricket tree. You'd have to think it would take an extraordinary effort from all involved with the team for it not to happen eventually—after all, it even happened to Australia in the 1950s and the West Indies in the 1990s. So perhaps it's appropriate to start looking for reasons why such a decline might occur. And before I start I must stress that if the team does start to decline, I'll be very surprised if it's the captaincy that causes the trouble.

•

My first concern is with the style of tours that the Australian team goes on. These days, they seem to contain only Tests and one-day internationals, which means there is little if any opportunity for 'fringe' players to push their claims. The England tour, for example, was once a vital ingredient in developing young players. Even those who did not play in the Test would get more chances on an Ashes tour than they'd get in three years of first-class cricket in Australia.

On my first tour of England, injuries to Colin McDonald and Richie Benaud gave me the opportunity to play in 26 first-class matches, and I ended up with 1947 runs and 51 wickets. On that tour, six batsmen scored more than 1200 runs and even Colin, despite missing some matches, scored 913. Eight bowlers bowled more than 450 overs, and they all took over 50 wickets each. Playing in so many matches ensured that every player had an opportunity to get into form and compete for a place in the Test team. Graham McKenzie celebrated his 20th birthday during that tour, and took five wickets in the second innings of his debut Test, at Lord's. He played in three Tests on the tour and took 11 wickets; in all first-class matches he bowled a total of 569.2 overs and took 54 wickets. How important was this education to Garth's future success? (Further, I wonder how the scientists of today would accept that such a young man did so much bowling, for it goes against their theory that teenagers shouldn't be allowed such a workload because they might break down.)

Gradually, the number of matches on an Ashes tour was reduced, and by 1989 the most first-class games played by any tourist was 18, by Geoff Marsh. Still, even that was a nice tally for Geoff to work into some form. In 2005, Brad Hodge, who would have come into the Test team if one of the batsmen dropped out, played the grand total of *one* first-class match for the Australians on tour! Stuart MacGill, the second spinner, bowled 44 first-class overs.

•

Part of the logic behind these shorter tours is that the lesser workload will extend players' careers. This brings me to my second concern about the future, and it relates to my strong belief that the standard of bowling not just in Australia but across the world is in decline, something I've referred to more than once already in this book. My belief is that rather than worrying about cricketers' futures, the people in charge of the world's best teams should be focusing on the present. The fact that teams can amass 434 in a 50-over game is certainly proof that the best batsmen in the world can hit as well as ever, but it is also strong evidence that 21st-century bowlers are simply not skilful enough to bowl line and length. The bowlers from my playing days and when I was

Australian coach could certainly do that. I know there is plenty of talk concerning the players' busy schedules, but I wonder if the bowlers are working hard enough in the nets, or whether they are being mollycoddled.

Back in the 1960s, there were countless medium-pacers in English county cricket who were relentlessly accurate, and all of them bowled many hundreds of overs per season. It didn't hurt them. In Australia, our blokes never relied on 'net' bowlers, whether they were at grade, Shield or Test practice—we preferred to do most of the work ourselves. As well as bowling all those overs in England in 1961, Graham McKenzie always worked hard at the nets. I can still picture Richie Benaud bowling for hours on end in South Africa in 1957–58 after normal team practice, trying to land his leg-breaks on a handkerchief while a local schoolboy gathered the balls and returned them to him so he could aim at that handkerchief again. Obviously, if you are a bowler and you do this amount of work in the nets you are going to learn how to bowl line and length. It will become a habit.

Today, I get really annoyed when I see Test bowlers being cut for four and two balls later they get turned off their toes for four. That just shouldn't happen, but it happens a lot. Genuinely accurate bowlers such as Shane Warne and Glenn McGrath are rarities. My primary explanation for this is that too many of today's 'elite' bowlers are not working as hard as they should and the result is that they've lost the ability to keep it tight.

Think of the contrast with the 'tailenders' of recent times who have worked hard on their batting in the nets and reaped the rewards. There are fewer cheap wickets in cricket today than there were in the past. Australians need only recall Jason Gillespie's unconquered double century against Bangladesh, how McGrath's batting has improved, and how well Warne, Brett Lee and Michael Kasprowicz batted in England in 2005 and in South Africa in 2006, for evidence of this.

The other explanation I have for the decline in bowling relates to the influence biomechanics have had on Australian cricket in recent years. I first heard the term 'biomechanics' in relation to cricket in my first or second year of coaching Australia. Peter Spence, then with the Victorian Cricket academy introduced me to a fellow whose name I'm afraid I can't remember. For maybe fifteen minutes this bloke used words that I'd never heard used before in relation to cricket, but I kept listening, listening, listening, until finally the penny dropped. He just had totally different terminology for what I knew as batting and bowling *technique*. When I put this to him, he didn't argue with me. 'I know what you are talking about,' I said. 'I've known about it for 30 years.'

'But this is all new,' he replied.

'No it's not new,' I said. 'I've got no problem with what you're saying, but I think you need to realise that the right technique for one player is not necessarily the right one for someone else.'

This is where I think things have gone awry, and why I have a huge problem with the coaching programs that are being implemented in academies across the cricket world. My strong view is that you cannot set up a blanket coaching pattern for all cricketers, but this is exactly what Cricket Australia and the other administrative bodies have done. In the end, they're still trying to teach technique, but what they are doing is foisting their favourite principles and theories on all their students, which leaves us with a situation today where nearly every fast-medium bowler runs up to the wicket and delivers the ball in much the same 'biomechanically correct' way. In doing so, the naturalness has been taken out of these bowlers. Too many batsmen have the same stance and pick up the bat the same way. The irony is that these young people are so keen to do their own thing, except when it comes to their cricket. Another irony is that in the 1990s the biomechanics argued that bowlers should use a 'front-on' action because that would minimise the risk of injury. As that hasn't worked out the way they thought (indeed I have been told that the number of injuries increased dramatically), the suggestion now is that 'side-on' is the biometrically correct way to go. The truth is, as excellent and durable bowlers such as Mike Procter, Neil Hawke and Max Walker demonstrated, front-on actions can work for some people, while Jeff Thomson was blistering proof that absolute side-on can work for others.

•

My third worry with Australian cricket's future concerns the Pura Cup competition, which for many years, when it was known as the Sheffield Shield, was always the prime source for the talent that went into building a strong Test team. Nowadays, however, a state side with plenty of players in the Australian teams is obliged to often play a virtual second XI in the Pura Cup. Have a look at New South Wales' averages for 2005–06: Simon Katich played in three games, Michael Clarke two, Brett Lee and Glenn McGrath just one each. When I was an Australian selector I found it difficult to judge how good up-and-coming players were if their only success had been in Shield matches when the Test guys weren't available. Things have become worse, not better, since then. I further wonder if a youngster's education is complete if they have rarely rubbed shoulders with the game's elite, either at practice or in matches.

The other problem I see with the Pura Cup is that players in their late 20s and early 30s are continuing to play well beyond their 'use-by' date. Part of this is a by-product of the reasonable wages first-class cricketers are receiving these days (you can make a pretty fair living these days), but the big downside is that there are fewer opportunities available, and 'promising' players are not making their debuts until later than they did in the past. It was once said in New South Wales that if you didn't make the state team by the time you were twenty you wouldn't make it at all. It is not impossible for a gifted teenager to break into state cricket these days, as New South Wales' 18-year-old Moises Henriques demonstrated in 2005–06, but maybe Moises also proves my point, because his appearances were restricted to two ING Cup one-dayers and three Twenty20 games. Thirty or 40 years ago, he would have been in the Shield team for sure.

More and more youngsters are winning a position in the Australian Under–19 team before they have even played first grade for their clubs. My gut feeling is that the emphasis being placed on youth cricket may well be backfiring and holding back the talented. At present, teenagers can win state and Australian selection at the under-15, under-17 and under-19 levels, but are they being 'held back' so they will all go through according to a specific program? I know that cricketers such as Neil Harvey, Richie Benaud, Alan Davidson and me played our youth cricket at school. On Saturdays, we were in men's cricket by the age of twelve and, interestingly, we all played Shield cricket before our 21st birthdays.

Ricky Ponting, of course, did the same, and what a bounty Australian cricket has won from bringing him on 'early'. If Ricky is to be ranked with Allan Border, Mark Taylor and Steve Waugh as being among our greatest captains at the end of his career, it might well depend on how quickly some quality, battle-hardened young players are found to share the Test-match stage with him. My fear is that the only way that is going to happen is if a few things change, and change quickly.

32

LUCKIER THAN MOST

These days, when the top cricketers are on tour, most of the team tends to be always looking for something better to do. But that 'something better' rarely happens, so they end up doing what they did every other night. Consequently, they don't go to shows like we did on our tours, and with a few exceptions they don't take in touring life as we did. It's also not cool these days to say, 'Gee, I enjoyed last night,' if 'last night' was a formal dinner.

This is the way it is nowadays, even though there are few of the grand functions that we used to go to, the ones that used to feature black ties and some of the best public speakers in the world. Back in 1961, special permission was granted for a Lord's Taverners' luncheon to be held in the Long Room at Lord's. Fortunately, the Australian team was invited, and when we arrived I looked at the seating plan and discovered I'd be on the same table as Harry Secombe, Boris Karloff and Eric Sykes. I immediately thought, 'This is going to be the greatest lunch ever.' Of course, I wanted to talk about their celebrated careers in the world of entertainment; all this famous trio wanted to do was talk cricket. Karloff, especially, was mad about the game. Why wouldn't young men want to spend time in this kind of environment?

I enjoyed this day at the Home of Cricket more than another that occurred on this tour. On the second day of the Second

Test, I was due to bat at No. 6, and as our first innings had just got underway I decided to go and have a quiet sit in the corner. Suddenly Neil Harvey, captain for the game because Richie was nursing a damaged shoulder and as usual due to bat at three, said, 'Simmo, I've got to go to the toilet, put the pads on.' Sure enough, Colin McDonald was dismissed immediately, and out I rushed to be caught Illingworth, bowled Trueman, for 0.

In 1964, before I went away to England I must have spoken to every Rotary and Apex club in Sydney, just for the practice. It came in very handy, because as captain I had to make thirteen speeches during the first eleven days after we landed in London! Fortunately, a fantastic bloke named Merv Fenn, by day and night a hard-nosed 'journo', had been very kind to me. 'Simmo,' he'd said, 'you'd better be prepared.' I'd write a speech and ask him to review it, and he'd say yes to this and this, but no to that. Though I was hardly the most inspiring speaker in the world, I was lucky that as captain of Australia, a bit like the best man at a wedding, it didn't really matter what I said, so long as I didn't really muck it up.

My first speech as skipper had actually been made during the previous Australian summer, after Richie broke a finger and suddenly I was in charge for the Melbourne Test. I had to speak at a Board dinner. Afterwards, no less than Prime Minister Sir Robert Menzies approached me. 'Well done,' he said, before adding, 'Remember Bobby, when you speak, don't imitate anyone. If you need any help I'm happy to do all I can for you.' Not long later, I received a package of Sir Robert's transcripts, and many contained references to cricket. He clearly knew the game, loved to talk about it with cricketers, and from my experience the old stories of him planning overseas trips to coincide with Ashes tours was very true. In England, it seemed as if Sir Robert was never too far from the team. From the time I became captain I was often receiving telegrams from him, always wishing the team the best.

Of course, Menzies has not been the only cricketing prime minister of my experience. During the 1970s I got very friendly with Bob Hawke when he was leader of the Australian trade union movement, to the point that Meg and I used to visit his home in Melbourne over the New Year, sometimes even on New Year's Day. A feature of these occasions was an annual tennis challenge between the two of us, in which neither competitor would give an inch. We are two very stubborn people. I can recall Bob's first wife Hazel saying at the time, 'Look at those silly old bulls out there.' It was 110°F but we were going hell for leather.

Bob took a genuine interest in cricketers' rights, and I know he gave the World Series Cricket players some advice during their dispute with the Australian Cricket Board (ACB). One suggestion I understand he gave was that the players form an 'association' rather than a 'union', which I thought was shrewd. Perceptions can count for plenty in certain environments.

My friendship with John Howard goes right back to the days when my brothers used to play cricket against his brothers in the Protestant Churches competition. I never played against John, who is three-and-a-half years younger than me, but I'm sure I would have run into him at the time. He was Leader of the Opposition in federal politics when I became Australian coach in 1986, and I remember saying to him about a year after I was appointed, 'John, we are struggling. The team would benefit if you sent the boys a telegram when they're losing. They only ever get telegrams from people in high places when they are winning. It's the sort of thing they won't forget.' Sure enough, a telegram arrived soon after. Since he became prime minister in 1996, I don't think John has missed a

Sydney Test match, and he has always been happy for the public to see his love for the game.

•

Back in 1968, I'd retired from international cricket for strictly commercial reasons. I had first done some newspaper work with the *Daily News* when I went to Perth back in 1956, and had my journalist's ticket, which saved me a few problems in England when some unionists objected to the idea of a player doing a reporter's job. The London *Evening Standard* had employed me to cover the fortunes of England in 1966 during the Test series against the West Indies, so I was aware there was some good money to be made if I swapped my cricket bat for a typewriter. In fact, I made a lot more money, perhaps as much as ten times more (before expenses), on that 1968 Ashes tour than Bill Lawry, the Australian captain, did by playing in the Tests, and soon after I was able to buy a really nice house. I had enjoyed sixteen seasons in first-class cricket, played in 52 Tests, and captained Australia 29 times. I was only 31 when I played what I thought was going to be my last Test, but the only time I regretted retiring even a little was when the West Indies came to Australia in 1968–69 and I saw how much Charlie Griffith and Wes Hall had slowed down. They'd bounced me so much in the Caribbean in 1965 I think I would have enjoyed scoring some of the runs Bill, Ian Chappell and Dougie Walters took off them that summer.

I must say, though, that while I made more money as a journo than I would have as a cricketer, I worked harder, too. I had around a dozen deadlines a day for papers around Australia and the *Evening Standard*, and I was also writing a 60,000-word book. I shared a car with Phil Tresidder, the same man who'd broken the news of my elevation to the New South Wales side back in January 1953, when we travelled around England. Phil was always a good mate of mine. At other times, I resided at a little apartment in Chelsea. Wherever I was, every morning I was up at 6 a.m., to punch out a few more words for the book, or to contemplate the first article of the new day.

That was the only time my association with the Australian team ended because of money. I'd been dropped in 1958–59 because of poor form. In 1978, I retired again because the ACB wasn't prepared to guarantee my place in the side for the First Test only (which is a little different to being dropped, I guess, but given the circumstances not a lot). In 1996, I was sacked as Australian coach after ten years in the job, but even now I'm not exactly sure why. I've never received a letter from the Board saying 'well done' or 'thanks for nothing'. They just informed me that my contract wasn't going to be renewed—after they'd already approached Geoff Marsh to take the job on—and gave me next to no chance to argue the case that I should have been retained.

I was aware that certain people at the Board were gunning for me. They hadn't been happy that I'd supported the players when Allan Border and the team were so upset that Shane Warne and Merv Hughes were fined heavily after a couple of incidents in South Africa in 1994. I also don't think they appreciated me being so adamant that they had to deal with the match-fixing allegations from later that same year. I also wasn't sure I had captain Mark Taylor's full support, though I did feel we'd worked quite well together since he took over from Allan Border in 1994. Between 1994 and 1996, Australia had won a home Ashes series, beaten the West Indies in the Caribbean and reached a World Cup final. Yet when I had a meeting with the ACB Chief Executive Graham

Halbish and Chairman Denis Rogers all they told me was that it was 'time for a change'. That was all. I've since learnt that a member of the ACB staff had been spreading false rumours about my health, which some Board members apparently accepted as fact, but I don't think that was the only reason I got the boot.

When I was sacked I received a lot of phone calls, and I was surprised by some of the people who did call and by others who didn't. If one caller stood out it would be Mark Waugh, who straight up told me I was going to be missed. 'All of us have got reason to thank you,' he said. Mark was never the sort of fellow to get overly excited if you helped him out, but at the same time he was a delight to coach because you could offer him some advice—perhaps he was trying to turn too many balls to square leg that were pitched on the stumps—and immediately you'd see a correction. Some blokes never listen. Most of the good ones do.

•

To be a successful Test cricketer you need to have a partner who's prepared to go along with the fact that often cricket will run first, second and just about everywhere. It's pretty tough for the partners these days, but it's nothing on what I put my wife Meg through so I could live out my dream and be a Test cricketer. These days, the Australian players do get time with their kids, and their partners are usually allowed to travel business class with the team at the expense of the Board. I think it is great that they are given specialised treatment. In the past, neither the Board nor the players could afford to do such things. Until the 1990s, wives weren't even allowed to stay in the same hotel as the players on tour. They certainly weren't permitted to travel on the same plane. I must confess that part of me supported this, because I knew how important it was for the team to bond, for the boys to get to know each other and share their love of the game. I also knew it could create potentially damaging inequalities within the team set-up if some players had their wives with them, because they could afford it, but others did not. The other side of this is that if a relationship you treasure is in trouble, you're hardly going to be in the right frame of mind to play good cricket, or to be a generous team-mate. During my career, I saw friendships break down, and quickly realised that unless you are going out with, engaged to, or married to a very special woman, the partnership isn't going to last very long.

In 1958, I left the team in Perth after we landed following the six-month South Africa tour, and caught a plane to Sydney so I'd have a couple of days up my sleeve before my wedding. In 1961, I was on board the *Himalaya* on the way to England when I discovered that Meg was pregnant. I certainly didn't know when we sailed, and it must have caused grave suspicion among the neighbours when they saw my wife's stomach expanding while I was on the other side of the world for eight months. I became a dad for the second time just a few weeks after the team returned to Australia from England. In 1965, before the tour to the West Indies, I was so churned up at the thought of leaving my young family again that I forgot to hand Meg the car keys before I headed for customs. When we landed in Fiji there was a message asking if I could arrange for the keys to be returned home. Back in Sydney, my wife had needed to find someone to break into the vehicle so she could get herself and her two children, aged five and three, home. What a nice bloke I was!

When my daughters, Kim and Debbie, were very young they hated going to the SCG or any of the major sporting grounds because they were not places for kids. The administrators didn't do anything to help a player's family in those days; they were there to run the cricket not crèches, or so they thought. They never even offered reserved seats for a player's immediate family. That attitude has changed now, thank goodness, but only recently. Grade cricket was different, because there was room for the youngsters to run around on the hills of the suburban grounds, but at the SCG the only amusement Debbie and Kim could find was at the turnstiles, where they helped the old attendants punch the tickets as the spectators entered the Members enclosure.

Meg and the girls made a lot of sacrifices for the sake of my career, so I never insisted on them being involved in cricket. Meg was a magnificent Latin American dancer, accomplished enough to win a championship on ABC television and also an Australian professional title, but it was just too hard for her to be both a single parent and a top dancer. She gave away her career so I could have mine. Knowing that, I could hardly complain that she was never a regular at matches, while I was never one to hang around for hours after play. If I was in Sydney I wanted to get home to my wife and daughters, and I resolved to never let the events of the day shape the atmosphere at home. Meg often said during my career that if she hadn't been listening to the cricket on the radio, she wouldn't have known when I came through the door if I had scored a hundred or a duck. Home with the family was the special place in my life.

We had started going out when Meg was sixteen and I was eighteen. Cricket brought us closer together in a weird way— someone suggested dancing would be a good way to improve my footwork and balance, so I went to a well-known ballroom in Pitt Street in the city to discover how dancing was done. I was pretty hopeless to begin with, but gradually improved enough for Meg to agree to share the floor with me. Had she not been there I probably would have given it away pretty quickly.

Earlier, I mentioned the days in England when I was playing in the Lancashire League in 1959 and the money was often tight. We had hoped to come home with £150, but a few days before we left I was advised that I owed the British tax man 120 quid, which meant we weren't really able to be too sociable on the voyage home. I needed the £50 a week Ron Roberts offered for the tour of South Africa with his Commonwealth XI team, which took place between the end of the English season and start of the Australian one, so I could pay Meg's hospital bills when she went in for the birth of our first child. An even bigger bonus was that I was offered a public relations position with the tobacco company, WD & HO Wills soon after that, and for the following few years they always paid me, even when I was on tour, even though I never smoked, whether we were living in Perth or Sydney. Meg and I were hardly rich, but now we did have some sense of financial security, which I'm sure helped my cricket. From then on my life seemed to be ever moving forwards, into the Test team, the captaincy, the first retirement, successful years in business and the press, the comeback during WSC, more business and media ventures, the coaching, working for the ICC, coaching consultancies in places as diverse as Holland, Nepal, Zimbabwe, Bermuda and India, and then in 2006 I was elected into the Australian Cricket Hall of Fame. It hasn't all been smooth sailing, but looking back, there is very, very little I would have changed.

I can understand how former top players can get a little bitter about the money today's cricketers earn, but I've never been like that. I think I played in one of the great eras of the game's history, when the tours were fascinating and the people around us were fantastic. I was luckier than most, because I stayed in the game and got to work with and enjoy the company of more generations of cricketers, not just the men I played with. It's not just that I've seen everyone from Miller and Harvey to Ponting and Warne, I've actually shared a dressing room with them, seen them close up, been able to learn what makes them special. Throughout, I've had a loving family with me on every step of the adventure. What stories I would have for Messrs Secombe, Karloff and Sykes if I could share another lunch with them now.